The Game of Nations

THE AMORALITY
OF POWER POLITICS

BY

Miles Copeland

SIMON AND SCHUSTER/NEW YORK

To my aunt "Sis,"
Mrs. Mary Armstrong

Contents

7

Preface

According to Edmund Wilson, F. Scott Fitzgerald was once inspired by Emily Post's *Etiquette* to write a play wherein the dramatic conflict would arise from stalemates between gentle people all trying to do the Right Thing. The conflict could be resolved only by the intervention of a cad who would bound on to the scene and set things right by behavior such as is totally outlawed by Mrs. Post. The situation is well known in diplomacy. Awful impasses arise between governments, each holding to its position on grounds of high principle or mere diplomatic propriety. The Guest No One Invites Again burrows under the strictures to break the deadlock and, at the same time, to save all the faces.

What caused the British and the Egyptians to come off their respective uncompromising positions on the Suez Base dispute in 1954? What brought about the fall of Mossadegh in Iran? How did the Nasserists wind up on top in the Lebanese civil war in 1958, doing so right under the noses of the U.S. Marines? Why did Nasser refrain from war in Israel at times when he had some chance of victory, yet propel his country toward war in May 1967 when he was least prepared for it? Historians leave these and other such

9

mysteries unexplained because, except in rare instances, the "story behind the story" is denied to them. Diplomats who have written autobiographically about the events were restrained partly by security considerations and partly because of a tacit understanding that there are some things about which it is ungentlemanly to disillusion the public. A diplomat to whom I showed the original draft of this book chided me for "revealing a lot of information which had best be forgotten" and for "needlessly" puncturing a view of our Government "which it is best for the public to have." I disagree with this outlook.

In the first place, I doubt that intelligent citizens really take comfort from the view of our nation's statesmanship that they get, for example, from Robert Kennedy's published account* of the Cuban crisis of 1962. Mr. Kennedy would have us believe that our Government's decisions in this case were made by "dedicated, intelligent men disagreeing and fighting about the future of our country and of mankind," sitting for hours in a room in the White House pondering "our heritage and our ideals" and having reactions of "shocked surprise" to the instance of Soviet disingenuousness that had just been shown them. I believe that most intelligent citizens would be relieved, not dismayed, to hear something nearer the truth: that there was not a man in that room who was capable of "shocked surprise" at anything, certainly not Soviet perfidy. Our statesmen are *not* the Pollyannas they try to appear in their published accounts of themselves. They would not be where they are if they were not fully aware of what a generally amoral world we live in; they get daily confirmation of this as they read the secret intelligence summaries.

In the second place, I think our citizens should know what it is they are admiring—or despising, or complaining about—however they happen to feel about our Government. I believe it is just as likely that they will have con-

* See *Thirteen Days*, Macmillan, 1969.

fidence in the Government as it really is as in the romanti-
cized version they infer from autobiographies of our nation's
leaders. Mr. Kennedy and others depict a lot of tired pa-
triots, of tremendous intelligence, integrity and courage,
wrestling with their consciences and with each other to arrive at decisions "affecting the future of their country and
of mankind." This might be a comforting image to anyone
not worldly enough to realize that our national leaders
(fortunately!) are neither supermen nor saints and that as
individuals they are usually reluctant to make decisions
about anything. Surely, though, most people living in a
Western economy know enough about *organizations*—General Motors, the Catholic Church, the Trades Union Council
—to grasp a more sophisticated image, one nearer to ac-
tuality, and not to lose confidence in the process.

The fact is that the key participants in top-level Government meetings where major decisions are made are not
there as tribal wise men but as heads of large departments
having at their disposal every means known to man for determining the truth of a given problem and for weighing
alternative means of solving it. Moreover, these means are
impersonal, objective and of proved effectiveness. With the
analyses that these means put before them, the top officials
of our country have remarkably little discretionary leeway.
Intelligence on foreign affairs identifies dangers and problems and indicates the variety of possible safeguards and
solutions; intelligence on domestic affairs, mainly on public
opinion, tells which of these safeguards and solutions are acceptable to our people. The job of our top decision makers,
essentially, is to match the two.

Sometimes the two are utterly irreconcilable. By an extraordinary exertion of leadership, a President can sometimes "change the input" on the domestic side of a problem:
that is, change some fundamental aspect of the problem
itself as opposed to solving the problem as it stands—the
way President Roosevelt dragged an unwilling nation into

the Second World War, for example. (This is almost never possible on the foreign side.) Usually, however, wherever domestic considerations prevent our adopting an only solution to some problem in international affairs our Government has to accept the fact of irreconcilability.

But what happens when it is a question of national survival? Here is where "cryptodiplomacy" comes in. While our citizens may take pride in the solid front of high morality that our nation presents, they can also sleep more easily at night from knowing that behind this front we are in fact capable of matching the Soviets perfidy for perfidy. We do indeed believe in honesty—although not so much as a great moral principle as because, as Benjamin Franklin said, it "is the best policy." And a policy, by official definition, is a standard solution to a constantly recurring problem and not an inviolable law. When we choose to violate any of our policies, from being truthful in our diplomacy to refraining from "interfering in the internal affairs of a sovereign nation," we find means outside the normal machinery of government. Our Government has such means. It is able to define a problem, to release forces which, largely on their own power, can effect a solution, and to disclaim any responsibility for what follows. These forces come into conflict with comparable forces of other governments, all of which have the same problems of moral "front," and a "game of nations" results.

That Game of Nations is what this book is about. I have concentrated on the Middle East, especially Egypt, mainly because I have often been there as The Guest No One Invites Again and have been directly involved in much of the "cryptodiplomacy" that accounts for the apparently illogical behavior of Middle Eastern leaders dealing with the West and of Western diplomats dealing with Middle Eastern governments. I regard the book, however, as a "case history": it is intended to reveal general truths about the relations between great powers and those small powers which, by techniques such as those of Egypt's President Nasser, are able to gain international influence out of all proportion to their inherent strengths—and even, at times, to win diplomatic victories over one or another of the Great Powers. In other words, its intent is the same as that behind the Harvard School of Business's use of the story of a particular corporation to illuminate general management principles. I hope to show that if things have gone wrong from time to time in our foreign affairs it has not been so much because of unwise decisions by our top officials as because of faulty understandings; and consequent misuse, of their own system for dealing with problems that are insoluble by ordinary means. The mistakes our Government made in dealing with President Nasser are ideally illustrative.

I wish to emphasize that this is entirely a personal account; although I got assistance from old friends in the diplomatic and intelligence services of various governments in checking details of half-forgotten events, I by no means "cleared" my manuscript with them in a way that would force on to them any responsibility for it. In deciding what to include and what to omit, I have been guided only by my central objective: to acquaint the readers, and future historians, with a facet of our Government's handling of its foreign affairs that is often the most determinative and yet is virtually unknown to the public. I have omitted information that is protected by governmental security regulations (both American and British) except where it is already in the hands of foreign powers because of previous leaks through espionage channels (e.g., Kim Philby, the British intelligence officer who defected to the Soviets) or because of exposés by journalists. I have not, however, withheld anything because of loyalty to the cabal.

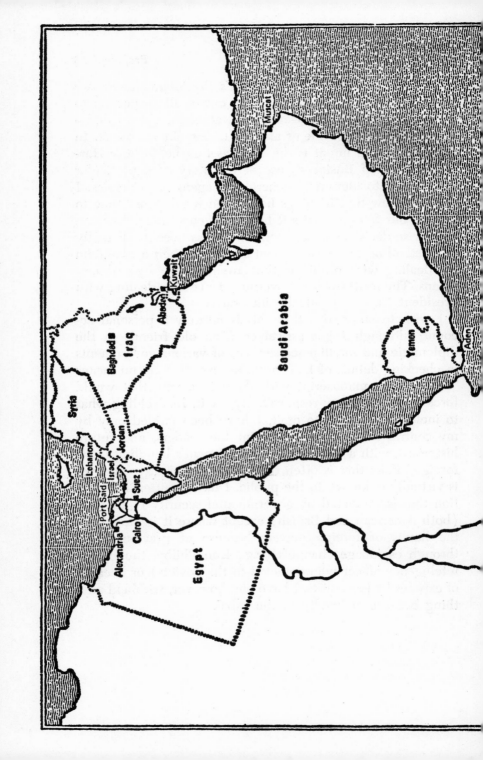

The Events
in Proper Order

Throughout, I have done a lot of chronological skipping about and overlapping. E.g., we have Nasser, Byroade and myself at dinner together on page 152 and again on page 211—the same dinner, although many earlier and later events are recorded between these two pages. There should be no confusion to the reader who sees each segment of the book as a single series of game plays; nonetheless, the following chronology should be helpful.

FEBRUARY 21, 1947: The British Embassy in Washington delivers its note on Greece and Turkey to the State Department—i.e., the end of "Pax Britannica" in the Middle East.

MARCH 12, 1947: The "Truman Doctrine" announced.

JUNE 5, 1947: The Marshall Plan announced.

JULY 1947: The Syrian elections reported in Chapter 2.

MAY 14, 1948: Creation of Israel, and beginning of first Arab-Israeli war.

MARCH 30, 1949: The Husni Za'im coup in Syria.

JANUARY 26, 1952: The burning of Cairo by mobs—"Black Saturday"; Kermit Roosevelt goes to Cairo to organize "peaceful revolution" under King Farouk.

MARCH 1952: Kermit Roosevelt gives up on "peaceful revolution" and meets Egyptian Free Officers.

15

JULY 22, 1952: Nasser's coup d'etat in Egypt.

MARCH 5, 1953: Eden, Dulles, and Eisenhower meet—the first discussion of "Middle East Defense Organization."

MAY 1953: Secretary Dulles meets Nasser.

AUGUST 1953: The overthrow of Mossadegh in Iran.

FEBRUARY 1954: Nasser removes General Naguib and openly takes over Egyptian Government—on the same day, incidentally, that President Shishakli of Syria is overthrown.

APRIL 1954: The Turks and the Pakistanis sign an agreement which leads to creation of the "Baghdad Pact."

OCTOBER 1954: The British and Egyptians sign an agreement whereby British forces evacuate the Suez Base.

NOVEMBER 1954: Colonels Eveland and Gerhardt visit President Nasser to discuss mutual-defense arrangements.

JANUARY 1955: The Baghdad Pact formally announced. Shortly afterwards Ambassador Byroade takes over from Ambassador Caffery in Cairo.

FEBRUARY 1955: Nasser's month of VIP visits—Nehru, Tito, Eden, etc. Also, the Israeli raid into Gaza, ending Nasser's "moderation" on Israeli questions.

APRIL 1955: Nasser's success at the Afro-Asian conference at Bandung, Indonesia.

JULY 1955: Shepilov visits Cairo to extend Soviet offer of arms to Nasser.

SEPTEMBER 1955: Nasser concludes the Soviet arms deal, and "Allen's Lost Weekend" in Cairo follows.

MARCH 1956: Troubles in Jordan, ending in the dismissal of General John Glubb by King Hussein, under pressure from pro-Nasser elements.

JULY 1956: Dulles announces withdrawal of U.S. financial aid to Egypt's Aswan High Dam; Nasser announces the nationalization of the Suez Canal Company.

OCTOBER 1956: The British-French-Israeli invasion of Cairo, the "Suez affair."

NOVEMBER 1956: The Syrians claim to have uncovered a "CIA plot" to overthrow the Government.

JANUARY 1957: The "Eisenhower Doctrine" announced.

APRIL 1957: Pro-Nasser coup against King Hussein of Jordan attempted and foiled.

FEBRUARY 1958: The Syro-Egyptian union: creation of the "United Arab Republic."

MAY 1958: Start of the Lebanese crisis.

JUNE 1958: Another pro-Nasser coup foiled in Jordan.

JULY 1958: The overthrow and assassination of the Iraqi royal family, Prime Minister Nuri, and other Government figures— the Qassem coup d'etat. U.S. Marines land in Lebanon and British forces land in Jordan to prevent coups in those countries.

MARCH 1959: Pro-Nasser military clique tries to overthrow Iraq's President Qassem, fails.

SEPTEMBER 1961: Syria breaks away from the United Arab Republic.

SEPTEMBER 1962: Coup d'etat in Yemen followed by formation of a republican government, Egyptian support to that government, Saudi Arabian support to the deposed royalists, and "Bob Komer's War."

FEBRUARY 1963: The fall of Qassem's government in Iraq.

OCTOBER 1965 to OCTOBER 1966: "Zakaria's year" in the United Arab Republic.

JUNE 1967: The Six-Day War between the Arabs and Israel.

NOTE: Several items have been omitted despite their historical importance because little mention was made of them in the book.

American ambassadors to Cairo during the period covered by this book were Jefferson Caffery (until January 1955), Henry Byroade (until September 1956), Raymond Hare (until January 1960), Frederick Reinhardt (until April 1961), John Badeau (until July 1964), Lucius Battle (until May 1967), and Richard Nolte for a few days in May until the U.A.R. broke relations with the United States upon outbreak of the Six-Day War with Israel.

THE GAME OF NATIONS

. . . differs from the other games—poker, war, commerce—in several important respects. First, each player has his own aims, different from those of the others, which constitute "winning"; second, every player is forced by his own domestic circumstances to make moves in the Game which have nothing to do with winning and which, indeed, might impair chances of winning; third, in the Game of Nations there are no winners, only losers. The objective of each player is not so much to win as to avoid loss.

The common objective of players in the Game of Nations is merely to keep the Game going. The alternative to the Game is war.

—From a lecture by Zakaria Mohieddin, the Vice President of the United Arab Republic, to the Egyptian War College, May 1962

1

The Washington
"Peace Game" Center

*The first prerequisite for winning a game
is to know that you're in one.*

One freezing afternoon in early 1956, word got around
Washington that a "limpet," an electric transmitting device,
had been found under the conference table in an important
State Department office. It was a Friday, and Government
employees were anxious to get away early, especially since
the sky was threatening snow, but orders went out that
skeleton staffs were to remain on duty in those offices containing secret information so as to be on hand while security
men "swept" the offices in a search for more of these de-
vices. This was a major scare. The limpet, no larger than a
double matchbox and requiring no wires, could in seconds
be stuck under any desk by a charwoman, a workman, or
any one of a dozen other categories of employees who are
given only light security checks.

The Games Center (working hours 5:30 P.M. to midnight)
was swept at about eight in the evening, when the "early
meeting" was just breaking up and its participants, some of
them in dinner dress, were looking out of the twelfth-floor
window at the stream of cars pouring down Connecticut
Avenue and wondering how they were going to make their
respective Georgetown parties. The later arrivals, who were

to keep the "board" until midnight, were removing their coats and rolling up their sleeves, ready for a rough evening. The security sweep took an hour. Nothing was found, but as long as the possibility lasted we amused ourselves with the thought of what some foreign intelligence service might make of its gleanings from a microphone placed under *that* particular conference table.

Normally, it is covered with papers and file folders and surrounded by an assortment of harassed-looking men, sometimes whispering to one another in small groups, sometimes shouting in debate, and sometimes sitting in tense silence while one of their number makes some astounding announcement. Telephones in the corners of the room, well away from the conference table, are either ringing unheeded or in the hands of men in shirt sleeves cupping the mouthpiece so that they can talk over the hubbub in the room. Secretaries run in and out. Occasionally one of the men at the table is called to one of the telephones, or leaves to be replaced by someone else, who slides into the vacated seat and begins briskly to remove papers from his briefcase.

Conversation going into such a microphone would include snatches such as these: "Has anyone checked these with the Kremlin boys?" . . . "Where the hell is De Gaulle? He should have been here an hour ago." . . . "We could lose half of Europe before Tito figures out how he should react to Nasser's Moscow visit." Monitors picking up the transmission could hardly have known that "Tito" wore a Brooks Brothers suit, a crew haircut, and a button-down collar. "De Gaulle" could have been Peter Sellers; "Anthony Eden," Sidney Greenstreet. "Konrad Adenauer" was a remarkably pretty girl who wore her hair straight and tied into a bun and hid behind horn-rimmed glasses. The "boys from the Kremlin," arriving later carrying expensive leather attaché cases, could have been the Yale Choir about to register at the Statler Hotel for a football weekend.

The foreign agents would have been eavesdropping on

what was known as the "Peace Game," years later to be travestied in *Report from Iron Mountain.* In this little-known "Games Center" a carefully selected assortment of superexperts under contract to the United States Government "gamed out" international trends and crises to predict their outcome. With the benefit of information teletyped hourly from the State Department, the CIA, the Pentagon, and other American Government agencies, teams "representing" the various countries of the world assessed their respective positions, worked out solutions, and took action— notionally, of course. "Action" was in the form of a memorandum stating what this or that "player" thought the real Tito, de Gaulle or Nasser would *really* do under the circumstances—or, more usually, a set of alternatives each of which had its "probability priority." These actions were fed back into the stream of incoming information by being put either into the computer or, in cases where the purely personal element was especially strong, on to the desk of players who had been drilled in the personal characteristics of the world leaders who would be most affected were the action real.

Rules of the Game were simple:

First, moral judgments are relevant only when they are in accord with the recognized moral standards of the various countries in the Game. Our own moral standards applied only when we were predicting what our own Government's actions and counteractions would be. "Good is good, and bad is bad wherever you go," a famous churchman once said. Such thinking was not allowed in the Game. We spent a lot of time trying to identify what the moral background of a national leader's actions *really was* (as opposed to what the nation's politicians, religious leaders, and newspapers *said* it was), but we let it go at that. We didn't label it "good" or "bad."

Second, we assume, unless it is proved otherwise, that a national leader's first objective is to stay in power or, if he cannot, to retire from power with a minimum of personal loss (however he views "loss") to himself. There are many patriotic leaders throughout the world about whom such an assumption is not justified: they would unhesitatingly sacrifice their lives, and even their reputations, in the national interest. But when we assumed that such leaders were rare exceptions our predictions seemed to come out much better than when we allowed ourselves to take a more roseate view of human leadership. Hence this rule.

Third, we assume, unless it is proved otherwise, that a national leader acts in his country's best interests as he sees them, and that he sincerely thinks he has a good case as he explains his actions to the world. Readers may remember the American congressman who got carried away in a patriotic speech and accused De Gaulle of being "un-American." So, as we played the Game, he was. But this did not make him a Bad Guy. We had no Good Guys and Bad Guys in our Game, only a lot of players each of whom was trying to win and to win according to what constituted "winning" by his own lights.

That was all the rules we needed. A "player" was given the known facts of a given situation—that is, the facts that were presumed to be known by the government that the player notionally represented; then, on the basis of his understanding of the assets at his command and the restrictions on his action, he decided what he should do. Before actually making his play, he stepped into the role of the national leader he was playing and, on the basis of his knowledge of the style and foibles of that leader, he took action—in the form, as I said earlier, of the "action memorandum" which was fed back into the system as raw information to be processed, along with other action memoranda and the material coming over the teletype machines from the State Department, the CIA and elsewhere, to make "decision information" on which players planned their subsequent moves.

Findings of the Game were not infallible, of course. Human beings, even heroic national statesmen, sometimes act unpredictably and fail to take courses of action that they seemingly have no choice but to take. But the Game performed remarkably in predicting, following, and assessing the results of Soviet moves in Europe as well as the countermoves of the various European countries and the countermoves of the Soviets to those countermoves. It was outstanding in its current assessments of the Sino-Soviet conflict: the Chinese would do this, to which the Soviets would respond that, and to which action and counter-action the rest of the world would react in such a way. After all, the Game had to be only about 85 per cent accurate (about what we expect of the U.S. weatherman) to be ahead of other means of prediction.

Predicting the general course of European politics, including the Russian, was easy. It could almost have been left to the computer—provided the computer was constantly fed high-quality up-to-date data about economics, public opinion, and other changeables. When we came to the Afro-Asian countries, however, the predicting was more difficult and we had to rely more and more on human sensitivities and instincts which we hadn't yet worked out how to program into a computer. It took more than a computer to predict the fall of Nkrumah (we thought the Ghanaian army too docile to rise), Qassim's coup d'etat in Iraq (all programmable evidence showed Nuri Pasha's Government to be virtually coup-proof), or the durability of the Viet Cong. Even after being cleared through the sensitivities and instincts of those playing the roles of leaders, Game calculations on these particular items proved wrong. I must add, though, that when Game conclusions were forwarded to the CIA, they started the CIA's analysts on the way toward *correct* estimates on these same items. The CIA, by means of highly secret information not available to Game players, was often able to know what national leaders and would-be leaders were *in fact* doing, and as the result to draw different conclusions from those produced by Game reasoning. This was as it should have been.

In general, though, it can be said that the best known methods of intelligence analysis—the Game, the CIA, the State Department, or whatever—have not proved up to predicting the actions of leaders of those countries of Africa, Asia, and South America where the economic situation appears hopeless, where the gap between expectations and realization apparently can't be closed, where the people are frustrated, and where the leaders, if they are to stay in power, must either resort to demagoguery or discover new ways of squeezing more aid from the rich countries or both. Except for those who rely entirely on demagoguery (and who are therefore easily predictable), leaders of frustrated peoples in economically hopeless countries do not play by the rules—or, rather, they make rules of their own. For example, as the Game's "De Gaulle" thinks he is playing chess with one of them he learns, to his sudden dismay, that he is not playing chess at all but "Chicken"—that remarkable contest between juvenile delinquents in the United States wherein two cars race head-on toward one another at full speed on a state highway. The winner in such a game is the one who does not "chicken out" by losing his nerve and pulling off the road to leave the way clear to the other. In "Chicken," the De Gaulle player does not have a chance. The advantage is on the side of a determined lunatic rather than that of the cleverer strategist. When players enter the Game who are prepared to switch to the rules of "Chicken" every now and then, the other players have to work out new ways of winning. Bluff is important in any game— poker, war, or business—but the "Chicken" ploy isn't exactly a bluff.

That is the first reason why the Game is a less effective instrument of intelligence when it is dealing with problems in what we might call the "non-Western world." There is a second reason. It is that the actions and reactions of our own Government are difficult to predict. Prejudice, ignorance, and other such handicaps, even on the part of some of our top officials, influence decisions to an unbelievable degree. We do not—perhaps we *cannot*—approach such questions as the Arab-Israeli issue, Vietnam, and Rhodesia with the same cold-blooded, self-interest Game considerations that we have in mind, to the exclusion of all others, when we ponder Soviet moves concerning the satellites. We cannot, for example, computerize a match between John Foster Dulles and Gamal Abdel Nasser the way we can computerize one between Joe Louis and Cassius Clay.

On many problems of the non-Western world, we begin by being confused at the apparent courses of action of the Afro-Asian leaders, and our confusion is compounded by doubt as to what our own action can be. Public opinion in general, pressures of special interest groups, Congressmen grandstanding to their respective constituencies (and who wouldn't sit still for a confidential briefing on the problems —or who, in the first place, could not be trusted not to leak such a briefing to the newspapers), and many other such factors: these keep us from taking what our Game procedures tell us is the "right" move as we face the problems with no more than cold-blooded appraisals of our national interests in mind. Thus, this or that "wrong" move by our own Government is a given factor in our calculations. We take it from there to calculate the move's effect on others, to predict their reactions, and to suggest "right" moves we might take in response to these reactions—provided, of course, that we are not prevented from so doing by these external considerations.

But one thing is certain: handicapped though we may be by ill-informed or apathetic public opinion, by pressures from groups who put their own interests above national interests, and by Congressmen who are themselves motivated by Rule Two of the Game, the top decision makers of our Government have no intention of letting our future be determined by "Chicken" proficients in Africa or Asia or anywhere else. There are limitations on what the government of a democratic country can do about its internal handicaps; there are none on what we can do in the country of others. Or rather, when our Government decides what to do about other countries it is limited only by considerations of effectiveness. If it works we can do it. When moral considerations loom up, the question is not "Can we do it?" but "Can we get away with it?" We teach our diplomats that "Our foreign policy, *to be effective,* must reflect the democratic principles and moral values of the people" (italics mine). If we do not lie about our intentions or enter into treaties we don't intend to honor it is because such behavior is ineffective—and the fact remains, of course, that we *do* lie about our intentions and fail to abide by our treaties when it is to our advantage to do so and when we can get away with it.

Naturally, I am not defending such duplicity: I have no feeling about it one way or the other. I only contend that it exists. Both games—the game of simulated circumstances we play in the Games Center and the Game of Nations that our diplomats and soldiers play for keeps in the world at large—assume this to be the case. For various reasons the innings we have had that involved President Nasser of Egypt provide the best case history to illustrate how our strategy of double morality works.

First, somehow a "Nasser" seemed all along to be essential to the drama. When we used to sit around the table during the period when I played his part, it became apparent to those with any sense of dramatic balance that a Game without Nasser would be like *Bonnie and Clyde* without C. W. Moss. In getting together the Case of Gamal Abdelnasser,*

---

* Nasser's real name is "Gamal Abdelnasser Hussein," but most of us who live or work in the Arab world have long ago stopped fighting the Western insistence on calling him by the last part of his middle name, "Nasser."

and in trying to arrange it so that it teaches lessons of universal applicability, I had the feeling throughout that had Nasser not been born our Game would have had to create him just to have on hand a kind of leader who, although nonexistent at the moment, was natural to the Game and was sure to pop up sooner or later. Nasser sees himself in the same way, of course: in his *Philosophy of the Revolution* he speaks of a "role in search of an actor" and of his attempts to fill that role. I once asked him if he thought he had succeeded, and he replied, "No, I haven't." It is true that he has not, but this is beside the point. He has come near enough to define the role. Despite the misleading description of it in *Philosophy of the Revolution,* it is by now clearly defined.

Second, that one or more Afro-Asian leaders of the Nasser type (as we will define it later) would in fact come along to fill the role was inevitable. There was no question of our dramatic sensibilities' being offended for long by the absence of a player in that particular place. In those countries where the economic and social conditions appear hopeless —or, at least, beyond the local resources of a government— the usual outcome is either for a local leader shouting "freedom from imperialism" to hold on by sheer demagoguery as his country goes to ruin, or for a practical type to take over the country with foreign aid and hold on, as a "stooge of the imperialists" or an "agent of Moscow," with foreign protection. From about 1960 onwards, however, neither type of leader has seemed capable of lasting for very long. By now, when we have seen the fall of Nkrumah, Sukarno and a long line of Syrian and Iraqi leaders, it seems safe to say that a leader's chances of sticking it out in conditions of economic and social turmoil often depend on the extent to which he weds his own style to the Nasser approach. For example, we might say that Nasser is a 90-percent "Nassertype" leader and that because this percentage seems more than enough for his particular circumstances he has managed to hold out. Nkrumah could be graded, let us say, as a 70 percent "Nasser-type" leader and, this being an insufficient grading for his circumstances, he did *not* hold out. We can go on with Sukarno of Indonesia, Qassim of Iraq, and the others—even to include King Hussein, who, although only 40 percent "Nasser-type," has managed to survive because in his particular circumstances this has so far been all he has needed. The point is that even though the perfect archetype of the Nasserist leader does not exist, a study of the nearest thing there is to one (Nasser himself) will show us much about that part in the power makeup of many other leaders which, to one extent or another, explains their ability to stay in power and to participate actively in the Game of Nations. More important, a study of how we have played the game with Nasser up to now should teach us valuable lessons about our own strategy in dealing with such leaders.

Third, despite all the objections to "leaders with a streak of Nasser in them" as Secretary Dulles once said, our Government has learned by now that they are often the least undesirable of the alternatives—from the point of view of our own interests, that is. Our Government will respect the independence of the new Afro-Asian nations to the extent that it can, and overlook instances of irresponsible behavior when our vital national interests are not concerned. But when our vital national interests *are* at stake, and when it is a question of seeing them endangered or bowing to some high moral principle, there is no question but that it is the high moral principle which will suffer. To put it more bluntly, while we normally make our plans on an assumption that certain leaders *are* in the game, whether we like them or not, situations sometimes arise in which we cannot "win" with this or that leader, and in which "loss" to him would gravely damage our national interests. In such circumstances we might seek to bring about the removal of that leader, and his replacement by another leader to whom we have a better chance of accommodating. The American view, and to some extent the British, has been that of all the alternative types of leader that might arise in the Afro-Asian world, the Nasser type is the one with which we have the best—or least bad—chance of winning our game. Winning over any one of the demagogues who come to the top in Syria, for example, would be a hollow victory: he would be thrown out and replaced by someone even worse. Nasser, however, can survive a "loss"; he can to *some* extent adjust to a "winning" of ours so that it is not necessarily a loss to him; he can get away with making an unpopular decision in instances in which we both would gain from it, but in which his populace see things otherwise—such as coming to an agreement with the Israelis. Better a wise enemy (by whatever standards) than a stupid friend.

I have for long been intrigued with the Nasser role, not only as it is played in the Washington conference room but as it is played in the real world by Nasser himself. I played the role in the Games Center off and on from the summer of 1955 until the spring of 1957, during which time I was also serving as consultant to a group called the Middle East Policy Planning Committee at the Department of State—a job that gave me the opportunity to visit Cairo and other Middle Eastern capitals where I had the chance to discuss Nasser's moves with Nasser himself and with other Middle Eastern leaders affected by them. Aside from this, I had already known Nasser for several years in the most favorable possible circumstances and was almost as well acquainted with the other important Middle Eastern leaders, both those who were against Nasser and those who were for him. There has always been some demagoguery in Nasser, of course (as there has been in every national leader, Eastern or Western, of any importance), but something other than demagoguery accounts for the way he has consistently won his game with almost all players, certainly with the United States and the Soviets if not with the Israelis. It always amazed me how, when I compared my moves in the Game in Washington with the moves Nasser actually made, my move was "worse" (in the light of Western interests) than his. When Frank Wisner, Deputy Director of the CIA, asked me a week before the Suez crisis if I did not think that Nasser, among other things, would nationalize the Suez Canal Company if the U.S. Government withheld financial aid for the Aswan High Dam, I replied, "Well, in playing his part in the Game I nationalized the Company months ago, but he didn't, so I don't know what he's going to do now." When I discussed the Suez problem with Nasser later, it became clear that he thought the Anglo-American reaction would be much *more* violent than we in Washington thought it would be, and that he was consequently more timid in his actions than he would have been operating on the basis of intelligence available to me at my Game chair.

It's the Nasser-type leaders for whom we need a winning formula. If we learn how to deal with Nasser we will thenceforth be a long way toward understanding how to deal with many other leaders who already exist in Africa, Asia and South America, as well as others who are likely to turn up during the latter part of this century. But first, let me try to clarify what is meant by "winning."

Nasser and his lieutenants tend to think of our game as being of the "zero-sum" sort—i.e., their gain is our loss, and vice versa. In poker, the perfect zero-sum game, if you add up the winnings (plus) and losses (minus) of all the players at any given moment, the sum will be exactly zero. When the United States Government and the Egyptian Government began their game over financial aid, the Americans were thinking of an amount in the region of $40,000,000 and Nasser wanted a much larger amount. Thus, if Nasser were to succeed in getting $60,000,000 from the United States he would "win" to the extent of $20,000,000 and the United States as he looked at it, would "lose" by that same amount. Needless to say, we do not think of it in quite that way.

Our concept of Games includes a wide variety of situations —e.g., a number of parachute troops losing contact with one another and trying to reassemble on the basis of calculating one another's probable reasoning and behavior, or two businessmen negotiating a deal from which both will profit. It also includes, as a tactless businessman once put it to Nasser's Minister of Industry, "the contest between a mother who wants a child to drink its milk and the child who doesn't want to do it." In any event, we regard our game as one in which, however bitter the contest, all contestants can come out all right in the end.

An objective examination of our Game of Nations behavior to date will show that the truth lies at neither extreme. When we set $40,000,000 as the amount of aid to offer Nasser we weren't putting in a "low bid"; the fact is that, had our State Department thought it could avoid a storm of protest from Congress, the figure would have been nearer $100,000,000. Moreover, we wouldn't have thought of the boost of $60,000,000—or, for that matter, the basic $40,000,000—as our loss and Nasser's gain. Instead, we honestly thought of it as an investment from which both sides would profit. On the other hand, once the $40,000,000 —or $100,000,000 or whatever—was invested we hoped it would bring gains that were strictly ours, even though they might have been at some cost to the Egyptians. The cost need not have been much, and it is good diplomacy to argue and pretend that it is nil, but when we plan our strategies in the attics of the State Department it is only benefits to ourselves that we ultimately seek. Benefits to the other side, real or imagined, are either incidental or bait by which to induce the other side to see things our way.

Zakaria Mohieddin, Nasser's most thoughtful lieutenant and until recently Vice President of the United Arab Republic, argues that even in the most clearly defined zero-sum game there are interests common to all and that Game of Nations players wanting to avoid war, to promote economic development, and to advance the brotherhood of man are no more than the equivalent of a table of poker players having a common desire to enjoy the game, to play by the rules and not cheat, to avoid fistfights as a means of settling disagreements, and so on. "We assume certain objectives to be common to all civilized mankind," he used to tell his classes at the Egyptian Army Staff College, "but we often —usually, even—have conflicting ideas with respect to how those objectives should be reached." This is as convenient a way as any of explaining the disagreement as to what kind of Game we and the Egyptians are in.

But it doesn't matter. The finely worked out theories of games, strategy of conflict, and decision systems of Thomas Schelling, Morton Kaplan and the others don't apply to this particular segment of the Game of Nations anyhow—although it might amuse these professors to hear that Nasser, Zakaria Mohieddin, and other senior officials in the UAR Government have done considerable homework on their theories. What matters is the understanding of the Egyptian leaders, shared by many of those American diplomats and businessmen who have dealt directly with them, that there is a kind of contest between us which has in it all the standard game elements: conflict of interest, rational decision making by each side as it seeks to advance its interests, and the use of bluff, deliberate misinformation, and all the other game-type stratagems. The central point of this book is that, while many excellent straightforward accounts have been written of American and British relations with the various unstable countries of Africa and Asia (we did this; they did that), insufficient attention has been given to actions and reactions back and forth as "moves" intended to "win" over the other side in resolving conflicting objectives. Less attention has been given to moves and aspects of moves that have been hidden because of their obvious departure from our publicly stated policies. The purpose of this book is to remedy the oversight.

To conclude this chapter, let me dispel any remaining notion that this is a book about Nasser. Rather, it is a case history—I hope, teaching lessons of general applicability—of relations between the United States and a "non-Western" leader of a particular kind that is likely to become increasingly prominent in international relations of the future. Although I have devoted much space to Nasser, I have tried to concentrate on aspects of his behavior that might be expected of any Afro-Asian leader, to the extent that he is the Nasser type, given (1) desperate economic and social circumstances like those in Egypt, and (2) the moves in the Game of Nations made by the United States and Britain to which he must respond.

2

The "Political Action" Experiments in Syria: 1947-49

*If you can't change the board,
change the players . . .*

On a cold and rainy February afternoon in 1947, one year before the Games Center was established, First Secretary H. M. Sichel of the British Embassy in Washington telephoned Loy Henderson, Assistant Secretary of State for Near Eastern and African Affairs. He had two messages from the Foreign Office which were "rather important." They were of a sort that normally should be delivered by the British Ambassador direct to the Secretary of State, George Marshall, but since General Marshall had already left the office for the weekend perhaps, Sichel suggested he could drop off the notes, have a "brief" chat about them, and allow Mr. Henderson a weekend of reflection on them before briefing the Secretary prior to meeting the British Ambassador on Monday morning.

Sichel arrived as State Department employees, after a comparatively dull week, were donning their raincoats and galoshes to take off for an indoor weekend. Loy Henderson, who habitually worked until eight or nine o'clock even on Fridays, had sent off all his secretaries and was alone in the office. The scene was the one of utter calm that skillful dramatists often establish to provide the psychological setting for a shattering announcement.

The announcement, which Mr. Sichel delivered in the course of his "brief chat," was certainly shattering. The two messages were official notification that the *Pax Britannica*, which had kept order in much of the world for over a century, was at an end. Specifically, His Majesty's Government could no longer afford the $50,000,000 or so that was required to support the resistance of the Greek and Turkish Governments to Communist aggression either, as in the first case, by guerrilla warfare or, in the second, by direct military action of the Soviet Union. Either the United States Government would fill the gap, or it would go unfilled— or it would be left to the Russians. Mr. Henderson, whose considerable diplomatic experience included assignments in Moscow and other capitals in the Soviet orbit, didn't need a weekend of reflection to realize that more than Greece and Turkey was at stake. The vacuum of which these two countries were a part extended throughout all of southern Europe that was not already behind the Iron Curtain, and through North Africa and the Middle East. With the British announcement, delivered so calmly by Mr. Sichel, the United States was given the choice of becoming an active world power—an "on-the-ground" world power, as a lecturer at the State Department's Foreign Service Institute was later to put it—or seeing the Soviets become a more menacing feature of world politics than Nazi Germany could ever have been. Mr. Sichel said, "I hope I haven't spoiled your weekend."

The cold and rain of that February afternoon were, in a way, symbolic. The winter of 1946–47 had been one of Britain's worst. There was a shortage of coal to start with, and a series of blizzards froze transport of what coal there was, besides killing the winter wheat and causing impossible working conditions. Many factories closed down and some five million workers became unemployed. The British Government of the day—which, blizzards or no blizzards, was preoccupied with old-age benefits, shorter working hours, and what American businessmen were calling "production de-incentives"—was ill equipped to deal with its domestic problems, let alone administer the bold approach to foreign affairs that the new Game of Nations required. Britain, like France and Italy (both of which, incidentally, were themselves in danger of Communist takeover), was in serious economic trouble. All she had to offer was sound advice— if, indeed, American diplomats and intelligence officials were in a mood to take it.

Secretary Marshall, it happened, had left his office early on Friday afternoon to take a train to Princeton, where he was to make his first major speech since assuming office, a speech in which he was to express his hope that young Americans would "fully understand the special position that the United States now occupies in the world, geographically, financially, militarily and scientifically" and that they would help their country to "develop a sense of responsibility for world order and security" and "a sense of overwhelming importance of this country's acts and failures to act in relation to world order and security." He delivered the speech the next morning with no knowledge of the diplomatic notes concerning Greece and Turkey. Meanwhile, in Washington, Loy Henderson had called Undersecretary of State Dean Acheson away from a dinner at a South American embassy, and the two of them discussed the problem until late into the night of February 21, then again the next morning with the heads of bureaus and staffs most directly concerned. By the following Monday morning, when Secretary Marshall arrived in his office, his principle subordinates had spent two days digesting the implications of the problem and were all set to define it. Mr. Acheson put in a call to George Kennan, who was enjoying himself intellectually at the National War College after a highly successful tour of duty as deputy chief of mission in the American embassy in Moscow, and later that day Mr. Kennan arrived at the State Department to join Loy Henderson in the formation of a special committee to work out plans to meet the changed circumstances.

The "intelligence community"—the Army, Navy and Air Force intelligence services and the newly formed "Central Intelligence Group," forerunner of the CIA—was not informed of the crisis until many hours later, about the same time that stories of it began to appear in the press. Here the problem was taken, more than anything else, as the occasion for getting in some good licks in the organizational squabble: the CIG and its personnel, mostly holdovers from the wartime Office of Strategic Services, was already being attacked by the military services for being "a wild-eyed bunch of intellectuals whose colleges don't want them back," and the new situation seemed to make the accusation even more appropriate and to add the argument that it called for "a highly practical approach, such as only services under experienced military discipline can provide," as one Pentagon memorandum put it.

Perhaps I am inordinately conscious of the organizational aspects of the February "Battle of Washington" because I was, at the time, a member of the management consulting team studying the organizational mess that then existed in the intelligence community and making recommendations to remedy it. I do remember, though, that a senior officer of Army G-2 (Military Intelligence) stated more or less publicly that the sudden necessity for the United States to get directly into the cold war that was developing could "save" our Government's overseas intelligence assets, which might otherwise be swallowed up by the new agency. At any rate, the then Director of Central Intelligence, Admiral Sidney Sauers, won the bureaucratic battle and won it so completely that the new group wound up with *all* the responsibility for creating the undercover apparatus, in both intelligence and "other activities," capable of doing its part in the overall program being devised by the State Department.

It is always easy for a historian twenty years after an event to see the folly of those involved in it. One must remember, though, that even events that are recognized at the time as being of major historical importance are dealt with by human beings who, regardless of their perspicacity, are motivated largely by topical considerations. "Everybody" knows that we wouldn't now be in the Cold War trouble we are in had we not been so weak at Yalta, had we insisted on keeping our troops in Europe at the end of the Second World War until Soviet intentions had become clearer, and so on. But anybody who was directly involved in the postwar decisions that now look so unwise will remember that, in the heat of the circumstances of the time, our decision makers could hardly have done otherwise. Similarly, the true shape of our game with the Soviets following the announced withdrawal of the British from Greece and Turkey now seems clear enough, but at the time our decision makers were restricted by handicaps that aren't apparent to historians of today writing about the period. There were two principal ones.

First, there was the necessary discrepancy between the publicly stated attitude of our Government toward world questions and the attitudes held in the inner sanctums of the State Department and the Pentagon. Early in 1946, George Kennan, during the last few weeks in his assignment as deputy chief of mission in Moscow, wrote a letter to the State Department which correctly outlined the shape of the oncoming Cold War and which was immediately accepted as the definitive analysis of Soviet intentions, outlook and behavior. At the same time, Mr. Kennan argued convincingly that if Europe was to be divided the blame should be placed on the Russians and not on ourselves. Winston Churchill, in a speech delivered at Fulton, Missouri, referred to the "Iron Curtain," and the presence of President Truman at his side implied official U.S. Government endorsement of such an attitude. Apart from this one lapse, however, official policy was still to pretend that the "spirit of Yalta" guided our actions and that the United Nations, with understanding and cooperation between the great "peace-loving" powers, would maintain order throughout the world by thrashing things out between themselves in a civilized manner. Internal Government communications, written or oral, that indicated otherwise were marked T O P S E C R E T. The fact that we were entering upon a Cold War with the Soviets was concealed in every possible way—even to the extent of application of misnomers to departmental units working on "Iron Curtain" questions.

The second handicap was the almost total lack of personnel equipped to fight what Admiral Sauers, director of the Central Intelligence Group, called "a war that isn't a war." The OSS had left an impressive array of secret intelligence assets in Europe, but there was little to replace those of the British in Greece, Turkey, and other countries that constituted the new vacuum. If our strategy was to be one of trying to stop the Cold War while at the same time fighting it—or, at least, of pretending to have only a defensive posture toward it—we would need a highly sophisticated kind of diplomatic-intelligence machinery that did not yet exist. The Near East and Africa Division of the State Department was weak enough; the assets of the CIG and the Pentagon intelligence services in the vacuum area were virtually nonexistent. There were a sprinkling of OSS agents of various nationalities, mostly archeologists and missionaries of odd sects, administered from Washington by retired college professors, and a miscellany of businessmen available for the odd chore of intelligence or cryptodiplomacy, and that was about all. Recruitment was obviously the item of first priority in assuming our new responsibilities.

Or, rather, it was priority number two. The first priority in any new program is to decide exactly what the program is to accomplish. In general, what we were trying to accomplish was to fill the vacuum left by the British departure from Greece and Turkey—a vacuum which, as I have said, included not only Greece and Turkey, but a larger area, the whole Middle East—and to do so in a manner that was consistent with our means and ways of doing things. We were entering into a new game, and as we saw it, the other players were mainly the governments of the countries in the vacuum rather than, as yet, the Soviets. And, as we said in the last chapter, it was to be a game that was partly a "game of cooperation" and partly a "game of conflict." Thus, the decision as to what, exactly, the new program was to accomplish was one of determining our precise objectives in the Middle East, with due regard to the extent to which these objectives would come into conflict with the objectives of Greece, Turkey and the other governments of the Middle East.

This wasn't easy. As a harassed planning officer at the State Department said, "We don't really have objectives; we only have problems"—problems arising from Zionist intentions to create a Jewish state in Palestine and Arab intentions to prevent them, from disagreement with our allies (and in the Pentagon itself) over what part the Middle East should play in future defense plans, and from the question of what official support should be given to American oil companies which were becoming increasingly active in the area. Later, our objectives shaped up as follows: (1) to prevent regional struggles that might involve ourselves and the Soviets, thereby turning the Cold War into a hot war; (2) to enable governments in the area to become sufficiently strong, politically and militarily, to participate effectively in the Free World's efforts to contain international Communism; (3) to effect environmental conditions favoring American commercial investment. In 1947, however, the only "regional struggle" on the horizon was the Arab-Israeli war, and both our Government and the Soviets were at that time far from decided where their sympathies lay; the possibility that the governments of the area wouldn't receive our political and military kibitzing gratefully and uncritically was not fully appreciated in Washington; and it seemed obvious at the time that "environmental conditions favoring American commercial investment" should be desired as much by the Middle Easterners as by ourselves, and that if these conditions did not exist already it was because of deficiencies in Middle Eastern leadership.

That, as we saw it, was the central problem: if the Middle Eastern countries only had leaders who were incorruptible and, as one ambassador said, "intelligent enough to know what they should do for the good of their countries and with guts enough to do it," then we would reach our objectives, *whatever* they turned out to be. But these countries, with one or two exceptions, had no such leaders. Thus, until we had time to formulate solid long-range objectives we were to concentrate our attention on finding means for ensuring the rise of "the right kind of leaders," as we referred to them in those days.

This is entirely according to the rules of the Game of Nations. You do the best you can to "win" (win *over* those with whom you are in conflict, and win *with* those with whom you are in cooperation), but when you see that this can't be done you either modify your ideas of what constitutes "winning" or try to change those players who block your way. It was implicit in statements in confidential memoranda of the U.S. Government in early 1947 that our diplomatic and intelligence services, such as they were, were to bring about changes in the leadership of certain Middle Eastern countries. But the historian looking back over the last twenty years to get at the reasoning behind our actions during that period is likely to forget this: although we were beginning to talk a "realistic" line—the need for espionage and covert political-action facilities, for facing up to the Russians on their own terms, and so on—the predominant thinking was still extremely idealistic. An examination of State, Pentagon and CIG (and later CIA) documents gives the impression that we were publicly idealistic and secretly Machiavellian. Anyone who participated in the early Game of Nations in the Middle East, however, will remember that we weren't really Machiavellian and that the current idealism was almost as prominent in our covert activity as it was in our overt.

The current got stronger as the recruiting got under way. To begin with, the holdover OSS officers, "staff" and "reserve" officers of the diplomatic service who were in cultural and informational assignments, and even some of the regular diplomats were mostly former missionaries and romantics inclined to believe that changing the leadership in Middle Eastern countries, especially the Arab ones, was a matter of removing certain artificial props which were keeping in power leaders who, by rights, shouldn't have been there in the first place. A lecturer in a joint State-CIG orientation course said, "Politicians in Syria, Lebanon, Iraq, and Egypt seem to have been elected into power, but what elections! The winners were all candidates of foreign powers, old landowners who tell their tenants and villagers how to vote, or rich crooks who can buy their votes. But peoples of these countries are intelligent, and they have a natural bent for politics. If there is a part of the world which is crying for the democratic process the Arab world is it." The lecturer was enunciating the commonly held view of officers already in the various services. The outlook was reinforced by new officers coming in from the outside world—from the business world, from Madison Avenue, from the colleges, and from other places where one is accustomed to view human intelligence and practicality with respect.

Our aboveboard response to the British diplomatic notes of February 21, 1947, was the Truman Doctrine, which was announced, after three weeks of hectic State Department and White House staff work, on March 12. Announcement of the Marshall Plan followed shortly; in July and from then on a flood of editorial, semiofficial and official comment (the latter mainly in the form of college commencement addresses delivered by top government officials) began to deal openly with the Cold War and our policy of "containing" Soviet expansion. Although this has all been covered by a number of excellent books, what has not been publicly recorded is the campaign that our Government waged beneath the surface to fill the vacuum. It is to this "war that isn't a war," as the Central Intelligence Agency was later to call it, that I will confine my attention.

The "war" started long before the creation of the CIA. The team of specialists who were to fight it were drawn from the State Department, from the Department of Defense, and from a miscellany of temporary bureaus, some of which were left over from the Second World War and some of which were created for the transitional period between war and peace. In them was a memorable mixture of overconfidence and overcaution, the former showing up largely in the shape of naïve criticism of the old masters, the British, and the latter in the shape of an inclination to lean on British diplomatic and intelligence resources to the maximum extent possible. At any rate, the prevailing view that emerged from the mixture was one of "we'd better try walking before we start running," and it was decided that our initial venture of interfering in the internal affairs of a sovereign nation would be a modest one, protected with a maximum of justification, and without the help—or even the knowledge—of the British.

Where to try it? With the Greeks and the Turks we had no quarrel; they wanted the same things we wanted and had adequate leadership to go after them. To the extent that we were in a game with them at all it was a "game of cooperation." With the Iranians, of whose leadership we also approved, our game was one of 90 percent cooperation (at the start, at least) and 10 percent conflict. It was with the Arab countries that we were almost totally in conflict—and this, we thought, was almost entirely due to mischievous or misguided leadership. We believed that under more enlightened and effective leadership they would be natural allies. The Arabs had every reason to fear the Soviets, and not us, and they should have welcomed our offers of protection. Our oil companies were going to make them rich. They would be the principal beneficiaries of an "amicable settlement of the Palestine question." The refusal of their leaders to see it this way was regarded by our planners as ample reason and justification for us to overthrow them—or rather, to enable their own people to overthrow them. If national leadership anywhere in the world was such as to justify our interference in its affairs, we thought, it was Arab leadership.

Iraq was the first possibility, tempting because it was a police state, with an unpopular government over it, and we could ease our consciences with the thought that we were only opening the way for a "popular" government. But this was one country where even an experienced political-action team, let alone a brand-new one, wouldn't be able to budge without British knowledge and acquiescence. Saudi Arabia wasn't (here we sought a less distasteful way of putting it but couldn't think of one) "ready for democracy." Lebanon, Jordan and Egypt were dropped for other reasons. By elimination, Syria was left. Syria was in good shape economically, it had a population untamed by years of Turkish and French subjection, and there were believed to be ideal conditions for democratic elections which would be won by intelligent and cooperative leaders. Finally, it appeared that the "artificial props which keep unrepresentative politicians in power" were especially vulnerable to the weapons that we intended to use.

In fact, the prevailing view was that we wouldn't need weapons at all—not, anyhow, in the sense that we contemplated for the more sophisticated operations we would launch after gaining experience. All that was needed was a discreet nudge here and there to encourage the more desirable politicians to campaign by fair methods, plus nationwide (but "unofficial") observation of the politicking and the polling to convey to the campaigners that incidents of pressure and manipulation would be found out and publicized. This would be accomplished not only by regular diplomats

—who, even when restricted by diplomatic proprieties, can manage impressive amounts of nudging and observing—but by foreign newsmen who were invited in for the purpose, and by various types of secret agents who avoided any appearance of promoting pro-American candidates but merely passed the word that "truly patriotic" candidates would be given a fair break. Protests of Syrian leaders were forestalled by means of a hint dropped by the American Chargé d'Affaires with the Foreign Ministry: "We believe that these elections of yours are going to be a model for all newly liberated countries, so I'm sure you won't mind our observing them." Private American companies and individuals, even the missionaries, did their part in intimidating those Syrians who had traditionally intimidated the citizens at election time and stood in the way of their voting according to their own inclinations. Landowners, employers, ward bosses, and precinct police chiefs were all warned, directly and indirectly, that "the people" must be allowed their complete freedom of choice, and that homegrown suppression was every bit as reprehensible, in the eyes of the world, as Turkish or French repression. The head of the Methodist mission extracted a promise from the senior Kurdish scribe "union" that they and their colleagues wouldn't take advantage of Kurdish voters' illiteracy to write in names of candidates of their own choosing.

The "discreet nudge here and there" (a phrase that I borrow from a highly circumspect "Personal and Confidential" letter written from someone in the State Department to the Chargé d'Affaires) also included the following: (1) a campaign, put on by the newly established American oil-company offices, to "get out the vote"—i.e., huge posters in public places exhorting the Syrian people, finally freed from centuries of foreign rule, to "go to the polls and vote for the candidate of your choice" (to the bewilderment of the Syrian people, no particular candidates being mentioned by name); (2) arrangements with *service* taxicab drivers to take voters to the polls free of charge—on condition that the drivers spurn tempting rewards from the candidates for them to be selective in their choice of passengers, or to influence the passengers' votes; (3) automatic, tamperproof voting machines, on the latest American pattern, were provided for all central metropolitan areas. The election, as the Legation political officer promised Washington, would be "as American as apple pie."

To say that the elections did not come up to our expectations would be an understatement. In Homs, the voting was a model of propriety, but only because the landlords had made it clear to their tenants that they were to disregard the "communist and imperialist nonsense" suggested by the posters in the town square and vote strictly according to instructions. Everywhere else, however, this first "free" election was an occasion for the Syrians, who had been brought up in the belief that *hkuma* (government) was an inconvenience imposed by foreigners, to exercise their native penchant for disruption and venality. There were gunfights and fistfights in which scores of people were killed or wounded. The simple voter saw in the elections a newfound opportunity to get a fair price for his vote, or to boost some relative into an office from which he could pass out largesse to his family. The *service* drivers banded together in a kind of union to sell their services to one candidate or another in order to get the maximum price for their cooperation. The Kurdish scribes broke their promise to the Methodist missionary. The voting machines, most of which didn't work properly to start with because of irregularities in the electric current, were sabotaged—all but two, that is, which worked efficiently enough except that, in the end, the losing candidates refused to accept defeat at the hands of "imperialist technology" and demanded, and got, recounts by hand which naturally settled the scores in their favor. And since ours was the only government of a major power that didn't give financial support, would-be "pro-American" candidates defected to the British, the French and the Russians, all of whom were astute enough to circumvent the "free-election" strictures our project had imposed—although they were inhibited by a feeling that we couldn't be all *that* naïve and a suspicion that our cunning Madison Avenue minds had concocted some novel approach to Syrian politics that involved subtleties beyond their Old World grasp.

I hasten to add that the Americans, official and otherwise, who were involved in the Syrian election project of 1947 were far from naïve; they were only new to the game. Neither our Government nor the private business concerns entering the Middle East had anyone who was experienced at this kind of operating, which was routine to the other powers. Accordingly, the State Department began training its promising personnel—in Arabic, Middle Eastern cultures, and all the rest—and to comb the country for the few Americans who were already qualified. Parker Hart, Rodger Davies, and Harrison Symmes (to name but a few) are officers who have since become stalwarts in the service but who would have left the Department from boredom had not the need for good officers been so great in 1947 and 1948 that they were shoved ahead into positions of responsibility. Charles Ferguson, a pioneer in "crash" language training, was brought in from Harvard University to set up courses in Arabic for young diplomats—with the result, incidentally, that within ten years the number of Arabic speakers in American diplomatic missions approached that of the British (allowing for difference in size of missions) and was roughly four times that of the Soviets. As a "coordinator of unconventional political activity" the Department assigned to Beirut Archibald Roosevelt, a grandson of Theodore Roosevelt, who had lived for months at a time with Arab, Kurdish, and Persian tribes; who spoke Arabic, Kurdish, Uzbek, Russian, French, Spanish and three or four other languages; and who had in past assignments shown himself to be a remarkable combination of an intellectual and a good organization executive. By 1952, our diplomatic service in the Middle East was as good as our Government was capable of providing.

But 1947–52 were lean years for our side in the Game of Nations. First, the sudden independence of nations that had for centuries been under colonial rule posed problems that were beyond the experience of our diplomatic service. Second, the problems were greatly exacerbated by the Arabs' belief—which, justified or unjustified, was sincere—that our Government was uncritically backing the Zionists and, later, the Israelis. Third, the quality of diplomatic talent being assigned to missions in the Arab world was not matched by the quality of that assigned to the Department of Near Eastern and African affairs in Washington where policy was made—or rather, as one of the desk officers used to tell us, "You fellows out there are field-oriented, whereas we back here have to be Washington-oriented," i.e., sensitive to the moods of Congress and the press, neither of which had much interest in the Arab world.

As the result, American diplomacy in the Arab world between 1947 and 1952 consisted largely in routine communication with the various governments whereby our chiefs of mission delivered occasional "our Government is concerned" messages and tried to convince the various Foreign Offices that our Government was not under the control of the Zionists. Cryptodiplomacy at the local level was confined to passing out campaign assistance, roughly comparable to what the British, French and Soviets were passing out, to candidates of our choice—in Syria, Lebanon, Iraq and Egypt. Our attitude was one of let's-wait-until-we-know-what-we're-doing. In the Game of Nations we were like the wise poker player who, coming to a table of unfamiliar faces, sits out for a hand or two or makes no more than token bets.

There was a later operation in Syria, however, which represented a departure from this attitude and which, for two reasons, is worth special study: first, it became a classic example of how *not* to interfere in the internal affairs of a sovereign nation and it provided a valuable catalogue of natural mistakes to be avoided in later operations of the kind; second, it throws some light on the importance—or unimportance—of the choice of individuals assigned to the operation as opposed to the advisability of the operation itself. At the time, senior State Department officials believed that the vacuum left by the British, plus our inescapable pro-Zionist position on Palestine, made success impossible, and that "minimizing failure" was all that could be hoped for. Consequently, instructions going to the various diplomatic missions from Washington were normally about as clear as prophecies of the Oracle at Delphi, allowing mission chiefs to interpret them as they chose—taking the blame for anything that went wrong for their so doing, while leaving the political appointees in Washington to grab the credit for anything that, by some fluke, came out right. Under such circumstances, the integrity, resourcefulness, and courage of the "field" officers were all-important.

The head of our Legation in Damascus, with the rank of Minister, was James Michael Keeley, a career officer of the highest integrity, who had been appointed to the post because he could be counted upon to remain calm in crises, to accept the delegation of authority, and to make decisions without referring to Washington on every detail. The Political Officer was Deane Hinton, age twenty-four, with an abrasive personality, a near-genius intellect, and a youthful kind of guts and integrity that matched the more mature kind of his boss, Jim Keeley. The man-of-action in the Embassy was the famous Major Stephen Meade, the Colonel Meade who will figure in a later chapter. The cryptodiplomat in the Legation was myself.

I had been sent to Damascus in September 1947 with instructions to make unofficial contact with President Quwwatli and other key officials in the Syrian Government and to probe for means of persuading them, on their own, to liberalize the political system. The first part of the assignment was easy. By the time Keeley reported for duty, some six months later, I had established an easy personal relationship with the President and with most of those around him who were worth persuading. The probe, however, produced only negative results: it was clear to Keeley, upon reading my report, that Quwwatli and his establishment had no intention of liberalizing anything and that they would remain blind to the increasingly apparent fact: that a serious political explosion was looming. "We have before us only two alternatives," said Keeley, "both of them undesirable"—by which he meant that either political opportunists, with covert Soviet support, would shortly stage a bloody uprising, or the Syrian army, with *our* covert support, would take over the Government and maintain order until a peaceful revolution could be brought about. Keeley disliked the latter alternative almost as much as the first, but he thought it would at least lessen the chances of bloodshed and give the responsible elements in the society a fair chance against those elements whose only strength was a capacity for violence.

The operation was the Husni Za'im coup of March 30, 1949. A "political action team" under Major Meade systematically developed a friendship with Za'im, then Chief of Staff of the Syrian Army, suggested to him the idea of a coup d'etat, advised him how to go about it, and guided him through the intricate preparations in laying the groundwork for it—a degree of participation which was only suspected by Syria's leading politicians and which was later written off as "typical Syrian suspicion" by Western journalists and students who interviewed the principal participants and examined the relevant documents. So far as the outside world knew, the coup was strictly a Syrian affair, although it was afterwards assumed, fairly generally, that Za'im was "the Americans' boy."

Details of the coup itself are not particularly relevant to our subject, but a few general observations are in order:

First, the State Department was informed of the coming coup as soon as it became a serious possibility. If details were not reported it was because the Department made it clear enough that it preferred not to have the details. References to the pre-coup involvement of Meade's political-action team were ignored. The tenor of the Department's replies was "If Za'im seems bent on changing the Government, the Department sees no reason to discourage him so long as we believe he will return to a parliamentary form of government as soon as practicably possible." Za'im, it happened, had made it clear that he had no such intention. Rather, he would (1) put the corrupt politicians in jail, (2) reorganize the Government along more efficient lines, (3) institute much-needed social and economic reforms, and (4) "do something constructive" about the Arab-Israeli problem—this last being what neutralized any inclination the Department might have had to give us explicit instructions to lay off.

Second, the attitude of the Minister, Jim Keeley, should be recorded. Keeley strongly believed in democratic processes—free elections, free press, and all the rest—and didn't share the Syrians' low opinions of themselves, their belief that they were unable to accept responsibility for their own actions but behaved honestly or dishonestly, intelligently or stupidly, leftishly or rightishly, only according to the dictates of "foreign influence." Nonetheless, he believed that the situation in Syria before the Za'im coup was so inherently disruptive that law and order was the first requirement, no matter how it was attained. Overestimating our influence on Za'im (as we all did), he thought that once Za'im ruled the country by sheer "naked power," as Bertrand Russell calls it, our persuasiveness, sweetened by a little military aid, would result in his introducing democratic processes as rapidly as the society would permit. Keeley loved the Syrians, and he persisted in a belief that they were "naturally democratic." He believed that a short period of dictatorship might quarantine them from "foreign influences," especially the imaginary ones, long enough to make them stand on their own feet and develop a truly independent outlook.

Keeley spoke for the representative chief of mission of the time: later, most of our other ambassadors and ministers in the Arab world were to tell me that had they been in Keeley's place they would have seen the situation as he' saw it. Similarly, Deane Hinton, our youthful political officer, spoke for the young idealists in the Foreign Service. He was devoted to Keeley, but he spoke up loudly and persistently when he disagreed with him, and he insisted on getting his disagreements on record. Hinton has since grown up, but in those days he was a devout Goo-Goo—one who believes that even in a country like Syria, Good Government is not only desirable but possible. On the matter of Za'im, he was entirely in opposition to Keeley, Meade and the rest of us—so much so that Meade convinced the Minister that Hinton should be left out of last-minute planning. The first Hinton knew of the actual coup was on the day it happened. As he, Meade and I were making a reconnaissance tour of Damascus that morning, he fulminated at length on the theme: "I want to go on record as saying that this is the stupidest, most irresponsible action a diplomatic mission like ours could get itself involved in, and that we've started a series of these things that will never end." He subsequently wrote a dispatch on the subject and sent it by slow boat to the Department, where it now gathers dust in the archives. Things have, of course, come out as he predicted.

The rest of us in the U.S. Legation thought we had opened the door to Peace and Progress. Za'im had been so "amenable to suggestion" (as we said in our reports) before the coup that it never occurred to us that things would change afterwards. For a while, until official recognition by our Government of the new regime came through, they did not change. Outrageous though it may sound, Meade spent the second day of Za'im's era telling the new dictator who should be Ambassador to the Court of St. James's, which officers should be promoted into diplomatic positions, and what diet should be given deposed President Quwwatli by his jailer so as not to irritate his ulcer. Immediately following recognition, however, Za'im became a new man—revealing himself suddenly one morning as he brusquely informed Meade and myself that we were henceforth to leap to our feet as he entered the room and to replace the familiar '*tu*' (Za'im spoke French; he had no English) with "*vous*"—or, better still, with "*Excellence.*" Except for this new note of formality, relations remained friendly enough for the rest of his tenure, but day by day it became clearer and clearer that certain *sine qua nons* had been left out of our plans and that we had better be thinking about a replacement for Za'im when he fell, as he surely would—shortly.

Za'im demonstrated, to all who would study his case, that being a stooge of the most powerful government on earth was not enough to ensure tenure. There was no magic in this widely (and correctly) assumed status, nor was there any magic in the mechanics of command in which he put so much faith. He hadn't learned the modern theory of command—that is, that the commander's principal function is to maintain conditions in which subordinates have no alternative but to accept them. A military man who had lived all his life under such conditions, Za'im took them for granted. He treated his immediate subordinates, his fellow colonels who should have been the shoulders of his "command structure," as though they had no choice but to carry out his instructions, and without question. After some months, it was clear that he represented no one but himself, whether dealing with his American patrons or with his own people, and other choices began to occur to his immediate subordinates. On the morning of August 14, 1949, a group of these associates, fronted by one Sami Hennawi but actually led by Colonel Adib Shishakli, surrounded Za'im's house, killed him, buried him in the French cemetery ("We are doing you the favor of treating him as a French agent," Shishakli told me) and took over the Government. Exactly four months later, Shishakli jailed Hennawi and ran the country himself through a succession of civilian front men until November 21, 1951, when he came into the open as Syria's "strong man." Shishakli fled the country in February 1954, in the face of yet another coup, and since then coups and countercoups have occurred so frequently in that country that even those of us who know it well are unable to keep track of which predator is currently in charge.

Perhaps we didn't learn all we should have learned from the Za'im experience, but in retrospect the following conclusions seem to stand out clearly enough:

1. The problem was not one of bringing about a change of government, but of making the change stick—to the end, of course, of having a new government that would become increasingly efficient and beneficial. A member of Syria's rotating oligarchy recently told a foreign correspondent, "The day is gone when a colonel can roar into Damascus with a few tanks and take over the city." Unfortunately, he is wrong. Syria remains the most coup-prone country in the Middle East—so much so that Western Governments would now prefer to see it settle down with one government, *whatever* its political complexion, rather than have more coups. If we were ever to interfere in Syria's affairs again, it would be only to bring about a government that had a chance of building a durable power base and of surviving.

2. However distasteful our idealists may find the idea of elites, in Syria we should have sought a potential new ruling group rather than a single leader. What Syria needed for a genuine revolution was not a leader in isolation—some unprincipled colonel in the Chief of Staff position, or one

who could get into it long enough to order troops about—
but an elite, inseparably bound to a sub-elite which, in turn,
had roots in the populace. Za'im held power (for four
months, anyhow) the way the leader of a criminal gang
holds power, and he lost it for the same reason—because
other members of the "gang" began to suspect that he was
going to sell them out. His successors fared somewhat
better only because they were better tightrope walkers and
were more successful at palliating the suspicions of their
lieutenants—or in some cases, at playing the lieutenants off
against one another. The politicians in alliance with them
have been so only as a *marriage de convenance*, not because
of any real affinity. And the politicians, in turn, have only a
pretense of interdependence with the populace at large in
the form of political dogmas which, having no real correla-
tion with the religion, native ideologies, or myths of the
country, are no more than propaganda. The politicians are
therefore mere camp followers to the Army; when the Army
goes they go—or rather, if they manage to survive it is
because of fast footwork and ability to alter their colors
rather than because of any independent strength. A political
structure of this sort (1) can't last; (2) is ruinous for the
country; (3) makes for a messy Game of Nations: although,
as adversaries, there is no danger of their winning over any
of the other players. (For all their noise, the Israelis worry
less about the Syrians than, say, the Jordanians.) It is un-
nerving for the other players to live with the constant possibility that a player, even a habitual loser, might kick over
the table.

3. The leader or leaders (i.e., the oligarchy) who can take
over a government, remain in power and thenceforth behave constructively are bound to be of a sort that precludes
them from being our agents, or even behaving in a fashion
that will be entirely to our liking. In short, in assisting to
power a leader who will provide the "good" we are seeking,
we must face the fact that there may be some "bad" arising

from what he has to do to stay in power after he gets there. The political structure that must exist under him, if "natural" (as it has to be if it is to survive), will inevitably have elements in it that are hostile to our interests. A basic point of this book is that our strategy in the Game of Nations, at least so far as the non-Western world is concerned, is largely a matter of accepting at the table a number of players who, inevitably, will not be entirely to our liking, and whom we can "win" over only by tactics that are quite different from those we use in playing with "game of conflict" opponents such as the Soviets and the Chinese, and from those we use with friends with whom we are in a "game of cooperation."

3

The Search for a True Leader in Egypt: 1951–52

. . . but settle for a true player, not a pawn.

During the let's-wait-until-we-know-what-we're-doing period (1947–52), especially after the Za'im fiasco, Department officials with bright ideas about how we could get some acceptable and influential Arab player to the game board kept such schemes pretty much to themselves. Except for a little harmless spying and routine election rigging, "We do not interfere with the internal affairs of sovereign nations" was still the guiding motto. Even after the Syrian elections of 1947, a top State Department official briefing a group of Foreign Service officers newly assigned to the Middle East could say, with apparent sincerity, "We only seek conditions wherein the people of those countries are free to choose, without pressure from anyone, whatever it is they really want." The belief persisted, despite mounting evidence to the contrary, that Middle Easterners, for all their fuzzy oratory, were too practical to "really want" Communism or any of the other political notions that would strengthen the positions of other powers at the cost of American interests, or generally disturb "the march of the area toward peace, stability and prosperity" which, anyhow, were "the only real objectives of the United States in this part of the world." Truly free elections, many State Department officials believed, could only result in the rise of high-minded leaders who would cooperate with the "Free World." Even the Arabs, whom these officials believed to be the most politically corrupt Middle Easterners, could and would work out their own destinies, and do so by democratic processes as we understood them in the West, if only foreign influences could be neutralized.

Secretary of State Dean Acheson, however, was not so sure. Publicly, he spoke exclusively of conventional diplomacy; privately, he believed that the possibility of some unconventional activity to help along the natural forces was at least worth considering. Accordingly, in late 1951 he borrowed Kermit Roosevelt from the newly formed Central Intelligence Agency to head a highly secret committee of specialists—some from the State Department, some from the Department of Defense, and some brought in as consultants from business concerns and universities (none from the CIA except Roosevelt himself)—to study the Arab world, with particular reference to the Arab-Israeli conflict, to identify the problems and assign priorities to them and to work out solutions, *any* solutions, whether or not they fitted orthodox notions of proper governmental behavior.

Within a month or so several ideas were developed, all of them unconventional. Someone advanced the idea of promoting a "Moslem Billy Graham" to mobilize religious fervor in a great move against Communism and actually got as far as selecting a wild-eyed Iraqi holy man to send on a tour of Arab countries. The project did no harm, and the managing of it taught the committee much about what was wrong with their basic planning assumptions—lessons that were put to good use years later when King Feisal's advisers put Feisal up to much the same kind of project, with Feisal himself as holy man. Subsequent projects, in more or less the same John Buchan vein, were just as harmless and taught even more about the do's and don'ts of rallying Arabs. Nothing as risky as the Za'im operation was attempted.

In early 1952, the committee of specialists finished a situation report on the Game of Nations in the Middle East, taking into account not only the positions of our friends, our enemies, and the neutrals, but also our previous experience and current capabilities. Our objectives were the same, as were (apparently) the objectives of the other players, and the same obstacles remained. There was, however, a big difference: since the Za'im lapse much soul searching and sober reflection had been done, and something like professional talent was beginning to become available—either through the developing experience and study of officials who had been in the business since the Syrian elections of 1947 or by being brought in from the outside. We thought ourselves ready for a major operation, and international pressures were such that we thought we couldn't put off action any longer.

There was much probing, and many false starts, but for various reasons, it was finally decided that Egypt was the place to start. Egypt was a country worth high priority on its own merit, and its influence on other Arab states was such that a turn for the better there would be felt throughout the Arab world. Operationally, it was thought to be a pushover, not only because of the nature of the people and their politics but because we had some operators of proved skill who knew the country well, including Kermit Roosevelt himself.

We believed that the Egyptian society lent itself to either of the following approaches: First, we could screen a number of possibles who were personality archetypes of the national ideal of some Arab country and select one with enough brains and reasonableness to be an effective front man, but no more. While we would do the selecting, actual recruitment would be done by elders of his own country with whom we could come to some sort of arrangement.

The elders, the "elite," would hear our suggestion, argue with us, drive some bargains, and finally succumb to our overall argument—sweetened as it would be by offers of economic aid and promises that once a constructive-minded oligarchy got into power we would be appreciative of what it had to do to stay in power and would stop short of actual pressure as we thenceforth made suggestions about how the country should be run.

Second, we could face up to some hard realities about political power such as were expounded by reputable political philosophers from Bertrand Russell to James Burnham. (The latter, by the way, came in to work with Roosevelt in early 1953.) These realities were:

1. We needed an Arab leader who would have more power in his hands than any Arab leader had ever had before, "power to make an unpopular decision," as we used to say. The only kind of leader who can acquire such power is one who deeply desires to have power, and who desires to have it primarily for the mere sake of power. It was argued by some in the Department that what was wrong with Za'im was that he was "power crazy," but a clinically dispassionate study of his behavior showed that he did not desire power enough—or, rather, that he desired it for the wrong reasons. He liked the perquisites and ego satisfactions of being the boss, but so long as we jumped to attention when he entered the room and addressed him as *"Excellence"* he would quite happily have remained an American puppet. We wanted someone whose obsession with power was less frivolous, and we realized that once we had helped such a person into office we would have forgone any moral right to fuss about his power complex—although, of course, we might one day do so for tactical reasons.

2. Second, we needed someone who, unlike Za'im, could share his victories with his followers. As Bertrand Russell

says, "When men willingly follow a leader, they do so with a view to the acquisition of power by the group which he commands, and they feel that his triumphs are theirs." Thus, we realized that besides studying the prospective leader we should also be studying the "followship" hierarchy under him—the elite immediately beneath him, the sub-elite below them, and the gammas at the bottom—and ascertain that, taken together, they would compose a package firmly held together by common interests and objectives.

3. Though we didn't much like the idea, we had to admit that no leader had much chance of really leading an Arab people (i.e., as opposed to finding out "where the mob is going, for I am its leader") unless there was some general fear affecting the populace. The Egyptians had had many centuries of leadership that was both foreign and corrupt, and all leadership was suspect. In this part of the world, Bertrand Russell's observation particularly applied: "A common peril is much the easiest way of producing homogeneity." Elsewhere, Arab leaders were using the fear of Israel to bring about a degree of national unity; we saw no way of avoiding use of the same means in Egypt, provided there was minimal danger of stimulating emotions that might get out of hand—and the likelihood of this seemed small in view of the terrible defeat the Egyptian Army had received from the Israelis in the war of 1948. Besides, there seemed little chance of successfully promoting a leader who would *not* make use of the Arab-Israeli issue.

Years later, these two possible types of leader (the handsome front man and the true leader) came to be known as the "Naguib" and the "Nasser" types. At the time, though, we knew neither Naguib nor Nasser, so the question was this: Is there a real leader to be found? If so, we would embark upon what came later to be known as the "Nasser approach"; if not, we would have to settle for the "Naguib approach." This was more or less the question that Kermit Roosevelt carried in his mind when he took to the field himself, in February 1952, to manage the first serious project of the committee of specialists. His mission, specifically, was first to attempt to organize a "peaceful revolution" in Egypt wherein King Farouk himself would supervise the liquidation of the old and its replacement by the new, thereby defusing the revolutionary forces which CIA agents had identified as much as two years earlier and which were by then reported to be on the verge of bubbling over. Second, if this failed, he was to look around for other possibilities—a handsome front man, a strong man, or some formula combining the two.

Kermit ("Kim") Roosevelt, a grandson of President Theodore Roosevelt and cousin of Archie Roosevelt, had parlayed a reputation for physical courage, the kind Middle Easterners most admire, into a virtually unique standing with both revolutionary and traditional leaders in the Arab countries and Iran—the anti-Shah Qashqai tribal leaders in Iran as well as the Shah himself, the progressive princes in Saudi Arabia as well as old King Ibn Saud, and so on. He had joined the CIA frankly for reasons of adventure, only to find that the CIA, as such, had so many restrictions on it that it was about as adventurous as the Fish and Wildlife Division of the Department of the Interior. Thus, when his old friend General Bedell Smith became Director of the CIA, he arranged to have himself lent to Secretary Dulles' personal staff to carry out missions in the tradition of Lanny Budd of the Upton Sinclair novels— the last of which was Operation Ajax in August 1953, when he almost single-handedly called pro-Shah forces on to the streets of Teheran and supervised their riots so as to oust Mossadegh and restore the Shah, who had fled to Rome. The "peaceful revolution" project in Egypt in 1951–52 was Roosevelt's first such mission.

King Farouk had developed a liking for Roosevelt during

the war during a tense period when the British were forcing him, Farouk, literally at gunpoint, to remove pro-Axis elements from his government and replace them with figures of British choice. While Farouk was fuming in his palace, as helpless as a beached whale, Roosevelt visited him almost daily to comfort him with the suggestion that after the war there could be a New Deal, an Egypt of true sovereignty of which he would be "the first ruler of a free Egypt in two thousand years." Farouk liked this kind of talk, and he liked Roosevelt well enough to receive him warmly when Roosevelt returned to Cairo in 1952. On the other hand, Farouk was not exactly Roosevelt's sort of chap. Though not stupid, he had a bird-brained lack of concentration which amounted to the same thing. In one meeting he would show an intelligent grasp of what was going on in his country, particularly as it affected his regime, and would agree to Roosevelt's remedies with all the efficiency and dispatch of a Pittsburgh business executive. The next day he would disappear, no doubt off on one of his famous orgies, and forget to make some move that he had agreed was essential to Roosevelt's plan. Then the next week, moved by a whim or pique of the moment, he would take an action that totally undermined the plan.

Roosevelt stayed in Cairo for the first two months of 1952, during which time Farouk: (1) played along with Roosevelt's scheme whereby the two strong men of the cabinet, Mortada el-Martaghi and Zaki Abd-el-Motaal, provoked a crisis to force the Prime Minister to resign, then put his secret police to work collecting evidence, to store away for possible future use, showing that these two were CIA agents; (2) agreed to appoint Neguib el-Hilali, a man widely respected for his ability and honesty, as Prime Minister, then invited him to take the position in such a way that he couldn't accept—not, anyhow, until Roosevelt pleaded with him privately in the name of the "peaceful revolution," making the point that the revolution did not have to remain peaceful if the King persisted in his obstinacy; (3) agreed to Hilali's cleanup of the Government, and banishment into exile of the most flagrantly corrupt officials, then replaced these officials with even bigger crooks of his own choice. By May of 1952, Roosevelt had thrown up his hands and agreed with the assessment of the then American Ambassador in Cairo, Jefferson Caffery: that only the Army could cope with the deteriorating situation and establish a government with which Western powers could talk sense.

Caffery, then the oldest Ambassador in the U.S. diplomatic service, knew Egypt well. Autocratic and aloof, he had ways of observing the Egyptian scene which were almost entirely apart from those of his Embassy staff and which depended on one or two Americans outside the Embassy and the one or two members of his staff whom he didn't hold in contempt —mainly the Assistant Military Attaché, one Lieutenant Colonel David Evans, and William Lakeland, the Political Officer. The regular Embassy staff, like most Embassy staffs of the day, considered Cairo and Alexandria among those posts which are pleasant enough for the upper classes—and, therefore, for the diplomatic corps—but which are politically hopeless and wherein one should relax and enjoy. In the manner of Woolcott Gibbs's instructions to the *New Yorker* staff, Caffery once ordered that his officers stop speaking of Egyptians as though they were mantel ornaments and henceforth eschew use of the word "little" in speaking of them (as in "a little man from the Interior Ministry was by to see me this morning"). One member of his staff told a visiting American newsman that the Ambassador's instructions would be fair enough if he, the Ambassador, would at the same time eliminate from his own usage the phrase "tame Egyptians" in referring to upper-class Egyptians who were especially available for diplomatic cocktail parties. In this Cairo and Alexandria of the "good old days," the Egypt of Lawrence Durrell's *Quartet,* only

Caffery himself and a few confidants were paying much attention to the Egyptian Army.

Roosevelt was distrustful of military coups, having seen the mess they were making of Syria, but he agreed to meet the officers whom the CIA had spotted as likely leaders of the secret military society known to be plotting a coup. This he did in March 1952, four months before Nasser's coup. Nasser, having spotted the CIA's reconnaissance of his organization, was ready for the approach and arranged to put in Roosevelt's path a number of officers who were far away enough from the center of the movement to be expendable, yet who could be counted upon to say all the right things while keeping the Free Officers' essential secrets. There were three such meetings, the third attended by one of Nasser's most trusted lieutenants. The large area of agreement reached by Roosevelt and this officer, speaking for Nasser himself, is noteworthy.

On three general items there was immediate agreement. The first was that a country's masses were not likely to rise in revolt because of the dismaying economic circumstances. Roosevelt had long argued this point at the State Department and had once passed out copies of Crane Brinton's *Anatomy of Revolution** to support his assertion that no major revolution in history had had economic causes at its root and that our Government couldn't get rid of a leader it didn't like by withholding grants of wheat from his people. Nasser realized even then what he was to have confirmed later from personal experience: that whenever the U.S. Government *does* seek to weaken his position by withholding economic aid he winds up in a stronger position than before, with his people blaming their deprivations on the United States, not on him.

The second was that the *Egyptian* masses were not likely to rise in revolt because of *any* circumstances. Two revolu-

* See Suggested Reading List.

tionary movements of the time, the Moslem Brotherhood
and the Communist Party, believed that the Egyptian
people—including the *felahin* (peasants), the workers, the
white-collar workers in the cities, and even the professional
classes—were at long last nearing a boiling point, and could
be brought to it by the right kind of appeal. Nasser didn't
agree. The point came up in the meeting between Roosevelt
and Nasser's representatives when one of these representatives remarked that "whoever rules this country will have
a hard time meeting the tremendous wants of the Egyptian
people." The senior member of the group, in his first complete sentence of the evening, replied, "On the contrary;
our problem is that the people don't want enough." Most
Egyptians, he went on to say, have lived at marginal sub-
sistence for thousands of years and could go on for another
thousand. "They aren't motivated to revolt," he said, "and
they aren't motivated to make the most out of their lives
after the revolution. After the revolution we will do our best
to motivate them, but we don't have time for it beforehand."
Thus, there was no question of a "democratic" or "popular"
revolution. It was understood from the start that the Egyptian Army would take control of the country, choosing a
time and circumstances that would ensure the support of a
politically conscious and active urban populace, and that the
rest of the country would be won over gradually thereafter.

Finally, it was agreed that in future relations between the
new Egyptian Government and the United States Government use of such phrases as "re-establishing democratic
processes" and "truly representative government" should be
confined to those exchanges which might be revealed to the
public and that between us there would be a private understanding that the preconditions for democratic government
did not exist and wouldn't exist for many years. The new
government's job would be to bring about these conditions,
which were: (1) a literate populace; (2) a large and stable
middle class; (3) a feeling by the people that "this is *our*

Government," and not an imposition of the French, the Turks, the British, or the Egyptian upper classes; (4) sufficient identification of local ideals and values so that truly indigenous democratic institutions could grow up, not mere imitations imported from the United States or Great Britian. Both Roosevelt and Nasser's representative realized that the American public, Congressmen, some journalists, and some State Department people, often including the Secretary of State himself, would soon be howling the old slogans. At the same time, they fully realized that any premature attempt at democracy would put the country back in the same old mess: elections between candidates who were supported by the U.S. and British Governments running against candidates supported by the Soviets, a rural populace (at 24,000,000 out of 28,000,000 by far the majority) voting as instructed by the large landowners, and the frustrated city populace reduced to riots and general troublemaking as their only means of exerting political influence, joining the Moslem Brotherhood and the Communist Party as being the only outlets befitting their energies.

There were other items on which explicit argeement was difficult, but which nonetheless formed a mutual understanding of what motivations would be behind the forthcoming coup. These were the items that involved looking beneath surface appearances—the way "motivational-research" analysts in the United States look beneath ordinary public-opinion surveys which show that the *Atlantic Monthly* and *Harper's* are read more than comic books, that there is no anti-Semitism in upper-middle-class America, and that the Kinsey report indicates the American sexual norm.

There were several of these items, of widely varying importance, but there was one worth special mention: Nasser's attitude on Israel. Politicians, writers and ordinary citizens in any Arab country—as well as most Western diplomats, scholars and writers who visit the various Arab countries—

will tell you that a determination to "regain Palestine" is to top priority to that particular country. Even such a discerning observer as Eric Downton of London's *Daily Telegraph* has been insisting all these years that Egypt's defeat by the Israelis in 1948 was a "traumatic experience" and that "hatred of Israel" was an important element in the thinking of those who put over the Egyptian revolution. After five years of tuning in on barrack-room conversation and talking individually to hundreds of officers, however, Nasser and his lieutenants decided almost the opposite. They realized that it might serve some later purpose to speak of "mobilizing Egypt's resources so as to redress the wrongs of Palestine," but that in early 1952 such talk would be irrelevant and harmful as a means of inspiring a revolution in Egypt. Nasser explicitly admitted to Roosevelt that he and his officers had been "humiliated" by the Israelis, but he insisted that their resentments were "against our own superior officers, other Arabs, the British and the Israelis—in that order." As the result of his talks with leading nonmilitary figures in Egypt, including King Farouk, Roosevelt arrived at a conclusion that accorded with Nasser's—a conclusion that Ambassador Jefferson Caffery had reached long before.

Then there was the even more ticklish problem of Arab nationalism. Getting an Egyptian leader, military or civilian, to state his true thoughts about Arabs was as difficult as it would be to get a straight answer out of a British Member of Parliament about his views on immigration. But rule number one for anybody planning a coup d'etat in an Arab country is this: make your appeals Egyptian (or Syrian, or Iraqi or whatever) and not, repeat *not* Arab. For all the talk of "we are all Arab brothers," the fact is that the loyalties of any group of Arabs are extremely parochial, and that in practical matters such as launching coups d'etat these loyalties are what count. This is true of Egyptians in general and of Nasser in particular. When he launched his revolution, this Egyptian, who has since become the nearest thing to a "leader of the Arabs" since the word "Arab" came into use, knew very little about Arabs (he wasn't—isn't—an Arab himself, and he hadn't then visited any Arab countries or met any Arab people), and what little he knew he didn't like.

Since 1952 he has visited *some* Arab countries, though hardly under circumstances that would teach him much about those countries, and the visits have served only to confirm his earlier suspicions: that the Iraqis are savages, the Lebanese venal and morally degenerate ("I picture Beirut as being one big night club," he once told me), the Saudis dirty, the Yemenis hopelessly backward and stupid, and the Syrians irresponsible, unreliable and treacherous.

I must emphasize that Nasser now denies that he ever had such attitudes (one could hardly expect him to admit them), and I believe that he has by now arrived at a genuine belief that there is such a thing as "an Arab people"—that is, the Syrian, Lebanese, Iraqi, Jordanian, Saudi and Libyan lower-middle classes who cheer him wildly whenever he appears on the television screen—who would cease behaving like Syrians, Lebanese, Iraqis, Jordanians, Saudis and Libyans if only they could rid themselves of their corrupt political leaders. I must also emphasize, however, that those lieutenants who helped Nasser to launch the revolution and who are to some extent responsible for keeping him in power today do not share this view and that they go along with his "Arab" postures only to the extent that they serve purely Egyptian purposes. As we shall see in later chapters, the Egyptian-versus-Arab conflicts have played a kind of counterpoint in Egypt's palace politics since 1955 when Nasser returned from the Afro-Asian Congress in Bandung, but whenever Nasser has serious internal problems he immediately becomes more Egyptian and less Arab. Certainly, when he has secret discussions of strategy with his closest advisers he does so strictly in terms of what is good for Egypt, with benefits for the Arabs in general being only a minor consideration.

These points, the unimportance of "regaining Palestine"

and the irrelevance of Arab nationalism to Egyptian revolutionary motivations, are worth mentioning only because there has been so much misunderstanding about them— misunderstanding which, as we shall see, has caused us costly mistakes in dealing with Nasser and similarly motivated leaders of the Arab world. The main specific to come out in Roosevelt's talks with Nasser's officers was the genuineness of their resentment of the British position in Egypt and of all Egyptians who accepted this position—the "tame Egyptians" of whom Ambassador Caffery spoke. About individual Britishers the officers were ambivalent, with admiration being the stronger feeling. (I once gave Nasser an American-tailored drip-dry suit; he thought it was the most ridiculous-looking garment he had ever seen. "What kind of tailoring do you like?" I asked. "British, of course," he replied.) They liked Americans, and fell in easily with our mixing-with-the-help camaraderie. But they respected and admired the British. It is for this reason that being treated by them as inferiors was so hurtful. Much later, when Wilton Wynn of the Associated Press was interviewing Nasser before writing his book about him, Wynn tried to get Nasser to admit that British administrators from Lord Cromer on had done much for Egypt—reforming its finances and law courts, installing sanitation facilities, protecting the peasants from forced labor and excessive taxation; Nasser would only reply, "No. They made us feel like second-class citizens in our own country." They patronized the Egyptians, in other words. In Roosevelt's talks with the revolutionary officers during the two months before Nasser's coup this was their main theme.

But there is a twist to the theme peculiar to Nasser and his officers—for that matter, peculiar to Nasser-type leaders and their followers: while they talk the loudest against the foreign foe (in this case the British), their really meaningful resentments—i.e., the ones that motivate them—are reserved for their own people whose weakness makes the position of the foe possible. Just as in the United States on Pearl Harbor day the leaders of our Government directed their animus to our own commanders at Pearl Harbor rather than to the Japanese, so Nasser and his officers resented the "tame Egyptians" in their ranks rather than the British. A little respectful treatment by some respected British Ambassador and all the Anglophobia dissolves. Resentment against the tame Egyptians, however, is permanent and deep. The difference is well understood by the Nasser-type leader. It has also been well understood by British Ambassadors from Humphrey Trevelyan to Harold Beeley; unfortunately, with one or two exceptions, our own diplomatic representatives haven't grasped the point.

Roosevelt grasped the point, and when he returned from Cairo two months before the coup took place, he reported to Secretary Dean Acheson (1) that the "popular revolution" predicted by the State Department and actively sought by the Communists and the Moslem Brotherhood was not in the cards; (2) that there was no possibility of "keeping the Army out of it," which was the hope of State Department planners who were especially conscious of the way Syria's military leaders were going, and that the Army was shortly to have a coup whether we liked it or not; (3) that the officers likely to lead the coup had only "standard" motivations, as opposed to the unmanageable ones attributed to them by most diplomatic observers, which not only would increase their chances of success but would make them more reasonable and flexible negotiators once they attained power; (4) that the U.S. Government would have to accept the removal of King Farouk, and perhaps the complete end of the monarchy, although there was no reason why some form of mild protest shouldn't be made to humor the pure in heart, and that it would be appropriate for Ambassador Caffery to show some concern for Farouk's personal safety; (5) that after the coup our Government should refrain from any but token attempts to persuade the military junta to hold elections, establish constitutional government, and all the rest, and should conduct its relations with the new government in the realization that democratic institutions would have to be built from scratch; (6) that for all these conspiratorial pre-coup meetings, no one in our Government must get the idea that it was *our* coup; it would be strictly an indigenous affair, almost totally free of our influence, which we could assist only by not opposing it. And as for the need of an enemy to fear (per Lord Russell's dictum), it wasn't to be the Israelis but Egypt's upper classes—and, whether we liked it or not, the British.

Roosevelt also had much to say about the kind of leader who should—or, rather, *would*, whether we liked it or not—come out on top in the prevailing atmosphere. First, he said that he agreed with all that his committee members had said about the need for a great charismatic leader (the need that had been agreed upon during the discussions of the "Moslem Billy Graham") but that the particular situation in Egypt at that very moment called for a leader of somewhat narrower appeal than had been previously thought. It required a leader who, in the words of Eric Hoffer, could "dominate and almost bewitch a small group of men," in this case the clique represented by the officers Roosevelt had met. Second, whether he turned out to be a great popular figure or remained merely a leader of a clique which, in turn, would lead the country, the leader could hardly be expected to fit criteria by which we Westerners measure our own statesmen. "He will be whoever he will be," said Roosevelt, "and if we don't know how to deal with such a leader we had better learn. If the one we bet on in these circumstances doesn't win out, then there will be another of the same type. And there will be others in many of the other countries in the same circumstances as this one."

4

The Emergence of Nasser, Our "Independent Ally"

That is to say, the new player you bring into the game will have his own objectives and policies . . .

Roosevelt's written report on his trip was composed in such a way that it wouldn't horrify some Congressional investigating committee of the future; it was therefore not an entirely frank explanation of our attempts to find a leader with a craving for power, a knack for Bonapartist-style leadership, and an ability to work up his people into a unifying attitude of fear. His oral reports were more frank. He told his superiors that anyone with a really strong desire for power would hardly sit around waiting for some American cryptodiplomat to come out and ignite him and that the other two qualities, similarly, were not only self-generating but of a kind that wouldn't come to the surface in a talent search. One conclusion, however, could safely be drawn from his meetings in Cairo: *someone* in Egypt, someone connected with the officers with whom he had met, had a highly sophisticated grasp of what it took to seize power in Egypt and to hold on to it. Also, that someone was going to do just that. All that could be hoped for was that his, Roosevelt's, remarks had reached the someone so that a mutual understanding could be worked out when the right time came. Certainly the someone would understand what we wanted and what we were prepared to pay for it. And from what Roosevelt gathered from those officers he met, our offer was eminently acceptable.

Our Government learned of the actual coup by reading about it in the newspapers the day it happened (July 22, 1952) following the usual flurry of CIA reports indicating that something was up but failing to pinpoint the exact time and movements. The press was entirely favorable: the coup had been bloodless, it was obviously acceptable to the Egyptian people, and no one seemed to regret the departure of the profligate king. The ostensible leader of the coup, General Mohammed Naguib, appeared as a genial, pipe-smoking type from whom mature judgments might be expected. His supporters appeared as clean-cut young officers, all of them slim and athletic-looking, who seemed to be ideal material from which to build a New Egypt. There were no wild statements such as invariably followed Syrian coups. The preoccupation seemed the same as that of intelligent, mature politicos anywhere: cleaning up corruption, building a more efficient government, reforming the political parties and so on. Nothing was said about Israel.

If the newspapers scooped the Embassy, it was only because they got their cables out at three in the morning, whereas the Embassy waited until the regular working day in order to get more facts. The delay wasn't the fault of Nasser, because, at a respectable hour of the morning, he sent one of his lieutenants to inform Ambassador Caffery officially. The lieutenant, Ali Sabri, who subsequently became the leading anti-American figure in Nasser's Government, gave Caffery a full, no-nonsense report of the events of the night before, together with assurances that the new Government wanted friendly relations with the United States. This was followed up by more public assurances from the coup's father figure, General Naguib, who at one point got carried away and passed the word to us that he "wasn't interested in Palestine," although he called Ambassador Caffery only a few hours later to withdraw the statement and substitute for it something less suited to public consumption in the United States, but more in line with what Nasser, and we, knew was required for the new Government to gain public acceptance.

Everything indicated that we now had at the board a new player who was exactly what we were looking for, and that the game we would play with him would have a high percentage of cooperation and a low percentage of conflict. Official Washington was delighted.

Various accounts of the Egyptian revolution have Naguib as its leader, the British and American Governments dealing with him as such, and Nasser taking over from him many months later. The truth, however, is that although Roosevelt had taken Nasser at his word when he insisted he was not the head of the revolutionary movement, members of the Embassy in Cairo, mainly William Lakeland, the Embassy's political officer, realized almost immediately that Naguib was only Nasser's front man. Lakeland first became friendly with Nasser's Free Officers through Mohammed Hassanein Heykel, who later became Nasser's closest friend and confidant but who was then a mere working reporter on the staff of a paper owned by Nasser's friend Mustafa Amin. Through Heykel, Lakeland met many of the leading Free Officers, including Nasser, and during the months following the coup he entertained them frequently in his apartment overlooking the Nile. While the Egyptian public and the outside world were cheering Naguib, the Embassy, through Lakeland, had begun to deal with Nasser as the one who really made the decisions.

Ambassador Caffery called on Naguib from time to time to pay formal visits or to deliver messages from Washington, especially if they were messages that he wouldn't mind having lost on the way, but the real business between the U.S. Government and the Egyptian Government was conducted through Lakeland and Nasser—or, rather, Lakeland and

Heykel and Nasser, Heykel getting more and more into the channel of communication because of his rapidly developing ability to sugar-coat Nasser's views as he passed them on to the Embassy and the Embassy's views as he passed them to Nasser.

After the coup, Roosevelt and members of his special committee refrained from any direct contact with Nasser and were content to watch developments in Egypt from afar. This was partly to avoid any suggestion of connivance, and partly because things were moving smoothly along predicted and approved paths. Similarly, major business concerns with an interest in the area were content to leave the new Government to solve its problems in its own way and saw no reason to identify the real powers behind the Naguib façade with whom to set up special relationships. It was after the Eisenhower administration came in (in 1953) that we decided to take a direct interest in the progress of Nasser's revolution. It was President Eisenhower's personal wish that we study this new player thoroughly: first, so as to assure ourselves that he was developing as we expected; second, to enable us to devise a strategy to "win" where there would be conflict; and third, to find means of making the game as much a game of cooperation as possible. We knew that to some extent, one day, any help we gave Nasser would increase his strength in that segment of the game which would inevitably be conflict, but we hoped that this would be more than balanced by an increasing ability—and willingness— to behave in a way that would suit both our interests.

Thus it was that on the eve of Secretary John Foster Dulles' visit to the Middle East in May 1953, Dulles decided, "It's time we looked into what these boys are really up to" and ordered Roosevelt to send to Cairo "a military man, one of their own kind," to size them up.

Roosevelt's choice was Steve Meade, who had just been brought in from the cold after such assignments as rescuing captured German scientists from Communist China, corrupting Kurdish tribal leaders on the Soviet border for military intelligence purposes, and, of course, introducing a Dark Age in Syria as described in Chapter 2. Roosevelt, whose experience with officers of modern Arab armies was limited, believed that Meade's adventurous background would favorably impress Nasser's Free Officers. He was, to some extent, right. During the weeks Meade spent in Egypt before the Dulles visit, Nasser's officers did indeed accept him as a man's man fitting the hero image they had developed from seeing American films. Actually Meade's virtues were those of an ordinary paratrooper of unglamorous pretensions. He had come to Intelligence only because a faulty anode in Army Personnel's IBM machine had caused "birthplace" on his classification card to be read "UKR" instead of "UKN," resulting in his being held by G-2 for possible parachuting into Russia rather than being sent into battle as he had hoped. His only unusual talent was a facility for learning difficult languages—among them, Arabic. His behavior was that of a model officer in anybody's army, including the Egyptian. His adventurous background made for interesting conversation in late-night get-togethers. That was all. And it even irritated Nasser and caused him to regard Meade's assignment to Egypt as an indication that Secretary Dulles considered his revolution as no different from a South American type of coup. When someone pointed out to Nasser, hoping to impress him favorably, that Meade was the only white man ever to have been made an honorary member of the Mau Mau, Nasser almost had him sent home.

From the U.S. Government's point of view, Meade's advantage was his extraordinary talent for measuring people, their motivations, and their intentions without getting himself involved in their politics. Despite his known friendship with various military-junta leaders in other countries (including, conspicuously, President Shishakli of Syria), no serious suspicion arose that he was trying to influence the course of the Egyptian Revolution. Nor was he. But he made observations about Nasser's Free Officers that history has proved to be true not only of Nasser's elite but of military elites in virtually all non-Western countries probably including Vietnam and certainly including West Africa and Greece.

Apropos of some country somewhere, Roosevelt once told Secretary Dulles, "We can't have a revolution without revolutionaries"—or, as Brian Crozier* put it some years later, "Men do not rebel because their conditions of life are intolerable; it takes a rebel to rebel." After some weeks of social mixing with Egyptian officers—which, after all, followed years of close association with Syrian, Lebanese and Iraqi officers—Meade believed the opposite. Syrian coups failed—or rather, they were quickly followed by other coups—because they had too many rebels in them. Meade believed that the Egyptian coup was likely to stick because it had been brought off as the result of Nasser's discipline, and because it was evident that Nasser's followers were amenable to his continuing the discipline. "These boys see themselves as Robin Hood's merry band," Meade wrote to Roosevelt, "and they are pleased to be billed as 'heroes of the Revolution.' But I haven't found a one who can explain to me what the revolution is all about. They aren't interested in politics, and, fortunately for Nasser and all of us, they want and require someone to tell them what to think and do. There'll be no difficulty in getting them back into the barracks."

The somewhat roisterous impression the Free Officers were making on the outside world did, however, give Meade and other friendly observers some anxious moments. Three or four days after Meade's arrival in Cairo, they tried to enlist his help in convincing Nasser that a long gallows, complete with some thirty-odd nooses and a grandstand to hold an audience of hundreds, should be built in front of

---

* See Suggested Reading List.

Abdin Palace to execute "enemies of the Revolution." Nasser put an end to this particular project by simply saying, "No. And I don't want to hear the subject mentioned again." But the officers did mention the subject again among themselves, until word of it leaked to the jittery general public. There were also numerous small examples of the officers' taking it upon themselves to harass a wide miscellany of persons whom they considered to be "enemies of the Revolution" or who they thought to be misusing their new authority for purely personal purposes. By such behavior they caused many observers to believe that they would get out of hand altogether one day and turn Egypt into another Syria. Meade suspected the same at first, but soon came around to the view that their behavior was due only to natural post-coup exuberance and was no more a cause for worry than was the behavior of De Gaulle's Free French troops after the Germans left France.

Meade's conclusions as to what the officers were really like were based in large part on what they told him about how they had joined the Free Officers in the first place. From a few days' talk, a picture emerged of a vast and complex secret military society, with esoteric creeds and pledges and all the rest. After more days of talk, however, the picture disintegrated, to be replaced by one less appealing to the Oriental imagination but more in line with observable facts; clearly, the Free Officers' movement, in effect, was what was left of the Army after the "fat boys" had been cleaned out—i.e., the deadwood at the General Staff, officers of upper-class families who had gone into the Army under the "dumbest-son" tradition, and other kinds of dilettantes who, despite their positions, weren't firmly in the channels of command because of absenteeism and general lack of interest. Nasser had singled out officers who were both serious and in key positions of command; his secret society consisted of these officers. His coup had not been a matter of upsetting discipline, but a matter of establishing it. His

pre-coup conspiracy was not concerned with building a rebellious force with which to seize power, but with easing
officers of his political persuasion into key positions so that
they could seize power by issuing orders through ordinary
administrative channels. Perhaps his greatest difficulty was
that of placing himself in a position relative to his key
lieutenants so that he could insert himself at the right place
in the chain of command when the big day came. The use
of Naguib served the purpose, but it had drawbacks.

The coup itself, as Meade learned about it in bits and
pieces (and as Nasser himself later explained it to General
Cabell, deputy director of the Central Intelligence Agency),
was not without farcical overtones: one of the principal officers failing to seize the communication centers because the
alert message arrived as he was out seeing a film with his
wife, Nasser's car getting stopped by a policeman on the
way to the rendezvous because one of his taillights was out,
Nasser almost getting swept off the street by one of his
own units because his identity as leader of the Free Officers
had not been revealed to the commander, news of the coup
leaking to King Farouk's security police because the mother
of one of the leaders saw her son take off in the middle of
the night "in a suspicious way," as she said, and called the
police because she "thought he might be getting into
trouble," and so on. Everything worked out in the end, of
course: the failure to cut the communications turned out to
be an advantage because it enabled Nasser to call Alexandria and set his forces there in motion (how he would
have accomplished this without the communications remains a mystery); the unit that almost arrested Nasser was
also turned into an asset—it arrived at a time when he
needed such a unit to seize the General Staff, which was
then meeting to discuss the tip-off it had received from the
distraught mother, via the regular police, via the security
police; even the tip-off itself proved to be a help, because
when news of the coup reached Intelligence headquarters

many of the officers there joined in and throughout the rest of the action, kept Nasser informed of moves against him.

For a coup that depended on the existence of a highly disciplined army within an army, this was possibly the most confused operation in modern history. Nasser told General Cabell: "You see, complete efficiency would have been possible only by relaxing security; the tight security which we needed could be gained only at the expense of efficiency. I thought it over and decided in favor of security, because I knew that if I chose the right time anything we did would come out all right. The real disciplines of the Army would take over, and even our worst mistakes would be swept away by the momentum we would gather if only we got things in motion."

How all this was possible was explained in Meade's report, later to provide raw material for many more scholarly studies on coups, which argued (in part) as follows:

1. The strength of any army, including the army of the non-Western country which serves mainly extramilitary purposes, depends on its being manned largely by what American sociologists call "good organization men": in other words, persons who like to give orders, to take orders, to know where they are in a "command structure," and to feel themselves parts of an organizational whole. Nasser realized that the success of his coup depended on the extent to which these "good organization men" could be brought into it. Nasser himself and some of his confreres may have been "rebels" in the Brian Crozier sense, but on down the line there were few or none. Nasser believed that the more orders launching and carrying out the coup could be in regular military form, going through regular military channels, the better.

2. The leader of a coup should be of the same social class, or able to pass himself off as such, as his principal followers,

and his relationship with them should be such as to enable them to share his victory. Indeed, Nasser's victory was thought of as the victory of all the Free Officers, with Nasser being only the one who made the victory possible. In turn, Nasser's principal followers had the same kind of relationship with those beneath them—and so on down the line. Ultimately, by the same principle by which a small holding company can control a great industrial empire, Nasser could control the whole country—or, at least, that part of the population which mattered politically (in Egypt, about 10 percent of the population at most).

3. Once the "holding company" had been activated, personnel changes had to be made that would ensure its continued operation on a strict basis of administrative hierarchy, not personal loyalty. After the coup, followers of Nasser's various lieutenants were known as "Zakaria men" or "Boghdadi men," thereby conveying the notion that their loyalty to Nasser was in proportion to their loyalty to one or another of his lieutenants. Nasser had to break this, although he had to do it in a way that would not alienate his principal supporters. Some of the lieutenants were extremely useful in affecting the coup, but were virtually useless in the post-coup situation (a problem common to all revolutionary leaders). These had to be placed in seemingly important sinecures. Others, who had useful talents and whom Nasser especially trusted, were placed in highly responsible positions which would keep them busy, while those who followed them on a basis of personal loyalty were transferred elsewhere. Meade, who had argued to Za'im that he should do this, believed that this feature of Nasser's technique should be a basic principle in anybody's manual on how to launch and consolidate a coup d'etat.

4. Nasser knew that for some time to come—that is, until he and his command structure had firmly established itself

in the post-coup situation—the "holding company" would depend on the Army, and on the Army's acceptance in the country. Pseudointellectuals, extremist politicians, and fanatics of all sorts would applaud the revolution and regard it as an opportunity to put over their kind of reforms. If allowed, they would demonstrate and give an impression of tremendous vitality—even, possibly, of representing some facet of public opinion. The temptation to enlist them in the revolution, however, was resisted. Their real value was as a counterirritant—that is, in making nuisances of themselves so as to justify the Government's disciplines. It was obvious that the common attitudes of the holding company, the ones shared up and down the line to such an extent that they were a principal factor in holding it together, were conservative. Nasser's main contribution, in the eyes of his military followers, was to make a respectable institution out of the Army, to bring real discipline into it, to make it into the kind of organization they had thought they were joining when they first enlisted years earlier. These "organization men" were against intellectuals, public disorder, permissiveness, social modernity (as opposed to technical modernity), sexual laxness, and other features of Farouk's Egypt which they saw as endangering their cherished institutions

Some of Nasser's followers believed that a student riot or two, which would be easy enough to arrange, might accentuate these feelings and make it possible for the junta to accelerate its hold on the country. Nasser vetoed the idea, however, as not being really necessary, but all his subsequent actions did in fact take these things into account.

In Syria, where the coup d'etat is regarded as an art form, Meade had seen Za'im come into power by a perfectly executed coup, then make every mistake it seemed possible to make; in Egypt he saw Nasser come into power as the result of a coup operation that would have been suicidal in any other country, yet succeed perfectly and, besides, provide a basis for consolidation that would make Nasser's new Government virtually coup-proof. He believed that the principles just stated were what made it possible. But there was one really fundamental principle that tied together all the others: Nasser's realization that solidfying his position was *all*-important and must take precedence over all other objectives. This realization caused Nasser to take actions that seriously disturbed Western observers: for example, he once allowed a situation to develop that seriously damaged Egypt's relations with the Sudan simply because it gave him a chance to blame it on one of his lieutenants who was becoming dangerously powerful. Meade argued, however, that such behavior was necessary and that we should not be too disturbed about it.

Also, Nasser's views on what he called the "natural elite," coming to our Government not so much through Meade as through the Heykel-Lakeland channel, bothered our planners. A natural elite, as Nasser sees it, is one that enjoys special influence and privileges in a country because of an obviously superior competence, and because the people so believe that it represents them and belongs to them that they do not resent it. All prosperous and stable societies, including Russia's, have such elites, and Nasser yearned for one in his own country. At the same time, he doubted the ability of his people to assess competence or to decide what was truly representative of them. Their long tolerance, in pre-coup Egypt, of an elite that was manifestly *un*natural caused him to believe that in a completely "open" situation only a carpetbagger kind of elite could arise. He was therefore becoming tempted by the idea of a military elite, even though it was in conflict with his conviction that the Army should be separated from politics. We found this growing notion of Nasser's disturbing, not because we thought it would make him a less desirable player at the game board (it might, in fact, have made him *more* suitable) but because of difficulties it would make for us on the American home front. The Eisenhower Administration was already being accused of favoring rightist military dictatorships; its rebuttal was that we sometimes had to tolerate them in the interest of law and order, but that we never did so unless they showed an intention to return to parliamentary government once law and order had been established. A "fascist military dictatorship" which clearly intended to remain as such, especially in the Arab world, would limit *our* maneuverability in the game.

Finally, we were worried at Nasser's apparent indecision as to what kind of social structure he hoped to establish. Nasser wanted time to think. Also, he wanted to give the Egyptian people time to think—or, rather, to develop the capability to think constructively about what they wanted. "Giving them what you call freedom too soon," he told Ambassador Caffrey, "would be like turning your children on to the street." And he believed that the country as a whole, if prematurely given Western-style freedom, would shortly become a battleground for carpetbaggers and fanatics. Above all, he knew that a completely free citizenry, at its then level of education and worldliness, would almost certainly disapprove of the actions on the international plane he foresaw himself having to take in Egypt's long-range interest. In other words, for the longest possible time he needed the maximum freedom of action without having to worry about public opinion. This meant that at least temporarily he needed a social structure, with elites and subelites on top, which could be held together by promises and cajolery.

These considerations did not worry Steve Meade, the expert on junta survival, but they worried Kermit Roosevelt. And when Meade reported that Nasser's shuffling of the command structure seemed aimed at establishing a military-fascist dictatorship, Roosevelt arranged with Ambassador Caffery for the assignment to Cairo of one James Eichelberger, a State Department political scientist who had written some impressive staff papers on military regimes in underdeveloped countries. Roosevelt had recommended massive economic aid to Egypt, and was about to argue for military aid. He believed that a study of the situation by Eichelberger would give him either a basis for justifying Nasser's budding policies to Secretary Dulles or, if he could not condone the policies, a basis for convincing Nasser that he should modify them.

Caffery assigned Eichelberger to work directly for him, apart from the regular Embassy staff, although he gave him access to information from the State Department, the service attachés, and the CIA. Eichelberger's task was to work out various situation estimates and recommendations for action, although Caffery made all the final decisions and was behind every word that went back to Washington, whether to the State Department, to the CIA, or to key individuals in the State Department or the CIA, including Kermit Roosevelt.

Eichelberger held long conversations with Nasser's military and civilian entourage, including in particular Mohammed Hassanein Heykel, the newspaper reporter who had been the "as told to" behind Nasser's book, *Philosophy of the Revolution*, building up a good assessment of what was genuine philosophy and what was for public consumption. Also, he talked at length to Heykel's then boss, Mustafa Amin, a highly intelligent newspaper editor who was as much an admirer of Nasser as was Heykel, but a little less enchanted. Most important, he talked to Salah Salem, Minister of National Guidance (or "Minister of Sweetness and Light" as he later came to be known by the irreverent) and to the various people whom Salem had brought into his Ministry to study public opinion—from the universities, from labor unions, and even from the old political parties. Finally, he talked to Nasser himself about a wide range of subjects and gained an idea of the extent to which Nasser understood the political forces at work beneath him. The result was a series of papers, some of which were translated into Arabic and passed to Nasser, pointing out what seemed to be the new Government's most important emerging difficulties and recommending policies for dealing with them.

The most interesting of the papers, *Power Problems of a Revolutionary Government* (included as an Appendix to this book) was translated into Arabic, commented upon by various members of Nasser's staff, translated back into English for further editing by Eichelberger, and so on back and forth between English and Arabic until a final version was produced. The final paper was passed off to the outside world as the work of Zakaria Mohieddin, Nasser's most thoughtful and (in Western eyes) reasonable deputy, and accepted at face value by intelligence analysts of the State Department, the CIA, and, presumably, similar agencies of other governments. Whatever may be said about its philosophical merit (and Eichelberger himself later came to think so little of it that he went to great lengths to disown any connection with it), as an indication of how Nasser, at that time, regarded the relationship between repression and popular support, it is extremely valuable.

Caffery, a practicing Catholic, had instructed Eichelberger to take a devil's-advocate approach as he surveyed the Egyptian scene. He did not agree with Meade's assertion that the Nasser Government was coup-proof. He believed that, one year after the coup, a "time of maximum counterrevolutionary danger" had arrived, and that trouble might be expected from three directions: certain individuals who had vested interests in the previous political system; political opportunists who thought they saw tendencies to instability which they could exploit; and outright political subversives such as the Communists who might pretend to go along with Nasser's movement but who would always be on the lookout for a chance to take it over for their own ends. A devil's advocate, deliberately being pessimistic in looking at the situation, could see three definite dangers:

(1) a factional coup d'etat, brought about by dissident members of Nasser's own entourage in cooperation with key Army and police officers—i.e., a coup very much like Nasser's own coup; (2) a counterrevolutionary coup d'etat, based on much the same kind of elements as the factional coup but supported by outside political forces, especially those having some capacity for getting mobs into the streets; (3) the penetration of Nasser's government by forces pretending to be friendly but actually hostile to its purposes. There was considerable information, from Nasser's own intelligence as well as from CIA and British Intelligence, indicating that the first of these two were at least possibilities, but Caffery and Eichelberger saw the third as the only danger to be taken seriously. Specifically, they saw the following possibilities: a subtle distortion of the new Government's program by any one of several top officials around Nasser who were loyal to him personally but who did not agree with his views; outright sabotage of the program by any one of a similar number whose loyalty to Nasser was in question; a more widespread, though just as subtle, penetration of the Government not so much for the purpose of influencing its policies as for weakening its ability to maintain power, thus preparing for its eventual overthrow.

Also a devil's advocate would have to consider the desire for popularity among Nasser's officers to be a source of danger. In an early report to Caffery which later, with language changed, was incorporated into *Power Problems of a Revolutionary Government,* Eichelberger said:

> Nasser is himself noncommittal, but in talking to Selah and Gamal Salem and some of the other Revolutionary Command Council members I get the impression that without quite realizing it they have embarked on a policy of drift and compromise. They do not feel that they have yet gained comfortable control over the instruments of government, and they do not have confidence in the efficacy of their repressive powers. They want popularity, and what they think they must

do to gain it invokes a kind of perpetual crisis psychology in the conduct of government affairs.

Eichelberger went on to give specifics, and then said:

> While trying to maintain power by trying to please one group in one moment and some other group in the next, they have to set aside their basic aims and let real progress look after itself. Before long it is going to be apparent to one and all that they are bankrupt of ideas, and further drift and compromise will become impossible. Too late, they will have to fall back on this "repressive power" that Nasser talks about, and we are going to see before us a nasty little tyranny.

But Eichelberger was underestimating Nasser. Nasser knew full well the elusive nature of "mere popularity," and he had no intention of chasing after it until his basic power was secure. Throughout the years he has appreciated the necessity for maintaining at least a *capability* for repression even at times when his popularity has been at its peak. As late as May 1967 he admitted to a foreign diplomat that "we could rule this country the way Papa Duvalier rules Haiti if things ever come to that, although, naturally, we hope that things won't come to that."

The appearance of drift and compromise was due not so much to Nasser's doubts about what he wanted to achieve as to indecision over how to go about it. His objective, then not clear to the Nasser watchers, was not to move from a military dictatorship to parliamentary government but to bypass parliamentary government, except for a pretense of it, and go on to Bonapartism—i.e., rule with a "mandate from the people" expressed through plebiscites and the like. In a country like Egypt, achieving such an objective requires a program of complexity and subtlety which, to one unaware of its purpose, necessarily looks confused. As we shall see, however, in Nasser's mind it was clear enough.

So far as *we* were concerned, all we wanted was a player at the board who met our specifications. What Nasser did about his internal political situation was his own affair, so long as it did not commit his Game of Nations strategy to channels endangering our interests. Whatever his real objectives, Bonapartist rule or any other kind, one defense of Nasser can be offered: During the period when he was consolidating his position his attitude toward his American friends was, "If you don't like the way I'm doing it, show me a better way. At least I'll listen." We never tested his sincerity because at no point along the line could we think of a better way.

5

The "Nasser-Type" Leader and His "Repressive Base"

... and his first objective will be to stay in the game—any way he can.

From time to time over the years, someone asks me, "If Nasser were confronted with a situation where he must either lose his power to save the country or let the country go to ruin in order to stay in power, which alternative would he choose?" My answer is that in dealing with any leader whose love of power for the sake of power is what we know Nasser's to be we must assume that he will do anything to hold on to that power, even though it means letting the country go to economic ruin or fighting a continually losing battle with the Israelis. This is an even safer assumption if the leader's power formula is Bonapartist and if the leader sees—or thinks he sees—that even the worst catastrophe will not break his "mandate from the people," enabling some rival group to emerge and wrest the power from him. This seems to have been a safe assumption at the time of the Arab-Israeli war of 1967: certainly no greater catastrophe could have befallen Egypt, and no greater opportunity for anti-Nasser factions to arise and take over the country, but Nasser's hold emerged stronger than ever.

Robert Michels, in writing about Bonapartism, speaks of a "psychological metamorphosis" that leaders like Nasser go through. As the result of having so much power, they eventually come to have an inordinate consciousness of their "personal worth, and of the need which the mass feels for guidance" which "induce in his mind a recognition of his own superiority. . . . He who has acquired power will almost always endeavor to consolidate it and to extend it, to multiply the ramparts which defend his position, and to withdraw himself from the control of the masses." Over the years, I have probably seen more of Nasser than any other Westerner. Even now, although it is no longer possible to drop in on him informally and stay for lunch, I manage a long talk with him every month or two, and under relaxed circumstances in which he is most likely to be himself. I have gone into these talks sometimes with no other purpose than a friendly social visit, sometimes with a mission to accomplish for one or another of my companies, sometimes briefed to the teeth by a CIA doctor, psychiatrist or ordinary intelligence officer to enable me to detect any signs of failing health or mental powers. Nor am I an amateur at seeing through poker faces. If I had to make a judgment on the current shape of Nasser's psyche, without regard to the game, I would say that his mental faculties and use of them are about what they always were. For game purposes, however, I would have to assume that what happens, sooner or later, to all Nasser-type leaders has happened to Nasser himself: whatever the endurance of his personality under the assault of sycophancy, blind adulation, uncritical loyalty, and ordinary fear, the barriers between him and the outside world have grown so thick that all but the information that attests to his infallibility, indispensability and immortality has been filtered out. Even if he were the greatest genius, the most stable personality, and the most perspicacious human being alive, it would be impossible for him to remain properly oriented for the Game of Nations given the shrubbery that inevitably grows up around his kind of leader. Thus, his opponents in the Game of Nations should assume that he makes wise moves in the light of his understanding of the game board, but that his understanding is warped—exactly *how* it is warped remaining a mystery. Nasser probably would not recognize the crossroads—personal power and ruin to the country versus loss of power and saving the country—if he came to it.

It all starts with the need to be insured by a "repressive base" as outlined in the Eichelberger paper. If Nasser had viewed leadership as no more than a mere matter of staying in front of the mob, *wherever* it is going, there would have been no problem—or rather, there would have been problems the solution of which depended upon fancy footwork rather than real leadership. Nasser, however, with our blessing, decided that "to be leader is easy. All you have to do is to identify the aspirations of the mob and shout them more loudly than anyone else. But to be a *good* leader is more difficult: you must influence the mob to aspire to what is really best for it." Remember, the whole point of our supporting Nasser was to have in power in one "key" Arab country a leader who would be strong enough to afford unpopular decisions—like making peace with Israel, for example. The first step, by our books as well as Nasser's, was therefore to establish order, by force if necessary.

This was no arbitrary, peremptory decision in the manner of the Greek colonels some years later. Nasser thought about the problem, discussed it with his own lieutenants and with leading politicians of the day, and conveyed his concern to his Western friends—who, incidentally, applauded his leaning toward an emphasis on law and order. Part of our thinking was due to a sentiment expressed later by as liberal a diplomat as we had in the service, John Davies, Jr., who said, "The basic issue is not whether the government is dictatorial or is representative and constitutional. The issue is whether the government, whatever its character, can hold the society together sufficiently to make the transition"—transition to modernity, that is. But part of our thinking was more down-to-earth: even then, we instinctively realized that the principal components of the repressive base—the Army, the police, and the intelligence services—would tend to be on our side, whereas Nasser's popular support was for a number of reasons likely to tend Leftward. The booklet *Power Problems of a Revolutionary Government* gives an indication of how we wedded the two views.

According to *Power Problems*—or, for that matter, according to common sense—the repressive power upon which a revolutionary government must rely is based on the following: legislation, police, organized intelligence services, propaganda facilities, and organized military force—the army. What Eichelberger and his Egyptian interlocutors agreed upon under these headings may be seen in the Appendix. Something should be said, however, about how development of the individual items worked out.

Legislation: Not even the most liberal observer disagreed with the proposition that a government which had come into power by a coup d'etat required a period of martial law and systematic steps to eliminate, alter or subdue institutions whose failure had made the coup necessary—and possible. No one denied that the new regime should use legislation as a means of defining "subversion" and "danger to the regime" and other such terms, and of prescribing preventive means and punishment. Nasser's legislation did just that: it defined the mission of the police and intelligence services; it gave them discretionary leeway to take the initiative in dealing with attempts to overthrow the government, incitement to violence, revealing official secrets, and even less serious versions of these crimes. The legislation, which reached the public by means of decrees of the Revolutionary Command Council, was intelligent and well written. Caffery's legal adviser proclaimed them first-rate—"unique in this part of the world," he said. "I've seen worse in France."

But the way the legislation was enforced brought the

Government in for serious criticism, criticism that even today forms the basis of the attacks against Nasser and his regime carried on by Egyptian groups exiled in Switzerland and elsewhere. Persons were arrested without charge, property was sequestrated, censorship was clamped on newspapers—all done in a very orderly fashion, but without very clear relation to the legislation. Then some of those who had been arrested were released and allowed to take up their old political activity, even encouraged to do so; some of the property was desequestrated; censorship was lifted when the newspapers least expected it. Then, after weeks of comparative freedom, there were more arrests, more sequestrations, more censorship. Back and forth, from complete repression to almost complete freedom, until Western observers friendly to Nasser thought he was causing an amount of fear and uncertainty throughout the country that would endanger his regime. There was no doubt that he was beginning to get a bad press outside his country, and most Western embassies were beginning to report increasing misgivings over the possibility that a "fascist military dictatorship is emerging," as one of them put it.

But if the American Embassy was critical it was not because of any serious distaste for the arrests, sequestrations, and muzzlings of the press but because of the inept way in which the government explained such actions to the public —bad public relations, in other words. The simple fact was this: whereas liberal-minded observers regarded legislation as something passive, something to be held up as a set of rules which one stayed out of jail by not breaking, Nasser had to use his legislation as something active, as a means for justifying the action he had to take, if he was to survive, against certain clearly defined elements of Egyptian society and specified persons. These elements and individuals were irreconcilable; no matter what he could have done they would have remained enemies of the regime—although, perhaps, pretending otherwise. Caffery and his staff, who had had plenty of contact with these Egyptians over the years, knew this as well as Nasser knew it. Also, these Egyptians themselves knew it, as did the populace around them. Thus, Nasser's cleanup caused no general fear and alarm. "Those who have cause to be afraid have been quarantined," as one of Nasser's security chiefs put it.

Police: The police, as such, took no part in the coup; one or two of the senior officers had tenuous contact with Zakaria Mohieddin, head of Nasser's shadow military-intelligence setup, but that was all. But Zakaria's men had thoroughly penetrated the police, and immediately following the coup a cleanup was easy. After removing some thirty or forty officers and some hundred policemen whose loyalty was in question, Nasser took over himself as Minister of the Interior and gave special attention to the police. In a matter of weeks it was as efficient a national security force as ever, and neutralized as a possible source of danger to the new regime.

At the Interior Ministry level, the Egyptian security system is manned, like security systems anywhere, not by the best brains of the country, but by the kind of people who join security services. One of Nasser's security chiefs once told me, "We operate on the principle that all people are basically loyal so long as they are made to understand that we will give the water treatment to anyone suspected of disloyalty." Perhaps someone will one day devise means for inducing gentlemen of finer sensitivities to become security officers, but certainly then no such means were known, either by Nasser or by his American advisers. The best we could hope for was to minimize the action part of security work and to emphasize surveillance.

Surveillance was accomplished by the famous "city-eye" system which Nasser inherited from the previous regime, and which has probably existed in Egypt for centuries. It is entirely unobtrusive. A CIA officer, formerly an FBI man, who had undergone the most sophisticated modern training in surveillance once went from one end of Cairo to the other and was prepared to swear that he had not been under surveillance for one moment, only to learn later from the smiling chief of security that every move he had made had been observed, every telephone call monitored, and every contact identified and recorded. The secret is simple: doormen, taxicab drivers, telephone operators, beggars, street venders, and hordes of other people know that they may be rewarded by a few piasters should they be able to give helpful answers to some security officer coming by to ask questions about a foreigner who has just passed. Such persons who work the blocks around the best hotels and other places where foreigners congregate have been rewarded so many times in the past that they have developed remarkable powers of observation and memories, together with an ability to spot the details that security police most frequently ask about.

Organized Intelligence Service: Nasser acted as Minister of the Interior for some three or four months, then passed the job on to his most intelligent lieutenant, Zakaria Mohieddin, who was at the same time the head of Military Intelligence. Nasser mapped out the shape of the new intelligence-security system. Zakaria designed some refinements and put it into operation. At the top of the system was the newly created "General Intelligence Agency," modeled after the American Central Intelligence Agency and staffed by Free Officers who had served under Zakaria in pre-coup days. They were of an extremely high caliber, clearly among those "good organization men" who would be useful after the coup as well as before. Using American management-engineering methods, they organized the new agency (in Arabic, *mukhabaret al-aam*) as an overall supervisory, coordinating body, then organized the operational agencies of the Ministry of Interior and the Army so that their relations with one another would be the right balance of cooperation and competition, finally setting up entirely new special intelligence and investigating agencies which were to report directly to the GIA.

Some of these operating units were concerned with foreign matters—training of guerrillas for Aden, intelligence on Israel, smuggling boxes of doped Israeli and Saudi Arabian double agents by air from Rome back to Cairo, etc.; most of the units were concerned with internal security problems. To the already effective—and unobtrusive—"city-eye" system they added impressive technical surveillance potential. They purchased the complete range of electronic equipment then being developed by American industrial espionage and counterespionage organizations and employed a number of former German intelligence officers (of whom more later) to train them in their use. For some months they were overpowered by the flood of information, and processing got so far behind that it was all virtually useless. Until they learned that processing tape recordings of the human voice takes exactly as long as the sum total of the lengths of all the conversations on the tape, with all the tiresome irrelevant details, they accumulated piles of unprocessed tape in the *mukhabaret* and Interior Ministry basements. Later, however, they learned to be selective. By 1960 they had the means for easy and quick installation of microphones in just about any hotel room, officers' mess, private residence or automobile in Cairo or Alexandria, for overhearing street conversations at a distance, and for various kinds of long-distance photography or for taking pictures in the dark. But at the urging of the Tourist Department and because of practical limitations (such as the time required for processing and the shortage of translators), only the most discriminating use has been made of the capability: enough, however, to spot sources of danger to the regime.

Propaganda facilities: Propaganda was the subject on which there was greatest disparity of view between the Americans (particularly Caffery and Eichelberger) and

Nasser. Nasser's military background was hardly ideal for preparation as a propagandist, or even for acquainting a leader with the problems of communicating with the public. At the same time, Nasser had seen enough of his own people to be aware how much was to be known about them, how little he knew of what there was to be known, and how leery he should be of outside opinion, however expert. Eichelberger had once been an account executive for J. Walter Thompson, one of the world's largest advertising and public relations firms, and he started with the assumption that one appeals to an individual or to the public in terms of their own interest. Nasser was ready to admit that he did not yet know how to appeal to the Egyptian public, but he was convinced that it should not be through self-interest. He strongly suspected that self-advancement was not likely to be, and should not be, a driving force in the revolution's appeal.

As a "repressive" tool during the phase when Nasser was consolidating his coup, the main argument was sidetracked in favor of the censorship question. Trouble quickly arose as the result of the to-be-expected inexperience of Nasser's military censor, who infuriated foreign correspondents by holding up their copy and operating on a principle of if-in-doubt-cut-it. This was disturbing to the friendly Americans, who wanted the regime to get a favorable press. Also, it was demoralizing to the friendly and highly articulate Egyptian correspondents whose help was needed in putting across an image of the revolution that would be suitable for local viewing, for the Arab world, and for the world at large—a subtle and difficult job.

The problem was solved the way a Nasser-type regime always solves such problems: by making a list of foreign and local correspondents who could be trusted to report favorably and a list of correspondents who could not be so trusted and by seeing to it that the former were given complete freedom and the latter given none. Also, the Government saw to it that the borderline cases—the foreign correspondents who were taking a wait-and-see attitude—were heavily courted and given information that would influence them favorably. Censorship, as such, became a routine matter—and except for the occasional unreasonableness that was due purely to administrative inefficiency, remained so until the war with Israel in June 1967. Only for a short time was it part of Nasser's repressive system.

Government-generated propaganda, however, was used very effectively as a means of exposing enemies of the regime in a bad light and of justifying harsh actions against them. Quite on their own, Mustafa and Ali Amin, the twin brothers who were heads of Cairo's largest publishing house, printed in their newspapers offers of rewards for persons coming forth with instances of corruption in the government or in the nation's political life. Instances were brought to the surface which enabled the Amin brothers themselves, Mohammed Heykel, and others to flood the papers with stories that were dramatically convincing of the evils of the old regime and all that went with it, and of the need for taking drastic measures to obliterate it. And the drive had the full blessing of the Americans: Ambassador Caffery arranged with Nasser for the loan to the Egyptian government of perhaps the leading practitioner of "black" and "gray" propaganda in the Western world, Paul Linebarger, the former OSS propagandist who during the Second World War had broadcast what were ostensibly German and pro-German newscasts but which were actually demoralizing to the Germans in effect. Linebarger showed the Egyptian propagandists how to damage hallowed figures (for example, General Naguib) while seeming to praise them—a technique that the Egyptians still use in Arab world politics.

The Army: Needless to say, the Egyptian Army is the bulwark of Nasser's repressive base. Nasser has kept it so by ensuring that there are no politically ambitious persons or rebels in key positions—or in any positions at all if they can be spotted. Those of his officers who were known to have political ambitions were taken out of the Army and placed in civilian posts which were either important-sounding sinecures or bona fide jobs where they would either make the grade or break themselves. Officers who might conceivably be entertaining notions of a new coup—those who showed signs of resenting having been excluded from the inner circle, or of lingering loyalty to the old regime—were given every opportunity to plot and otherwise incriminate themselves, or even goaded into it by *agents provocateurs,* then rounded up by the secret police. There remained, with a few unavoidable exceptions, only officers who were susceptible to discipline and whose loyalty could be ensured by catering to their healthier wants: prestige, a few harmless privileges, a few inexpensive perquisites, and, above all, a service of which they could be proud. So long as they were not *too* outraged by Nasser's association with intellectuals, leftists, and other objectionable persons—or, rather, so long as they were not allowed time or reason to think about such matters—they could be counted on as a loyal force to fall back on in case of need.

The question of Western—and Soviet—military aid to Egypt is more appropriately discussed in a later chapter, but apropos the American attitude toward Nasser's use of the Army as a repressive force the following should be said: In the early days when Nasser was asking for military aid there was no question of his using it for ordinary military purposes (e.g., for fighting the Israelis or the Yemenis or anybody else) or of large amounts' being supplied; the need was entirely for internal security purposes. Nasser made it quite clear to our ambassadors that his regime relied on the military for its insurance, and that he regarded a "shabby army as a potentially disloyal army." The amount of military aid for which Nasser asked the United States Government in the early days of his regime was first $40,000,000, then later $20,000,000, and finally "just two or three million dollars' worth of parade items"—helmets, pistol holsters, and various kinds of shiny equipment which would look good when the Army was parading through the streets of Cairo and give the officers and soldiers a feeling of pride. As I will show later on, it was the State Department's delay in granting this comparatively small amount that caused Nasser to turn to the Soviets—with the result that he got many times over the $40,000,000 he originally asked from us.

Although it will not contribute much to the main theme of this book, the picture of our aid to Nasser's repressive base will, by omission, be misleading unless we include a few remarks on our part in bringing in the German advisers.

During the Second World War it served the purposes of the Allies to exaggerate the omniscience of the German intelligence services and to pretend that one could not have a friendly discussion in a Piccadilly coffee shop without some German agent's overhearing it and cabling a brief summary to Berlin. British Intelligence and OSS suspected then, and confirmed the suspicion later, that German Intelligence was virtually nonexistent as a widespread network but survived on a few high-level operations—many of which were controlled by western deceptionists who used them as channels through which to send misleading information to Berlin. As the result of exhaustive postwar studies, it now seems safe to conclude that the only really clean operation of the Germans was that of the famous "Cicero" who stole secrets from the safe of the British Ambassador in Turkey. But this didn't come to much because German Intelligence headquarters was so overwhelmed by contradictory information (presumably sent by its agents who were under British or American control) that his reports were discounted.

Our contempt for German Intelligence was shared by many German intelligence officers themselves, and a good percentage of these made deals with Allied intelligence agencies as they saw the war coming to an end—some of them long before the end. Many more who never actually became Allied agents established in one way or another good relations with Allied officers and, as a result, received special protection. But with good people in the United States and Great Britain—not to mention France, Holland, Belgium, and other European countries including Germany itself—howling for Nazi blood, no American or British officer in his right mind would be expected to speak up in behalf of some ex-Nazi merely on the ground that he had been an intelligence agent or (an even weaker defense) that he would be valuable as an intelligence asset in the coming struggle with the Soviet Union. Nevertheless, with the Soviets taking the best German brains—including deep-dyed Nazis on whom they had sworn vengeance—we simply could not bring ourselves to let valuable non-Anglo-American assets (who, as Nazis, were under perfect "cover") go to waste. As a G-2 American colonel put it, "Believe it or not, some of us are still able to put future American interests ahead of the delights of revenge." If he had made such a remark publicly, in 1945, he would without doubt have been cashiered.

At any rate, right or wrong, good or bad, between the years 1941 and 1947 the Department of Defense, presumably with some kind of joint responsibility with the State Department, had on its hands a number of Germans who were not—or in some cases not *quite*—war criminals, and whom it was to our advantage to have absorbed, with a minimum of fuss and embarrassment, by various countries of the world where they could live inconspicuously and earn a living. There was an effort within an effort: we combed files of these Germans in a search for talent which could be put to good use, in some cases in the United States itself (Wernher von Braun, the space scientist at Hunstville, Alabama, is the best-known example) but mostly in other countries. This effort was well on the way to being completed when, in 1953, it became apparent that Nasser needed outside help for his intelligence and security services and our Government found it highly impolitic to help him directly.

For reasons connected with his own politics, Nasser most

of all wanted a military expert, a person who could bring Prussian discipline to his somewhat casual army. An American military attaché suggested Lieutenant General Wilhelm Farmbacher, who was eminently available—as his Nazi standing was well enough known to make him unwelcome in Germany and yet he had no particular talents, certainly none commensurate with his high rank, that would put him in demand elsewhere; he was "a placement problem," as the American G-2 officer in charge of him put it. Farmbacher's military prowess during the Second World War was far from remarkable, but perhaps he was up to the comparatively simple military problems of Egypt. "He might even screw things up," the G-2 said. (He did. In the course of the first maneuver planned for the Egyptian Army by Farmbacher the "reds" and the "blues" couldn't even find each other in the desert for the mock battle; it turned out that Farmbacher had given each side the wrong maps, but the accompanying directions were so complicated that they were unable to realize the mistake.) However, he was of impressively high rank, and we gained some kudos from Nasser for producing him.

Next was the famous Otto Skorzeny, the SS officer who took credit for rescuing Mussolini from imminent capture. Otto was a particular favorite of American Counterintelligence, having made friends with several of his captors before escaping from them, and was believed to be especially suited, in temperament and personality, for getting along with Nasser. He was approached in a routine manner, then at a higher level, then through a personal visit from a certain well-known Major General of the American Army, and finally through his father-in-law, Dr. Hjalmar Schacht, Hitler's former Minister of Finance. Although he had lost interest in security and intelligence work, and had moved on to bigger things, he finally agreed to visit Egypt to see what could be accomplished in the course of a short visit. Certain writers have reported that Skorzeny stayed in Cairo for many months to serve as "Nasser's chief military and geopolitical adviser," to quote one book on the subject, but this simply isn't so. Skorzeny stayed in Cairo long enough to lay Nasser open to the charge that his regime was being controlled from behind the scenes by "unrepentant Nazis," but then could not get out of Egypt fast enough—to stop off at his newly purchased farm in Ireland, then to return to his engineering business in Spain, which has since become a highly profitable enterprise.

But Skorzeny did, in a halfhearted manner, manage to bring in about a hundred Germans, the ones that all the unfavorable publicity has been about. To set the record straight, here are the essential facts about them: first, with one or two exceptions they are all small fry; second, they are not "unrepentant Nazis"—unfortunately, it might be argued, because as mere survivalists rather than men of principle, even wrong principle, they find no difficulty in adjusting to Leftish influences in Nasser's Government; third, the Egyptians made very little use of their advice— often keeping them waiting for hours to meet the Egyptian officials through whom they were to deliver their advice; fourth, the Egyptians paid them a fraction of what they paid advisers of other nationalities, including British and American, who worked for them. Lieutenant General Farmbacher, for example, received the equivalent of £50 per month plus a dilapidated house. (There were several Americans who received more than £500 per month plus an excellent house and a car with chauffeur.) Skorzeny had done the best he could under the circumstances, and to this day remains on the best of terms with Nasser—and, for that matter, with the American friends who were instrumental in getting him to Egypt in the first place. Skorzeny has long ago been cleared of any war crimes.

The fact is that Nasser and Zakaria, despite all their foreign advisers, built the intelligence and security services with remarkably little outside help. And so far as Western intelligence agencies can tell from their penetrations of these services, they did a remarkably competent job. Finally, with his legislation, police, intelligence services, propaganda, and Army, Nasser has a "repressive base" which can indeed enable him to "rule Egypt the way Papa Duvalier rules Haiti" if he ever has to do so, and which meanwhile enables him to make necessary, constructive decisions without having to fear popular rebellion. Much has been made of Nasser's running a "police state" without freedom of speech and other such liberties. The fact is, however, that apart from having to endure perhaps the dullest newspapers in the world and the inconvenience of relying on the BBC and the Israeli radio for news, the average Egyptian does not feel deprived by Nasser's occasional clamp-downs on such liberties—he does not have anything in particular to say anyhow. The anti-Nasser Egyptians are irreconcilably anti-Nasser whether or not they have free speech and the other freedoms, so Nasser and his supporters argue that he has all to lose and nothing to gain by allowing such liberties.

It has been distasteful for Western observers to see property confiscated at random, people jailed on mere suspicion, the press muzzled and foreign correspondents sometimes roughly handled. It has been particularly unpleasant for Nasser's friends in the diplomatic community, whose normal social contacts are with the "tame Egyptians" who have suffered most. On the other hand, the fact is that Nasser's repressive actions, however they appear to the outside world, have *not* been random, but rather coldly calculated, and this has meant that only a few easily identifiable elements and persons have suffered, not the general population. Nasser justifies his actions with the argument of self-preservation similar to that used by the Israelis for not tolerating large non-Jewish communities in their country; and having decided that totalitarian controls are necessary, he has to accept the inescapable fact that they will be administered with the same inefficiency with which everything else is administered, and that by the very nature of things security police in an Oriental country are even more stupid than their counterparts in Western countries. On the other hand, it can certainly be said that the Egyptians achieve more security with less ostentation than any other country in the Middle East.

As the years went on, Nasser retained his repressive base in one form or another, although to the inexperienced eye it was obscured from time to time by his bringing on to the scene a number of agencies whose purpose appeared to be repressive but was really something more Machiavellian— the "counterfeudalist" police, the Arab Socialist Union's "investigators," and others whom Nasser put at each others' throats to cause a little calculated chaos at a time when he needed it for some purpose of palace politics. The most important things for the diplomatic observer to understand about Nasser's repressive actions are these: first, despite any temporary appearance to the contrary (including the appearance of friction between Nasser and the Army), the repressive base has always been there and always enjoys Nasser's highest-priority attention. Many of his actions on the international scene which foreign observers find so opposed to the Egyptian mood as they understand it can be explained by some need of Nasser's, not apparent to the outside world, to maintain his repressive base. Second, although Western officials who dislike Nasser have spoken up from time to time to call him a fascist dictator, in actual fact the American Government, and to some extent the British Government, kept a sharp eye on Nasser as he built his repressive capabilities and condoned his actions.

In his excellent book *Nasser's New Egypt,* * Keith Wheelock expresses a view of the revolution that is representative of most well-informed outside observers when he speaks of Nasser's "indecision," gives accounts of the Revolutionary Command Council's apparent wavering between parlia-

* See Suggested Reading List.

mentary government and military dictatorship, deplores the Free Officers' "abandonment of the principles which they had held aloft," and concludes that "a historian, looking back on this turbulent period, will find cause to indict Nasser and his group." As we shall see, Nasser was throughout far from indecisive, and his apparent wavering between parliamentary government and dictatorship was carefully calculated. Moreover, it was calculated with the full knowledge of American officials and private individuals who are as liberal as anyone but who were close enough to the situation to see that Nasser could not do otherwise and that a premature attempt to move toward the "principles they had held aloft" would have resulted in chaos. If we didn't actually assist Nasser in his coup, in his consolidation of the coup, and in the laying of "repressive" foundations, it was only because, aside from occasionally heeding some of our gratuitous advice, Nasser would not accept our help. And we certainly offered no complaint, believing as we did that Nasser would as soon as practicably possible set about creating the conditions that Roosevelt and Nasser had agreed were prerequisite to genuine democratic government: a literate populace, a large and stable middle class, a feeling by the people that "this is *our* government," and sufficient identification of local ideals and values so that truly indigenous democratic institutions could grow up, not mere imitations imported from the United States or Great Britain.

But, regardless of how it got there, we must always remember, in dealing with Nasser, that the repressive base is all-important to him. We should not be surprised when, after the most catastrophic defeat in recent military history, Nasser and his lieutenants sit down not to talk about how to rebuild Egypt, but about how to rebuild confidence in the Army. This continues to be the Egyptian idea of priorities.

6

The "Nasser-Type" Leader and His "Constructive Base"

His second objective will be
to strengthen his position by constructive *means.*

Early in 1956, President Nasser, Ambassador-at-large Eric Johnston and I spent a long evening in Nasser's garden discussing what Nasser could and could not do to help Johnston put over the Jordan River Plan to other Arab leaders. The plan, designed to tempt the Arabs into at least limited cooperation with the Israelis, was a third-rate idea with at least a second-rate chance of success because it had a first-rate negotiator, Eric Johnston, to advocate the plan. Its only advantage was that it made sense: some three hundred thousand acres of Syrian, Lebanese, Jordanian and Israeli desert land would be reclaimed, and enough electric power would be generated to provide industrial employment for all the Palestine refugees who would otherwise live in privation for years to come. Nasser was tempted by Johnston's practical arguments, but the political obstacles were too great—even for Nasser.

Still, it was an interesting subject for discussion. We spent the first half of the evening exploring the ways in which a "Jordan River Authority" constructed along the lines of the Tennessee Valley Authority could fit into the more grandiose regional development schemes then being contemplated by the Arab League and others. (At this stage of his career, Nasser was suspicious of regional development, the "Arab common market," and other ideas of Arab economic cooperation, but he liked to talk about them.) We spent the last part of the evening on the unpalatable political implications of the scheme. Nasser seemed genuinely sympathetic to the scheme as a whole, "but you find me at a time when I am unable to take an unpopular action," he said. He then launched out on a lecture, peppered liberally with such phrases as "policy flexibility" and "tolerance parameters," in which he explained that at times of high popularity he was free to think only of what was good for Egypt, but that at times when he was less sure of himself he had to do what his supporters expected of him, no matter what the effect on Egypt.

Johnston listened with growing impatience and finally said that he had spent the previous week listening to a number of lunatic alternatives proposed by Lebanese and Syrian leaders and that he was frankly disappointed to hear the undisputed leader of the Arab world go on about what he could and could not get away with in the eyes of such demagogues. He stood up to go. He shook hands with Nasser, strode to the door, then turned dramatically and said, "Mr. President, I am reminded of the words of the French revolutionary leader: 'The mob is in the streets. I must find out where it is going, for I am its leader.'" Nasser beamed delightedly. "Exactly!" he said.

Nasser's literal acceptance of Johnston's *mot* was mostly facetious (he was not prepared to let the American master salesman get away with such an exit line), but he was also serious: he wanted to remind Johnston that any leader anywhere, and especially a leader in a country like Egypt, who does not have a firm understanding of "where the mob is going" is not likely to remain a leader very long. At a later meeting, he told Johnston, "The first task of a leader is to be the leader; only after you have ensured that you *are* the leader can you start thinking about becoming a *good* leader," and went on to argue that he, more than anyone else, realized that his "mob," if left to its own instincts, would destroy itself. "This doesn't mean, though, that I can disregard its compulsions entirely," he said.

At that time there was probably no chief of state in modern history who had a better idea of "where they are going" than Nasser, or a more realistic understanding of the sad fact that "they" were not in actual fact going anywhere —not on the basis of their existing wants, anyhow. They did not want the right things—that is, those things which would give them true satisfaction and not merely satisfy grievances of the moment. Nasser's job, as he understood it, was to play upon satisfaction of the short-range wants as a means of buying time, while awakening long-range wants only as he developed the means of satisfying them.

It is to his credit that this understanding didn't come easily. When he was planning his revolution he had an idea of what the Egyptian people *ought* to want (what he wanted himself), but he knew well enough that their actual wants were something beyond his comprehension at the time—and, for that matter, beyond the comprehension of any Egyptian leader. In other words, the mob was *not* in the streets. That was his problem. The Egyptian people had a fitful sort of "potential for fanaticism," as Paul Linebarger used to say, which was motivation enough for burning down a foreign embassy every now and then but not enough to support sustained revolutionary activity. Nasser knew that he had to engineer an environment that would awaken motivations in the people in the same way that warmer or colder water—dissatisfaction, in other words—motivates an amoeba. Only a motivated people could respond to the leadership with which Nasser hoped to provide his movement.

There was no shortage of expert advice as to how to go about it. With a bit of kibitzing from an American adviser whose name I am not at liberty to reveal, Salah Salem, the Minister of National Guidance, launched a public opinion

survey which provided the basic propositions upon which
Nasser could plan his whole campaign to "wake up the
Egyptian people." Taking as its starting point an excellent
study made by two ladies from the Bureau of Applied Social
Research at Columbia University, Salah's researchers went
carefully through the whole country examining farmers,
workers, students, professional people, and others. At first,
the researchers—three Egyptians, one Englishman and one
German—used the direct-question, Gallup Poll approach,
only to find that the respondents told the interviewers what
they thought the interviewers wanted to hear (to the Egyptians, "We hate the British, imperialism, and the Israelis";
to the Englishman, "We like the British and hate to see them
leave"; to the German, "We are sorry that the Germans lost
the war"). They then tried the "motivational-research"
method in which they would talk casually to the respondents
about which films they preferred, their favorite colors, their
attitudes toward nonpolitical social subjects, in this way
coming to sound conclusions about their *real* feelings for the
British, the Arabs, Israel, and so on.

The CIA was also involved in these researches. The head
of the CIA apparatus in Egypt at the time was under what
is known as "ethnic cover" (when the personal appearance,
language, habits and passport enable an intelligence officer
to blend with his surroundings physically) as opposed to
"cultural cover" (under which an agent is accepted for his
presumed political and social sympathies). Using a network
of informants as impressive in its way as the much larger
"city eye" of the Egyptian security system, he concentrated
on the subject "The Susceptibility of the Egyptian People
to Soviet Communism," attempting to identify specific attitudes of the people—by occupational classification (farmers, workers, professionals, intelligentsia)—that the Communists would be able to play upon and, putting himself
in the Communists' place, to determine the means they
would probably use. Although they were forbidden by CIA

headquarters to engage in outright espionage (penetration of the Egyptian Government, acquiring official secrets of the Government, or inducing an Egyptian citizen knowingly to serve a foreign power), the fact that his apparatus worked under cover enabled it to hear frank talk, in all quarters, which was not likely to come the way of Salah's interviewers or even to be picked up in an interpretable form by the "city eye."

In January 1954, Paul Linebarger, the Pentagon's leading authority on "black" and "gray" propaganda, visited Cairo, and Salah Salem was replaced by Colonel Abd-el-Qader Hatem, who remained Minister of National Guidance (or, later, Deputy Prime Minister for Culture and National Guidance) for the next ten years. Findings of the CIA edited by Linebarger and turned over to Colonel Hatem, combined with those of Salah Salem's researchers, were expanded by some highly astute observations by Nasser himself on the basis of his experience during the preceding year and consolidated in a large study which Nasser put under lock and key in his own desk drawer. As we shall see, Nasser understood that the various positions he would have to take up in the Game of Nations required that the world at large have a picture of Egyptian motivations other than the correct one.*

* The problem of reconciling Egyptian "private opinion" to the "public opinion," that Nasser wants to present to the world persists to this very day. As we shall see in a later chapter, the one clear revelation of "private opinion" in 1968 showed that there is little or no enthusiasm in Egypt for "redeeming the honor of the Arabs in Palestine" or for "improving" Nasser's single political party which the Egyptian people, according to their privately expressed opinions, would like to see disbanded altogether. But for the sake of objectives with which the Egyptian people *are* in sympathy, Nasser has to pretend that the public is clamoring to reopen the war with Israel, to strengthen the Arab Socialist Union, and to give a hard time to the "defeatists" and to "those who allow themselves to be bewitched by enemy propaganda."

Nasser's views as to how leadership can be reconciled with this situation are of particular interest. And here it is necessary to discuss more recent history than is actually relevant to our main theme, because of misconceptions of the Nasser-Naguib relationship given the public by writers who had no choice but to take appearances at their face value. Even Professor Lerner, in his essentially accurate book *The Passing of Traditional Society** contrasts the "Naguib style" and the "Nasser style" as a way of explaining the Egyptian people's receptivity to public communication as an instrument of social change. The points he makes are all valid. But the fact is that Naguib had no style other than that of those other handsome figures in TV commercials who look their various parts. As an Englishwoman talking to Ambassador Caffery about a meeting she had just had with Naguib put it, "He is so delightfully *evil,* so divinely *corrupt*-looking, but with such a warm smile. A perfect father figure for the Egyptians."

From the two long meetings I had with Naguib I got the same impression. He managed to exude what passes for charisma in parts of the Middle East and to project that image which Egyptians generally find so lovable, that of a kindly old crook. He was the sort of idol Egyptians tend to fall back on in their quieter moments between sprees of violence incited by more austere leader types. But his style in thinking and speaking was hardly that attributed to him by Professor Lerner.

Naguib's book was written by a very intelligent American named Leigh White, who was, in addition, the author of many of the wise *mots* attributed to Naguib. Leigh had personal reasons for wanting to be abroad for a year, in the most practical version of Shangri-la he could find, and he arrived by chance, in Egypt at a time when Naguib was becoming good copy in the international press. He secured

* See Suggested Reading List.

an advance from his publisher, easily gained Naguib's enthusiasm for the project (and Nasser's tired assent, which was necessary), and settled in Cairo for a year of following Naguib about: lunching and dining with him, waiting in his anteroom, actually sitting in on many of his meetings, and drawing him out in long conversations.

Leigh White was a first-rate raconteur, and the stories on Naguib with which he regaled Ambassador Caffery, me and others gave a wonderful picture of a sly and lovable village chieftain who had time for anyone with troubles—a wife with an alcoholic husband, a religious man who had seen a vision and wanted funds with which to erect a temple on the spot (as a tourist attraction), a landlord complaining about the vices of his tenants. But when he talked about Naguib's philosophy he was talking pure Leigh White, a frustrated liberal who had not found such an outlet for his energies since the Spanish Civil War. White and the local CIA chief (who, as we have mentioned, was under ethnic cover) loathed one another (although I doubt that Leigh knew the man was employed by the CIA), and many of the sensible and democratic utterances that Leigh attributed to Naguib first appeared as his own rejoinders in arguments with the CIA man—who, incidentally, was a Nasser man through and through. I once tried to engage Naguib in a conversation by asking him about one of these pieces of wisdom, and it rapidly became perfectly clear that he didn't have the faintest idea what I was talking about.

I think I have heard all the principal versions of how Naguib got into the coup, not only from the key figures themselves but from officers lower down. Three points appear to be common to all versions: first, while Nasser and his lieutenants were organizing the Free Officers network they hinted at the presence of a great leader, "one whom you all know and respect, and will be happy to follow to the ends of the earth once you know his name," though they carefully refrained from mentioning a particular individual

—indeed, at the time they had no particular individual in mind. Second, Naguib was far from the only choice; he was one of several possibilities, and right up to the last minute, when Amer finally convinced Nasser that recent events made Naguib the logical choice, he was not even first on the list. Third, although Naguib had an excellent record for courage and was extremely popular with the officers, his primary qualification was his apparent lack of ambition or desire for power. The officers thought they could handle him.

As indeed they could. The events that made Naguib the only choice were almost certainly rigged by the Communist member of Nasser's entourage, Khalid Mohieddin, and others who thought that they could handle him better than Nasser could and who would eventually find him useful if Nasser got out of hand. Nasser was probably aware of this —anyhow, he now claims that he was—but he had no fear of Khalid and the others and found it useful at the time to let them think they had a leader of *their* choice. At any rate, once Naguib's leadership did take hold as the revolution got under way it was not Naguib's Egyptian followers, whom Nasser could handle, but Leigh White who began to give Naguib the idea that he was history's gift to Egypt. One of the lieutenants wrote Naguib's speeches, but it was Leigh who polished them (after having them translated into English) under the pretense of "making them suitable for posterity," that is, for the autobiography of Naguib which Leigh was writing.

Nasser's ideas on the place of leadership in the revolution —his own leadership, that of anyone else, or that of a figure-head leader which he or anyone else might place in ostensible charge of the revolution—are interesting not only because of the insights they provide on Nasser as a historical figure in his own right but because they were endorsed by the American advisers around him at the time and are therefore an indication of how our cryptodiplomats see the role of leadership in non-Western society. Although Kermit Roosevelt and the advisers he sent to Egypt—Steve Meade, James Eichelberger, Paul Linebarger, and others—did not "control" Nasser any more than the Russians control him today, the fact that their ideas on the subject of leadership coincided with his own makes his whole leadership philosophy deserving of sympathetic understanding to an extent that his Western critics haven't realized. The extent to which Nasser would have done what he did regardless of Western approval or disapproval does not matter so much as the fact that what he did, at least at the time, had the approval of Westerners who were totally loyal to the interests of their own countries and who were guided by principles that are generally accepted in the West.

To start with, Nasser believed that you get anyone, a single individual or a populace, to do what you want him to do not by persuasion or by coercion but by creating circumstances that will make him want to do it. People are motivated by their own wants, not by the wants of their leader. Leadership, in other words, is essentially a job of motivation. First, you *motivate* the people (make them want something); then, you *direct* them (show them how to get it). Or, if you can't really show them how to get it (and this is usually the case, since nobody really knows a way to prosperity—or to any acceptable substitute—that is open to the people of a so-called "underdeveloped" country), you show them what *appears* to be a way, and this will enable you to hold on to leadership until they find out differently or until someone else turns up with a more plausible avenue.

As Nasser, before the coup, took a good look at his country, he saw people who didn't really want anything, who weren't really motivated in any direction. He saw that it was necessary to surround them with an environment that would stimulate the motivation; the "leader" was merely a part of the environment. And it was not necessary to Nasser that he be the leader himself, so long as he could engineer the environment and retain control of it. As Nasser has since openly become the leader, instead of remaining a manipulator behind the scenes, this argument is bound to be questioned. But those who know Nasser well believe it, and believe that what changed things was not Nasser's growing thirst for power so much as a thirst for power awakening in Naguib. Nasser wanted a figurehead, and Naguib could have stayed on indefinitely as long as he was content to remain one. And "engineering an environment," rather than Hitler-type personal leadership, is the Nasser style. If he has learned to like being the idol of a personality cult—and I, among others who know him, doubt this—it is coincidental.

Naguib was chosen as the leader because of his qualifications for at least the first of three stages of development that Nasser foresaw. Under Farouk, the Egyptian people were moderately discontented and engaged in a certain amount of grumbling, but they were generally no more dissatisfied than at any other stage of their history, including the present one. In those days the communal framework of society had not disintegrated. The ordinary Egyptian felt himself to be part of a family, a clan and a community, and he was "content" in the sense that a member of even the poorest family is content when he feels that he is not alone in his deprivations and when he has endured the deprivations for so long that they seem natural. Only a few Army officers, intellectuals and communal outcasts had felt the Western influence, which emphasizes the freedom—and independence—of the individual. Only these had personal independence, knowledge and imagination enough to be dissatisfied. Nasser knew that he would have to break up the traditional, "feudalist" society and to rearrange the entire authority structure of the country—as colonial powers had done in many countries of Africa and Asia but only partly so in Egypt—then face the consequences of a suddenly "awakened" populace. Later, as a coldly calculated act, he wanted to make his people discontented, turn them against their stultifying traditionalism, and infect them with a craving for self-advancement, but not until he was in a position to satisfy this craving. Under "Phase One," presided over by a Naguib, Nasser thought he could remove the forces that perpetuated the old society—the old political parties, the absentee landowners, and foreign-controlled commercial companies—yet leave the social structure essentially intact until he had gained confidence enough to start tinkering with it. Apart from his purely negative quality (his supposed willingness to remain a figurehead), Naguib was chosen precisely because he represented a father figure in the old pattern—a "nonrevolutionary" father figure, in fact.

Nasser envisaged "constructive motivation" as Stage Three in the "awakening" of his people. He knew that it might be some time before Stage Three could be reached, but he did not accept a thoroughly pessimistic view of his chances until one of his American consulting teams, the Arthur Little Company of Boston, told him: "Even if you get the one billion dollars you need for your Five Year Plan; even if your Five Year Plan goes off without a hitch; even if everybody in Egypt works to his maximum capacity, guided by the best you can borrow in foreign know-how; after all this the best you can expect is to keep your country from going backwards." In other words, Nasser would have to exert his maximum motivational skill on his people, and they would have to respond with 100-percent efficiency, just to keep the situation as it already was. All this effort and there would in fact be not one more mouthful of bread for any *fellah,* not one more luxury for the common Egyptian, no better education, no better anything, because the maximum growth in national production that could be achieved was about equal to the annual population growth. And no one—not Nasser, not the Arthur Little Company, not anyone else who had a realistic view of Egyptian society—believed that birth control would be accepted to an extent that would make an appreciable difference.

But Nasser did not *entirely* accept the hopelessness of the situation. As he told Eric Johnston, there must be a "different way of living on this earth" whereby countries like Egypt (and there were many of which the Arthur Little Company could have said the same thing) could "make a kind of progress, progress which will not look like much to you Westerners or to our own people who see Western films, but which by our own terms will nonetheless be real progress." He did, however, know well enough that his people *did* see Western films and that once they had been emancipated (i.e., thrown out into the cold from the communal home to which they were accustomed), their cravings would be beyond the criteria for the "new way of living on this earth" which he needed time to devise. Therefore, he realized he must settle for an intermediate stage, a Phase Two: a phase of motivational development in which the vast disparity between desires and chances of satisfying those desires was palliated by substitutes.

It is this "Phase Two" that is of most interest to us in understanding the Nasser-type leader, because this is the phase that contains the dilemmas which most account for the behavior of a high percentage of non-Western players in the Game of Nations today. The phase contains the following ingredients: a rejection of Western values and the Western view of the future of the world; a renunciation of self in favor of a cause; a determination to get rid of the present "system" without any idea of the new system to replace it; and a willingness to die rather than submit to the "disciplines of good sense" that Phase Three considerations demand. To understand what horrors such disciplines hold, it is necessary to contemplate *The Year 2000,** as envisioned by the Hudson Institute, as it appears to Middle Easterners who, perforce, must remain in Phase Two.

The "awakened" Egyptian—or Pakistani or Afghan or

---

* See Suggested Reading List.

Yemeni—*sees* that the year 2000 will bring a drastically reduced supply of food and raw materials, a vastly increased population to compete for them, and the power to decide who gets what increasingly in the hands of scientists who will discover how to achieve greater results with less material. The two social features of the science-fiction society that the awakened Egyptian sees looming most menacingly are, first, the continued ascendancy of a Western elite which already has near-monopolistic control of scientific knowledge; second, increasingly oppressive disciplines on everybody else, the vast majority of mankind, which the Western elite will impose in order to ensure a "fair" rationing of space, food supply, and everything else that is required to sustain at least marginal existence. Nasser has a keen mind for scientific possibility. He, more than most non-Westerners, appreciates the inevitable approach of these conditions and the unique Western capability for dealing with them. He envisages a world in which the Anglo-Saxons are an impregnable elite, living like the Americans he sees in the films and on television, while the rest of the world (possibly excluding Japan, which he hasn't got around to thinking about yet) is barely able to stay alive on the largesse of whatever is left of Western liberality. In fact, he sees the world as the student rioters see it. He cannot prevent it from coming, but he can nonetheless "reject" it and stimulate his lethargic people to action by pointing out its horrors.

During Phase Two, the leader must, first, so discredit the old order that the people will be ashamed to have been a part of it; second, hold out benefits, psychological as well as material, which are their "natural right" but which they are prevented from getting by an "enemy"; third, mobilize against the enemy all the energies of frustration. So long as the people generate *some* energy (in Phase One they were motivated only to avoid the expenditure of energy), and so long as this energy is not turned against the government, there is hope that it might later, under Phase Three, be redirected toward constructive purposes. This, in any event, was how Nasser—and Nkrumah and Sukarno and others —so calculated.

Essential to the energizing and mobilization of passions in Phase Two is the abnegation of self. The average Middle Easterner, who sees himself as a second-rate person (much more clearly than the most racist Westerner sees him as a second-rate person), simply cannot be moved by appeals to individual pride such as we Westerners use in political speeches, newspaper editorials and commercial advertising. I had this brought home to me by one of Nasser's lieutenants after he had several times heard me trying to put over my ideas by Madison Avenue sales methods which frankly appeal to self-interest. "In this revolution," he said, "you don't get us to do what you want us to do by telling us how we will benefit as individuals. We have given that all up long ago. We are all servants to the cause. Tell us how we can help the cause."

A "fanatic" is one who will sacrifice his own interests for a cause. It follows naturally that a cause *against* something, against an "enemy," is the kind which best gains a fanatical following. It would obviously be pointless for anyone to be willing to give up his life in order to gain something for himself. Rebellious students who want better conditions, and who have a clear idea of what better conditions consist of, are quite a different sort from those who want to "tear down the institutions" without any idea of what should replace them. The Nasser-type leader prefers the latter if only for the reason that he has no idea of how to provide the better conditions. But there is an additional advantage: the latter can be fanaticized; the former cannot.

Thus, for Stage Two purposes, Nasser wanted an amount of controlled fanaticism in his country—just enough to wake everybody up, but not so much that it would be beyond his capacity to channel its energies. And here is where Nasser began to get into his first domestic difficulties. As we shall see, Nasser's moves in the Game of Nations call for an amount of fanatical support at home (a willingness to sacrifice self-interest for the cause), and the Egyptian simply does not become a fanatic easily. Certainly he cannot be turned into a fanatic by a leader who is suspicious of fanatics anyhow (unless they are in somebody else's country, helping him to embarrass uncooperative leaders) and who is organizing a great cause not out of conviction (or demagoguery, which is just as suitable) but out of expediency. The Egyptian man-in-the-street is not so quick-witted or well educated as his Syrian cousin (who is highly responsive to such an appeal), but he is wiser, ordinarily less emotional, and less likely to believe everything he is told.

There is a certain degree of popular support—which, by the nature of the situation, must be *fanatical* popular support—that Nasser requires to support the moves he makes in the Game of Nations, and the amount of energy he and his Government must expend to gain this support is many times more than the Syrian leaders require. Foreign observers cannot understand why so much of the national energy must be occupied with a thing called "the Arab Socialist Union," Nasser's political party (the only one allowed in the country), because they don't understand the *kind* of popular support that Nasser needs, and the outlandish amount of energy that must be used to get it.

Phase Three is more appropriately handled in a later chapter. I may say here, though, that Nasser's Phase Two appeals to his public are strictly for Phase Three purposes—perhaps this is why they don't ring true, and why Nasser has to shout them so loudly. Egypt, if left to its own resources, simply isn't a viable concern—as American advisers have eloquently pointed out. Egypt must get aid from abroad. By experience with the United States Government and with the Soviets Nasser has learned that you get aid from abroad in direct proportion to the extent to which you become a "factor to be contended with" (a phrase used by former American Ambassador John Badeau in arguing for increased economic aid to Egypt) in the Game of Nations. And one becomes a "factor to be contended with" not by means of exemplary constructive behavior but by advancing a cause which is frightening to the Great Powers or which, at least, they have no choice but to take seriously. It is conceivable that Nasser could have brought his nation to life by promising them better lives economically, but (1) it wouldn't have taken the people long to see that the promise wouldn't be fulfilled, and (2) the national awakening wouldn't amount to enough of a "factor to be contended with" to gain the foreign aid he needed.

Nasser's Phase Two problems call for behavior that would make anyone appear a demagogue. As I have already said, Nasser has as much of the demagogue in him as other successful politicians, including American Presidential candidates, but there is this difference: the ordinary demagogue finds out where the mob is going, then gets in front of it; the persuasive, charismatic leader influences the mob to want to go where he thinks it should go. The Nasser-type leader, mostly by *indirect* means, causes the mob to want to go where he thinks it should go, then gets in front of it by means that approximate those of the ordinary demagogue. We might even go as far as to say that Nasser, by these indirect means, creates public moods that actually *restrict* him to courses of action that he wishes to take. To this extent, he is using a technique that is relevant to the Game of Nations. "I do what I do because public opinion won't allow me to do otherwise," he tells the American Ambassador. "But Mr. President," replies the Ambassador, "who caused public opinion to be what it is?" Nasser smiles benignly.

We have touched on these indirect means, but by way of summary we may recapitulate them here. They are:

Propaganda: The propaganda that was instituted as part of the repressive base is extended to gain popular support and to become a part of the constructive base. Its objectives are:

1. To discredit the internal enemies of the country by making them appear corrupt and immoral by the actual standards of the society—that is, as opposed to its ostensible standards. Egyptians say they are against financial corruption, but they are not; thus it had little effect on a politician's career to prove that he had taken bribes. To show him as being sexually degenerate or irreligious, however, was another matter. Thus, the campaign of smut, which Nasser tolerated during the first year or two of his regime, was launched as the only effective way of pulling the former Egyptian ruling class off its pedestal.

2. To break the social taboos which protected these upper classes, and which persisted even after they had been exposed as immoral. Respect and fear of a person of the upper classes is so ingrained in a member of the Egyptian lower classes, that it takes more than revelations about the upper classes' sexual habits to make him shed his habit of subservience. "Egyptians love a VIP," one of our Embassy officers used to say (as an explanation, by the way, of why they liked British diplomats but did not respect their American counterparts). Nasser broke the habit of subservience to Egypt's traditional VIPs by numerous subtle means, including films and television plays depicting a humble man "rising to his rights" and striking down a landlord. Scenes of this sort in the local theaters at first brought shocked disapproval, but the crowds soon got used to them. Now the staged sight of a workman rising against his boss or a mob of *fellahin* throwing stones at a former landlord brings loud cheers from the audience—although in real life, of course, authentic scenes of this sort are discouraged.

3. To cause and nurture an undercurrent of real fear of the dispossessed upper classes, for example by arousing suspicions that they are secretly connected with foreign groups who intend to invade the country, re-establish the old order, and punish the lower classes for their insubordination. Since no foreign group in its right mind would think of using upper-class Egyptians to bring about a coup against the Nasser Government, "evidence" against the alleged plotters must be actually fabricated. A few select stories, backed by skillfully spread rumors, apparently gained the desired results. At the time of the Suez crisis—which, to the ignorant majority, finally provided irrefutable proof of an imperialist fifth column—a public-opinion survey conducted (with Nasser's permission) by a highly qualified group of foreign experts found that there was a genuine widespread fear of Egypt's dispossessed upper classes, especially those with known or suspected foreign connections. The fear not only was enough to break a large part of the population away from traditional social ties which inhibited their acceptance of the revolution, but was almost enough, when combined with other fears, to be the "unifying fear" that we spoke about earlier.

The single political party: Many intelligent foreign diplomats and newsmen who ought to know better fret about Nasser's one-party political system and the accompanying restrictions on civil liberty. Given Nasser's Stage Two objectives, which ought to be obvious enough to any informed observer, it is surprising that they expect anything else. How could a two-party system possibly serve such objectives? How could it fail to cause the very confusion which, at all costs, Nasser must avoid? It is all very well for Westerners to argue, with De Tocqueville, that free dissent is essential to the evolution of a civilized political community, but to expect Nasser to accept such an idea strikes me as naïve. Rightly or wrongly, it is at least *natural* for Nasser to believe that a multiparty system would result, as he has told many Western visitors, in "a continuing contest between the party supported by the Americans, the party supported by the British, the party supported by the Soviet and, if we could compete with such wealthy sponsors, a party supported by the regime." Moreover, he well understands the affinity of the more vocal elements of Egyptian society for extremist movements and the tendency of extremist movements to be against the ruling government, whatever its character. Finally, without approving or disapproving, the informed Western observer ought to understand readily enough that Nasser's Stage Two, as *he* saw it, called for a period of political, economic and social regimentation during which he could mobilize the thoughts and energies of the people for the formidable Phase Three. A "free people," to Nasser's way of looking at things, may accomplish wonderful things in the typical Western country, but in the typical Arab country it is likely to expend its energies counterproductively.

For the reader interested in the details, I recommend P. J. Vatikiotis's *The Egyptian Army in Politics.** For present purposes, all we need to agree upon is this: according to the way the Nasser-type leader sees things, what the citizenry needs is the freedom to vote without the freedom to argue about what is being voted upon—except, that is, within the confines of the one party set up by the state. In Western democracies the party is an instrument of its members who want to influence the government to their way of thinking. In a country like Egypt the party is an instrument of the state whereby the state influences the people to think the way the leader of the state wants them to think. To expect it to be otherwise is naïve.

Big government: When I and my team of management engineers went to Egypt in 1953, our mission was strictly administrative: to bring about a governmental organization

---

* See Suggested Reading List.

that would perform the greatest service to the public with the smallest possible number of personnel—good government, in other words. It didn't take us long, however, to learn that the British colonial system (or, for that matter, the American system under Franklin D. Roosevelt) is highly preferable for a country like Egypt. When one of my colleagues showed the head of Customs how he could streamline some unwieldy procedure, give better service to the shippers, lessen the chance of tax evasion, and, at the same time, do the job with ten men instead of thirty, he shook the poor fellow's sense of security to its foundations. Later, an English friend of mine, teasing me about the recommendation, said, "If the job were left to me I believe I could manage to use fifty men on it." The purpose of government according to a more enlightened philosophy is not so much to serve the public as to keep a large segment of the public off the streets—a segment that could become extremely dangerous if left unemployed. If Britain had not applied this philosophy in its colonies, such countries as India, Pakistan, Nigeria and Ghana would have been deprived of a large part of their white-collared middle classes—and Nasser would not have had anyone to join his Arab Socialist Union.

By early 1967, Nasser had almost one million civil servants in his bureaucracy, excluding the armed services and nationalized companies. Booz, Allen and Hamilton, whose public-administration specialists are possibly the most respected in the world, said that the Egyptian Government could not possibly employ more than two hundred thousand persons without their getting in each others' way. Thus Nasser has paid a price in administrative chaos, but he has a million white-collared members of the middle class, most of whom are located in Cairo and Alexandria, who can join the Arab Socialist Union and otherwise serve his cause. As for the problem of corruption which must necessarily accompany such overemployment, Nasser has harnessed it the way the Damon Runyon Cancer Fund harnessed theater-ticket scalping. Instead of merely lining their own pockets, Nasser's bureaucrats in contact with the people (mainly the Ministry of Social Affairs, the Ministry of Interior, the Minister of Education) serve the people, and regime, much in the way Tammany Hall once served the Democratic Party in New York.

The myth: Before the coup, Nasser patiently sat through innumerable political discussions with his co-plotters which were at the two-legs-good-four-legs-bad level, but he always realized that even the most unsophisticated people require an appeal that is much more substantial than they are capable of articulating. Nasser needed a unifying motivator which would be to his movement what the general strike was to the French syndicalists and what the catastrophic revolution was to Marx. He needed what Georges Sorel, some seventy years ago, defined as a "myth:" "A body of images capable of evoking instinctively all the sentiments which correspond to the different manifestations of the war undertaken by Socialism against modern society"—although, for "Socialism" we must substitute "the Revolution" and for "modern society" we must substitute "enemies of the revolution," whatever Nasser may mean by these terms.

It is not important if he does not mean anything precisely: a myth may be just as effective in mobilizing emotions against some great unknown because, after all, the myth is an appeal to emotions, not to reason. All that is necessary is that, in Sorel's words, "men participating in a great social movement must picture their coming action as a battle in which their cause is certain to triumph." The myth may be so vague, so lacking in details, or so dreamlike, as to defy analysis; there need not be an important—and, to the rational man, obvious—connection between observable facts and "the picture people had formed for themselves before action." "Myths are not descriptions of things, but expressions of a determination to act." "A myth cannot be refuted since it is, at bottom, identical with the convictions of a group, being the expression of these convictions in the language of movement; and it is, in consequence, unanalyzable into parts which could be placed on the plane of historical description." I don't know whether Nasser ever read Sorel, but, without using the word "myth" (or its Arabic equivalent), Nasser has from time to time expressed much these same thoughts. There was a difference, however. In the manner of the headmaster of a *nouveau riche* prep school informing his staff that "We must decide what traditions to institute," Nasser dispassionately decided upon what myth to adopt. His new myth was not representative of the aspirations and convictions of his people, but of what Nasser thought could become the aspirations and convictions of his people.

This is not to say that he started from scratch: he started with an understanding of the fantasies of young Egyptians. In the way that a Western adolescent dreams of saving a beautiful girl from a burning building, or a browbeaten clerk imagines himself, in the manner of Walter Mitty, bettering a bullying boss, the young Egyptian thinks of himself somehow overcoming the Europeans who have for so long debased him. I have heard Nasser's Free Officers, for hours on end, exchange detailed stories, all patently false, of exploits against the British occupying forces. Nasser knew very well what it took to make himself a hero in their eyes. As Daniel Lerner says, "Only optimists in the West interpret his (Nasser's) seizure of Suez, for example, in such petty terms as canal tolls." Nasser knew how to become a symbol of the downtrodden Egyptian rising, as Morroe Berger says, to "humiliate those who humiliate the Arabs." To put it more simply, Nasser appears as the first "winner" to have come along for many years in a nation of people who have become accustomed to thinking of themselves as "losers."

But in being a "winner," Nasser has managed to maintain a show of humility, which may be largely genuine, by representing himself—and, probably, by thinking of himself—as an agent of a higher power. He is Moses, Cromwell, Lenin. His exceptional self-confidence, which is strongly communicated to anyone who meets him, arises from his belief that, like these prototypes, he is merely one who happens to fill the "role in search of an actor," as he explains it in his *Philosophy of the Revolution.* Thus, his playing of the role is absolutely righteous—an essential feature of the myth. His followers, probably in their subconscious as well as consciously, see in him *their* contact with this superior force—undefined certainly, but as we said, this does not matter. It is a force that brings Egyptians on to a par with Europeans (and many sociologists think that this ambivalence about Europeans is a highly important part of the Egyptian's emotional makeup); and it puts them a peg or two above other Arabs. (It is important to understand here that "Arab nationalism" as such is *not* a part of Nasser's myth; Egypt's being the *leader* of the Arabs, however, has become a very important part of it.)

To put it another way, Nasser's myth is the body of images that surround the battle between the colored man—Arab, Moslem, African (Nasser's "three circles")—against the European (Soviet as well as Western), a battle in which the colored man is sure to triumph in the end. Nasser's use of his other "constructive-base" assets—propaganda, political-party organization, and even big government—are mobilized to perpetuate this myth. Although we shall see in later chapters how Nasser has over the years moved on to Bonapartism, this view of Nasser continues to be the one best serving our purposes as we try to calculate how his attempts to gain and hold on to popular support affect his maneuverability in the Game of Nations.

7

Nasser's
"Positive Neutralism"

*The strategy of the weak player is to play off
the strong players against one another . . .*

By early 1953 it was clear enough to Nasser, even though
the Arthur Little report had not yet appeared, that Egypt
would not survive economically without substantial aid from
abroad, and that the amount of aid he would require was far
in excess of amounts then being considered by his most
likely source, the United States Government. Moreover, he
saw clearly what role he must play on the international
stage in order to induce the United States Government to
revise its aid policies in his favor. And he saw that the role
was one which didn't fit his domestic situation—anyhow,
not in Phase One. As we saw earlier, this was the reason for
Phase Two. Western observers are inclined to take Nasser's
Phase Two actions and stated objectives at face value, and
therefore to judge them a failure. The fact is that Nasser
gained just the popular sentiment he wanted: not so fanatical as to put the populace beyond control, yet fanatical
enough to discourage practical-minded Egyptians from articulating any "Egypt first" rebuttals which would play into
the hands of Secretary Dulles. Thus, when it came time to
sit down with the American Government to discuss financial
aid he was restricted by public opinion to the policy he
wanted to follow.

The preliminary exchanges between Egypt and the United States on the subject of aid were characterized by the usual banalities about "peace and stability in the area" and quotations from the speeches of President Eisenhower. ("Our nation was born because of the dedication of its people to liberty and justice") and from official memoranda of Secretary Dulles ("We seek a just and universal peace for all people") and they continued for so long that Nasser began to entertain the frightening suspicion that perhaps the Americans really meant all this (to him) nonsense. He was beginning to take it as an indication that either we were fools or we thought he was. When the Americans got down to details, however, they lapsed into a kind of language that Nasser and his lieutenants better understood. President Eisenhower, for all his pious talk (which he meant, from the bottom of his heart), was an old-fashioned Yankee nationalist with a no-nonsense understanding of foreign policy in pursuit of strictly American interests. As such, he saw the danger of "Communist ambitions"; as a military man he saw these ambitions being furthered by military means, comparable to those by which the Nazis overran Europe. The proper defense against them was military defense, first through the North Atlantic Treaty Organization (NATO), composed of European countries, and then by similar alliances in other parts of the globe. "MEDO," the Middle East Defense Organization, was the first to come after NATO.

On March 5, 1953, Anthony Eden and John Foster Dulles met with President Eisenhower to discuss the whole question of "Middle East Defense," which to Eisenhower meant the creation of a MEDO and to Eden meant no more than the retaining, by the British, of bases in the Middle East which would be required in the event of hostilities—*any* hostilities, from local war which might interrupt the use of the Suez Canal to World War III, from war between third parties (the Arabs and Israel, for example) to a war of Great Britain and her allies against the Russians. The specific

question at hand was Egypt: Nasser and his Revolutionary
Command Council were more interested in defending themselves from the British than in defending themselves from
the Soviets, and they didn't see the Middle East as being
in danger of military attack anyhow. Nasser did not want
any part of MEDO, nor did he have any particular interest
in whether or not the British had bases in the Middle East—
so long, that is, as none of them were in Egypt. On the
other hand, he did want military aid—from the United
States. He wanted it for purposes of internal security, to
turn his "shabby Army" (as he later told Secretary Dulles)
into a "proud Army," so that it could be a reliable mainstay
of his internal-security system. If his Army was to have any
military mission at all, it would be against the Israelis or
against one or another of the uncooperative Arab countries,
not against the Soviets or any European power.

Neither the British nor the Americans were under any
illusions about Nasser's attitude. Indeed, Nasser's attitude
toward "area defense," as the British and Americans used
the term, was spelled out in detail in contemporary national
intelligence estimates. Nevertheless, the meeting of March
5 proceeded on the basis of an assumption that in pursuit of
a "just and universal peace for all people" we needed either
(as the Americans believed) a regional defense arrangement like MEDO or (as the British believed) a simple
agreement with the Egyptians whereby the British, or the
British and the Americans, would have bases in the event of
any kind of war or uprising which endangered the Canal.
That Nasser had no interest in seeing us attain either objective was not unknown; it was simply ignored. Why? Because that is the way things are often done when two
sovereign powers are attempting to reach an agreement,
and when it is more important that an agreement be reached
than that it make sense—*any* agreement so long as it is at
least barely workable.

What happened between the British and the Egyptians in

arriving at a Suez Base agreement is amply recorded elsewhere—for example, in Anthony Eden's *Full Circle*.* But there is one aspect of the story that is worth mentioning in this context: first because there is no published account of it elsewhere and, second, because it bears on the question of cryptodiplomacy. In *Full Circle* Eden said, "The Egyptians rejected the idea that the Americans should participate [in the negotiations], and the President [i.e. President Eisenhower] had made Egyptian acceptance a condition for taking part." Later on, he says, "It was unfortunate that the United States Government and, in particular, their Ambassador in Cairo, were not prepared to put any pressure upon the Egyptians to bring this about." The Japanese, I believe, have a phrase, "to see without seeing," to indicate what happens when naked male and female bathers in the same pool disregard one another's existence for reasons of form while retaining the physical ability to see so as to avoid bumping into one another. We need a similar phrase, "to know without knowing," to explain autobiographical accounts of honest men who were at the time of some political happening fully informed about the behind-the-scenes actions which oiled the machinery of negotiations but who later brainwash themselves so that their memories retain only pictures fitting to their ideas of propriety. (In *Full Circle*, the reader will remember, Eden disclaims any discussions with the French and the Israelis prior to their move against Egypt in 1956.)

The fact is that during the March 5 (1953) meeting President Eisenhower agreed to send Lieutenant General R. A. Hull, an officer in whom he had particular confidence, to Cairo to assist the British negotiators and that Sir Anthony showed little enthusiasm for the idea—or rather, that his assistants showed little enthusiasm for it during the follow-up sessions which always take place between staff

* See Suggested Reading List.

officers of both sides whose job it is to pick up the pieces after their respective bosses have got carried away at historical meetings and made God-knows-what commitments. The lack of enthusiasm of Eden's assistants was matched by that of the American ambassador in Cairo (Caffery) when he received cabled news of the idea: Caffery lost no time in pointing out that the American Government enjoyed a close, personal, "unofficial"* relationship with the Egyptians which could be of greater assistance to the British than could the presence of an American negotiator, however competent, at the conference table. Moreover, a Great White Father coming out from Washington would undermine Caffery's position in this relationship. Finally, the staff officers in the State Department who had followed up the suggestion to send out General Hull also undermined it because they feared that General Hull, like Eisenhower, would take MEDO as a serious proposal and discuss it as such without suitable winks being exchanged between himself and Nasser.

On the Egyptian side, Nasser understood very well that treaties between Great Powers and Afro-Asian nations were at most highly fragile affairs, and that he could subsequently wriggle out of any disagreeable features—*after* receiving the military aid which would be a part of the deal. His generals, however, were less sophisticated. Nasser—like Caffery, and like knowledgeable staff officers on both sides of the Atlantic—had visions of General Hull and the Egyptian generals straight-facedly discussing the pros and cons of a regional defense agreement until they lost patience with one another, with an Anglo-Egyptian agreement getting lost in the shuffle.

With varying degrees of frankness, the whole problem was

---

* In the language of cryptodiplomacy, the word "unofficial," used in quotes, applies to persons or actions which can become "official" when success is in sight but which, with an appropriate gesture of moral indignation, can be denounced as "totally unauthorized" in case of failure.

discussed between the Americans and the British (at the "staff," or "working" level), between the Americans and the Egyptians (Caffery and Nasser), and, presumably, between the British and the Egyptians. Under the circumstances, it seemed that the best way to put the idea to rest was for the Egyptians to reject it officially. By the time he got around to writing *Full Circle*, Eden had apparently forgotten it, but the fact is that he was told at the time that the Americans would give "unofficial" help but, for the reasons that he of all people would appreciate, could not participate in the actual discussions.

Secretary Dulles' talk with Nasser in Cairo (May 1953) served the purpose of getting MEDO out of the way—or, at least, of turning it into "a future rather than an immediate possibility"—and Ambassador Caffery was then free to get on with the job that he considered to be the important one: getting a military agreement between the Egyptians and the Americans that would provide our Government with the basis for giving Nasser the arms he needed for his internal-security purposes and at the same time further the chances of the British's getting whatever kind of agreement with Egypt it took to satisfy them. Contrary to what Eden remembers, the former was firmly contingent upon the latter: as Nasser understood then and understands now, harmony between the Americans and the British on world-wide defense policy takes higher priority with our planners—from those of President Eisenhower to those of any President likely to be elected in the immediate future—than relations with any Middle Eastern leader.

In August, Ambassador Caffery buttonholed me as I was on my way to lunch with Nasser to suggest that I, as an unofficial American, might be able to get some idea of the ultimate position Nasser would take in negotiating with the British and also an idea of some shortcut we might take past all the haggling to arrive at that position, or at a position fairly between the British position (which Caffery already knew) and Nasser's ultimate. "Find out his maximum desirable and his minimum acceptable," Caffery said, "and make him understand that we will keep his answer to ourselves."

This was the first time I had been asked to discuss politics with Nasser—or, rather, *international* politics; touching upon internal politics had been unavoidable since it related to some extent to the public-administration questions which concerned me—and I felt myself unprepared to do more than suggest that Nasser should *have* a firm idea of his "maximum desirable and minimum acceptable" whether or not he chose to communicate it to me. In fact, when I got around to bringing up the subject during lunch, I said that he should *not* communicate his position to me since, considering the state of my knowledge of the subject at the time, it would go in one ear and out the other. My suggestion was that he and I select some responsible businessman with interests in the Middle East—and an interest in seeing the matter settled, one way or the other, not necessarily in favor of the British—and enlist his aid in getting the best possible deal.

We couldn't think of any suitable businessmen, so we began to discuss Kermit Roosevelt, whom I considered an excellent choice but whose CIA connection I considered a handicap. Nasser did not agree. "He can be as official as we want him to be," Nasser said. Nasser believed that a senior CIA official would have the advantages of a private citizen since he would not "represent" the United States government in any normal sense and would be under no obligation to tip off the British to his real position, yet he would also have the advantages of top security clearances in the United States Government and therefore be in a position to know what he was talking about. His closeness to the Dulles brothers was also important to Nasser, and he knew that Caffery would go along with the choice.

Nasser didn't really believe that Roosevelt wouldn't keep

the British informed; it was inconceivable to Nasser that any official of any country, regardless of what oaths he might take as a person, would not break confidence as he saw fit in the best interests of his own country. But earlier experience had led him to believe that Roosevelt was the kind of man who would know how to keep up the pretense of being privy to the inside story of Nasser's "real" bargaining position—which, needless to say, Nasser had no intention of revealing to Roosevelt or to anyone else—and thereby to get a better deal from the British than his own negotiators could. As it happened, however, Roosevelt was able to be entirely straightforward with both sides. I reported my talk with Nasser to Caffery immediately after the lunch; Caffery cabled the idea to Washington that same afternoon; Roosevelt arrived by the end of the week, after stopping off in London to get a general briefing from the Foreign Office to see what items in the negotiations were important and which ones were not. In his first meeting with Nasser he simply got himself brought up to date on the state of Phase One and Phase Two, a subject with which he had familiarity almost amounting to vested interest and which, to Nasser and the Americans, provided the proper context for a military settlement or any kind of settlement between Egypt and Britain and America. From then on his job was one of determining exactly what it was the British and the Egyptians really wanted, as opposed to what they had to *say* they wanted, then working out a formula by which each side would give in on the really important (but sometimes obscure) points but allow the other side to win on the unimportant (but sometimes seemingly important) points. Thus, the trick of cryptodiplomacy is often no more than dragging out on to the table, and forcing frank discussion of, a number of questions in a way that cannot be part of a regular diplomatic exchange or allowed to get into the record.

Although it would serve no purpose in this context to go

into the details of the Suez Base settlement, for purposes of this book it is important for the reader to understand enough to see what is meant when I say that such and such a point is "really" important, although it may not receive any particular emphasis in negotiations, whereas other points over which a lot of fuss is made are relatively unimportant. In earlier discussions the British proposal had contained three alternative solutions to the Suez Base problem: Case A, Case B and Case C. Under the first, the British would turn sovereignty of the Suez Base over to the Egyptians (in the way the Spanish have sovereignty over American bases in Spain), but the Egyptians would allow several thousand British servicemen to remain in Egypt to run it. Under the second, Egyptian servicemen would run the base, but under British supervisors. Under the third, the Egyptians would run it under their own supervisors with the British having only the right to inspect it from time to time. Before Roosevelt's exchanges with Nasser, negotiations were a matter of haggling between Case A, which was the British "maximum desirable" and which was totally unacceptable to the Egyptians, and Case C, which was the British "minimum acceptable" and which was eminently acceptable to the Egyptians because, except for the sake of appearances, it was meaningless. Had the negotiations continued on this basis the Egyptians would conceivably have accepted Case B, but Roosevelt argued that the whole approach was irrelevant anyhow.

I am not trying to say that Roosevelt brought about a settlement of the Suez Base question—which, of course, was actually brought about by a highly competent team of negotiators working under the then British Ambassador, Sir Ralph Stevenson—or that he was the first one to think of the irrelevancy of the Cases A, B, and C approach. I am only saying that, like the little boy who cried, "But the king *is* naked," Roosevelt helped the British negotiators to bypass a lot of irrelevant haggling and therefore contributed more than the "American participation" which Eden claims to have missed or the "pressure" which, in *Full Circle*, he says he would have liked Ambassador Caffery to exert. Anyone in the Foreign Office who knew anything at all about the way the Anglo-American worldwide defense picture was developing understood that: (1) MEDO was an anachronism, just as NATO was becoming an anachronism, and the only reason it was being discussed at all by the State Department (with only affected seriousness) was because of Secretary Dulles who, brilliant man though he was, simply could not rid himself of the idea. If Cases A, B and C were to be considered at all they had to be considered not in connection with Anglo-American "area defense," but frankly, in the context of Britain's (not America's) East-of-Suez defense problems. (2) In *any* event, general redeployment of British forces from the Suez Base eastward was going to be necessary for a lot of reasons, having nothing directly to do with defense. (3) The Egyptians were not going to live up to *whatever* agreement was worked out, and were arguing hard for Case C or its equivalent only because of its propaganda advantages. Had the Egyptians agreed to Case A, they would have started clamoring for its abrogation one month after the signatures, and would have launched a wave of sabotage against the Base to underlie their dissatisfaction. Case B would have lasted until some incident provided Nasser with the excuse to put the British supervisors on a homebound boat—daring the British Government to take counter action, as he later dared the British Government when he nationalized the Suez Canal Company. The fate of Case C, which was the one finally decided upon, is public knowledge. The point is that everyone concerned with the negotiations—the British, the Egyptians, and the American kibitzers—knew all this quite well but couldn't come right out and say so. Roosevelt could. And did.

For his part, Nasser knew that Anglo-American relations

—which, so far as they affected him, were as close as ever—were suffering somewhat from family frictions, resulting mainly from personal animosity between Dulles and Eden. He did not understand, however, how such politics alone could account for the terms of reference within which they were conducted: NATO, "Middle East Defenses," bases, and all the rest. He understood enough about the Russians—and he knew that the British and the Americans understood even more—to see that the chances of their challenging us militarily as Hitler did in the Second World War were about nil, and that what we seemed intent on doing to oppose such a nonexistent danger would make us look like the warmongers Soviet propaganda was claiming us to be. Nasser saw the Soviet attack on the Western world, and even more so on the Middle East, as being political and subversive and as being so conducted that the presence of military "imperialism" in the various countries would actually be helpful to them. Also, he could not imagine our taking seriously the idea of treaties. Surely we, with our long experience and diplomatic sophistication, knew well enough that when moments of crisis arose all nations behaved in accordance with their best interests at the time, treaties or no treaties, and that the crises that were likely to arise in the future would be political in character (with riots, guerrilla warfare, and assaults by ostensibly "internal" elements, rather than military invasions, to supply the physical element) and beyond the reach of treaties. He frankly admitted to Roosevelt that in even bothering to discuss the provisions of the Suez Base agreement sought by the British he was "only humoring Dulles and Eden," because all he wanted was to get the British out of the country and he was willing to make any promises to get them out so long as his own people did not get the idea that he intended to keep the promises.

For our part, the only Americans and British who understood Nasser's attitude on the subject were those who had followed the revolution from the beginning and who had observed its problems along with its developing aspirations. We understood that Nasser had irrevocably committed himself to a policy with which meaningful alliances with Great Powers were totally incompatible. He was committed to breaking any Suez Base agreement—or any other such agreement—he might, for tactical reasons, decide to make. As he told both the British and the American ambassadors, as he told Roosevelt and the various specialists Roosevelt sent to Cairo, and as he told me and others of his Western friends who dealt with him on management, economic and financial questions, his key objective was this: to get into a position where he could decide individual questions of international politics on their merits, and not in accordance with whether or not they fitted into one or another of the Great Powers' scheme of things. Until the Russians or anybody else attacked the Middle East he wanted to retain the freedom of deciding whether to oppose them or to side with them, and how to go about either, while keeping us all guessing to the last minute as to what his decision would be. Naturally, it was part of this objective that both we of the West and the Soviets understand this to be his position, accept it, and deal with him accordingly—court him, in other words.

Apart from the bargaining power he would gain from such independence, there was also the matter of catering to the awakening pride of the Egyptian people which his Phase Two was bringing to life. This matter of pride should not be underestimated. When one sees Palestinian refugees (whose "Phase Two" comes naturally from their predicament, rather than from the inspiration of any leader) take all their tents and blankets, on the coldest night of the year, put them in a pile and set fire to them, one begins to understand that to a frustrated people the satisfactions of pride are more important than even food and shelter. After Nasser had established a dependable "repressive base" for his power structure, and had begun to work on his "constructive base," he thought that satisfactions of pride were a suitable substitute for the economic satisfactions which he could not yet provide. He soon learned, however, that they were more than mere substitutes. As late as January 1968, a few months after Egypt had been beaten by the Israelis and when the country had worked itself into its worst economic plight ever, an Egyptian of undoubted intelligence, Mustafa Amin, who had spent over three years in jail because of Nasser, could say, "Nasser has done a lot to harm me, my friends, and my country, but I must admit that he has made me proud to be an Egyptian." By the time Nasser's position had been established as "permanent" (in the peculiar way we use that word in the Middle East), he and the Westerners who dealt with him had already learned that the "awakened" Egyptian would forgo any economic benefit in order to satisfy his pride.

Becoming a truly independent country, with freedom to decide on questions of international politics entirely on their individual merits, without having to do so according to a framework laid down by London, Washington or Moscow, went a long way toward satisfying the Egyptians' awakened sense of pride. And at the least, it gave Nasser the basis for other steps which furthered his more practical objectives while satisfying the same craving. Nasser wanted national backing to push for a new deal in Arab unification which would give Egypt greater advantages than the old Arab League, Greater Syria, Fertile Crescent approach to Arab nationalism which the British had inspired. Only a truly independent Egypt, with no Lawrences of Arabia directing it from the back rooms, could put Arab nationalism on the new basis that Nasser envisaged. It was essential to Nasser's plans that Egypt should at least get the Arab countries interested in the subject so that they would judge their own politicians by the criteria that the "new Arabism" would generate. It was *not* essential that an "Arab nation" actually be brought about. Once Nasser was free of the "British occupation," as he called it, he was on firm ground from which to inspire Egyptian pride in terms of leadership in the Arab world.

How this was a cold-blooded, unidealistic, *practical* intention of Nasser is the subject of the next chapter. At this point, I only want to point out that Nasser's true intention was recognized, if not by Secretary Dulles himself, then by working-level officers at the State Department and the Defense Department. These officers, despite any distractions of their superiors, moved relentlessly toward the formulation and application of policies that took into consideration the facts of life as they understood them, however unpalatable they were. And the facts of life seemed to favor the rise of the leader—if not Nasser, then some other leader—who would know how to use the East-West conflict to his own advantage, thereby gaining power in the Game of Nations out of all proportion to his country's military and economic strength.

The British and the Egyptians signed their Suez Base agreement in October 1954, and one month later the Pentagon sent two colonels, Albert Gerhardt and Wilbur ("Bill") Eveland, to Cairo to see what basis, if any, could be found for an Egyptian-American relationship that would allow our Government to give the Egyptians the arms they required for internal-security purposes. The meeting was to be with Nasser himself, flanked only by his top-level aides, and was to be secret and off the record. Ambassador Caffery asked me to arrange the meeting, to attend it and to report back to him what happened. My role, of course, was entirely that of an observer with no official status.

The meeting took place at eight o'clock one evening at the suburban home of Hassan Touhami, Nasser's senior aide, and was attended by Nasser, Chief of Staff Abdelhakim Amer, the two American colonels, Touhami and me. The atmosphere was friendly and informal—deceptively so, because despite all the off-the-record exchanges our Government had had with Nasser up to that point, this was to be the first meeting where fundamental Egyptian-American differences were brought to the surface and where the game board between Nasser and Dulles first began to take shape. Coats were removed and hung on the backs of chairs; first names became in order—"Al," "Bill," and even "Gamal"; a delicious home-cooked meal appeared, and we sat at a round table and ate it family style. After an hour of soldierly conviviality, we settled down to what came to be known in later years as "frank talk such as we used to have."

Al Gerhardt began by explaining the philosophy behind NATO: "to give the Allies a chance to band together as equals before the outbreak of war," he said, "so that there won't be all the misunderstandings over difference in responsibility and who-owes-what-to-whom such as we had in the last world war." Nasser, prophetically, replied that the idea of banding together "as equals" was attractive enough, but he wondered if the French, for instance, would think much of the idea ten years hence.

Bill Eveland then explained that equality was not so important as effectiveness, and that anyone who had been in on NATO planning up to that time could see that the total military capability had become more than the sum of its parts. Turning to Amer, he said, "As a military man, you've got to admit that regional defense is the only kind that can be effective in the Middle East. The individual military capabilities of all the Middle Eastern states, simply added up, won't serve anybody's purpose, least of all your own."

"A regional arrangement might serve *your* purpose," Amer replied, "but before we can say what serves our purposes we've got to know whom we're going to be fighting. Whom *are* we going to be fighting?"

There followed an argument that was a credit to both sides in that the Americans did not once mention "the Free World" and the Egyptians did not mention "the imperialists." Colonels Gerhardt and Eveland argued that it made no sense to talk about "Arab unity" or any other kind of regional unity so long as the states of the area insisted on individual defense programs. Amer kept asking, "defense against *whom?*" Gerhardt and Eveland admitted that it was a "planning assumption" in Washington that the Russians would be the enemy, but that this did not have to be spelled out in regional plans. "Our position is that your regional defense arrangements would be against any enemy that appears," Gerhardt said. "We would take our chances that you and we would recognize a common enemy when the moment of real danger appears."

Nasser sat quietly throughout the exchange, until he finally interrupted to say that all this theoretical ambiguity about identifying the enemy might suit sophisticated discussions of the kind we were having, but would become meaningless once it reached the Arab military planners. In Arab strategy sessions the enemy would be identified readily enough as Israel, and it would be recognized that to the Americans the enemy is Russia. "The Arabs will say you are trying to get them to unite to fight *your* enemy," he said, "while they know that if they show any intention of fighting *their* enemy you would quickly stop all aid. Any regional military agreement that did not take this attitude into account would be a fraud."

There followed an exchange centering around a statement that Secretary Dulles had reportedly made a week earlier to the effect that the Arabs "ought to realize that their real enemy is international Communism." Gerhardt and Eveland halfheartedly defended the Secretary's argument that a fear of Communism should provide the Arabs sufficient motivation for forming an alliance to repel military invasion by the Soviet Union, and Nasser replied with a bored dissertation on the distinction between the threat of Communist penetration, which was a country-by-country security problem, and the threat of Soviet military invasion

—which, if such existed, would indeed provide motivation for a regional defense arrangement. "But," he said, "in this region we know of only two enemies: the Israelis, with whom we are still technically at war, and the British, who occupy Arab territory. The Arabs don't know anything about the Russians. It is foolish to try to stir them up to a fear of Soviet invasion."

Each side had said what it had come to say. The exchange was ended. In his summation for the Americans, Bill Eveland made a statement which implied, without saying so explicitly, that whether it made sense or not our military planners wanted to see a workable area defense plan and that all military and economic aid to Middle Eastern countries would be proportionate to their respective degrees of enthusiasm for the idea. In his summation for the Egyptians, Nasser made a statement enunciating what has become not only a key objective of his foreign policy, but the stance he uses to face the Great Powers in order to get what he wants out of them in furtherance of his other objectives. "Nuri Pasha may be willing to make his decisions on a basis of whether or not they fit your world strategy," he said, "but I am not." Nuri, then Prime Minister of Iraq, was Nasser's *bête noire* of the moment. "I intend to judge issues on their merits, and to make my decisions only on a basis of what's good for Egypt. Having this kind of freedom is as important an objective to us as economic prosperity. Furthermore, in spite of what you say, I believe that your Government will in the long range be more helpful to a free nation than to a satellite."

That was that. The party broke up in the same mood of informal good cheer with which it had started: parting jokes, arrangements for rides back into town, all the features of the end of any pleasant purely social dinner. I had not the slightest feeling of having been present at the opening move of the game in which the American Government and Nasser have been locked ever since, through the Arab-Israeli War of June 1967 down to the present.

The next morning, however, I got some inkling of this when I asked Bill Eveland, "What did you think of Gamal's pronouncement?"

"Crap," he said. "There is no such thing as complete 'independence' for any country in this world, least of all a country that is as dependent as Egypt on outside aid. If we give him the economic aid he wants, he's damn well going to have to give some consideration for our interests. If he won't go along with us, there are others who will."

"But what if he lines up the others—I mean, the way a labor union lines up the workers to face management with a united front?"

"He's too late. We've already got Iraq, Lebanon, Jordan, Saudi Arabia, Turkey, Iran and Pakistan."

So Secretary Dulles had already taken the High Road. In getting the colonels off to the airport, I had a chance to look at Bill Eveland's passport and I found that he had indeed visited Lebanon, Iraq and Jordan. Knowing of Bill's excellent relations with President Chamaoun, Prime Minister Nuri Sa'id and King Hussein, I had no doubt that he had lined them up for some kind of MEDO—although Bill would not have been above making me think he had done so just to get me to put some pressure on to Nasser. If he had said, "Please don't tell Gamal," I would have been sure that he was bluffing. The calculated indiscretion was as standard a ploy in those days as it is at present.

The "High Road of Statesmanship and Diplomacy," known to the Pentagon and the CIA simply as "HORSE-SHIP," was based on the assumption that all the nations of the world aspire to a better way of life economically and socially and that the way to establish mutually beneficial relations with them was to offer irresistible amounts of economic and technical assistance. The High Roader can only look on in bewilderment when (as we have already mentioned) he sees a mob of Palestinian refugees, on the coldest night of the year, pile up the blankets given them by Western charities and set fire to them—or, more recently, when he sees the Egyptians, after a catastrophic defeat at the hands of the Israelis, sit down with the Syrians and the Algerians to work out how they can go through the same exercise again, at the same time doing as much damage as possible to alienate the Western powers whose help they need. A prominent High Roader remarked recently, "I just can't believe that the Arabs will forever go on cutting off their noses to spite their faces."

The Low Roaders, on the other hand, believe that the Arabs—and, for that matter, peoples of many other developing countries—may go on indefinitely doing just that. The reason why the prospects for such countries are so bleak, they argue, regardless of the amounts of aid poured in, is that their peoples have become dropouts—dropouts from a system to which they can never belong except as second-class citizens. An American ambassador in an African country recently told me, "These people will never, never make transistor radios, or refrigerators, or anything else as cheaply as they can buy them from abroad, nor can they have any role in the Western—or Soviet—economy other than that of supplying raw materials for us to manufacture into finished products. No matter how fast they advance, with all the help we can give them, the Western countries are going to advance that much faster. After twenty years of watching their frustration, I can hardly be surprised to see them reject Western logic and Western values even when they have nothing better to turn to." This is the Low Road view, which amounts to a conviction that the peoples of the underdeveloped countries are frustrated to the point of irrationality and that Western policy which assumes that they will act in their best material interests is bound to fail.

Secretary Dulles had, then, taken the High Road, and we were to see more of it before it collapsed, but the working levels at the State Department and the Pentagon were well advanced down the Low Road and right under Secretary Dulles' nose were putting across subsidiary policies which were almost totally inconsistent with the Secretary's key policies but which nevertheless determined the forthcoming chain of events. To come to the point: within days of Gerhardt and Eveland's assuring Nasser that his chances of aid depended upon his agreeing to an area-defense policy, and Nasser's making it clear that he had no intention of doing so, Nasser *got* the $40,000,000 in economic aid that had been held up, and exchanges between the U.S. Government and the Egyptian Government were started whereby Nasser was to be allowed to purchase $20,000,000 worth of military aid at reasonable prices and on easy credit terms.

Although it may divert us for a while from our main theme, we must now consider the person of Henry ("Hank") Byroade, the Assistant Secretary of State who was in Washington during the latter part of Ambassador Caffery's tenure and who, in January 1955, replaced Caffery as Ambassador to Egypt. Byroade was then thirty-nine years old, the same age as Nasser, and before coming to the State Department had been a highly successful Army officer, having become a brigadier general before he was thirty. He was also a democratic, informal person whom everybody liked and whom Nasser was sure to like. He was trustworthy, loyal, helpful, friendly, courteous, kind, obedient, cheerful, thrifty, brave, clean and reverent. In short, he was what the writers of *The Ugly American* would call a model ambassador.

The $40,000,000 in aid was announced in November; the beginning of the military agreement that Bill Eveland had mentioned was announced six weeks later (in January 1955); Byroade arrived the following week. The military agreement, which came to be known as the "Baghdad Pact," started as an agreement between Prime Minister Adnan Menderes of Turkey and Prime Minister Nuri of Iraq, and later included Pakistan to comprise the "northern-tier" arrangement which Secretary Dulles had come to favor over the regional defense arrangement as a means of containing the Soviets. It included only one Arab country, Iraq, but it was nevertheless disturbing to Nasser because it stood in the way of his forming a neutralist Arab front. Jim Eichelberger and I delivered the news to Nasser the afternoon after the agreement was signed. Although Gerhardt and Eveland had warned him that such an agreement was in the cards, discussions on the $40,000,000 in economic aid with $20,000,000 in easy-credit military aid had caused him to believe that Gerhardt and Eveland were only bluffing. He was therefore most upset and informed us that he would like me to tell Byroade that he hoped to see him immediately upon his arrival.

This proved difficult; Byroade had come by ship, and characteristically, he had made friends with everyone on board—the aged tourists, civil servants on the way to their posts, the crew, everyone—and had invited them all to Cairo for the weekend. Then there was the matter of the presentation of credentials: according to diplomatic custom, ambassadors must ceremoniously present their credentials and have them ceremoniously accepted by the chief of state before they can legally speak for their governments. Still fuming from the Baghdad Pact announcement, Nasser intended to take his time about going through the ceremony, but he still wanted an early meeting with Byroade. It was arranged that Nasser and Byroade, plus Abdelhakim Amer and Hassan Touhami, would come to my house for dinner.

This dinner began the Byroade-Nasser relationship which was to initiate the Nasser-is-the-wave-of-the-future era of Egyptian-American relations. It was followed a week later by an outing attended by Hassan Touhami and myself besides Nasser and Byroade, during which the whole range of questions between our two countries was reviewed, with emphasis on these points: (1) A truly independent Egypt would be a friend worth having, whereas an Egypt so bound to us by treaties as to appear, by the criteria of the "awakening" Arabs, to be our satellite, would not. (2) The Arabs, being Moslems, have a "natural antipathy to Communism." Besides, the Russians could not possibly match our economic might when the contest as to who could give the most aid got started. Therefore, we should not be afraid of Russian competition. (3) A strong and independent Egypt could take the leadership in a *meaningful* movement toward Arab unity—i.e., a movement that would fit the Cold War, or whatever kind of East-West rivalry might replace it, as opposed to the kind of unity that "the British and Secretary Dulles" spoke of in connection with military alliances and with an outdated, Lawrence of Arabia kind of understanding of the Arab mentality. (4) Moreover, a strong and independent Egypt could take the leadership in reducing the tensions between the Arabs and the West since the creation of Israel. "Only when you are in a strong position can you afford to take unpopular decisions," Nasser said. (He actually hinted that if he was strong enough he might even take positive steps to reduce the tensions between the Arabs and Israel.)

Needless to say, Byroade was not completely convinced by these arguments. In the course of that day in the country, however, he did become convinced that what had been said did in fact constitute Nasser's position and that Nasser was not going to be talked out of it. Moreover, thought Byroade, the position *did* have much to be said for it. At least, in the light of the oncoming wave of irrational Arab nationalism which Byroade—and the State Department and the CIA and everybody else who understood the situation— foresaw, it was preferable to the alternative policies that were beginning to appear. It even had advantages over the "pro-Western" positions of Nuri of Iraq and Chamaoun of Lebanon: namely, the advantage of survival through the days ahead when, by the nature of things, American and British actions would appear to the Arabs to be increasingly pro-Israel and anti-Arab.

It was on the basis of a partial acceptance of Nasser's position that Byroade took up the cry of arms for Nasser.

As a military man, he knew that there was nothing to fea
from the possibility that Nasser might use the arms in som
way that would run counter to American interests. Havin
been Assistant Secretary of State for Africa and the Middl
East, he knew that there was a lot in what Nasser said abou
the kind of beneficial influence Egypt could exert through
out the area if Nasser had a mind to. Also, he was move
by an impression that Nasser was one leader in the Aral
world who was representative of the new mood and witl
whom at the same time a Western diplomat could hold ar
intelligent discussion. One could discuss any subject witl
Nasser, including the possibility of peace with Israel, witl
the feeling that he was listening intelligently to what wa
said and was using his brains rather than his emotions a
he offered his rebuttals. For this reason, along with many
others, Byroade wanted Nasser to survive. And he believe
that turning his "shabby Army" into a "proud Army" wa
essential to his survival.

As I have already mentioned, before Byroade's arriva
our government had granted Nasser $40,000,000 in economi
aid and had agreed in principle that he would be allowe
to purchase $20,000,000 worth of military equipment a
reasonable prices and on easy credit terms. (Incidentally
it is a fallacy to think of "economic aid" or "military aid"
strictly as such, even when the tightest strings are attache
to it, because aid to a government for any specific purpos
frees the government's own funds that have been set asid
for that purpose, and these funds can be used for any othe
purpose of the government's choice.) The only question
were: Which items—new, obsolescent, obsolete—could
we release for sale? How much would we charge? Seemingly, these were details. The Egyptian Defense Ministry
made up a list and sent it to Washington; the Pentagon
made a few changes and sent it back; the Egyptian Defense
Ministry made a few more, and so on. There is always the
question of prices: the Pentagon people have some kind of

sliding-scale arrangement which I have never been able to understand but which seems capable of coming up with *some* price which can be haggled over. In this case, however, both the final list of approved items and the list of prices to match it somehow never got past the penultimate stage.

Meanwhile, there was no indication that the problems, whatever they were, would not· be resolved in the end, leaving Byroade and Nasser to work out a solid Egyptian-American friendship and an arrangement for co-operation whereby the pressing problems of the whole area could be solved, leading to that era of peace and prosperity which our idealists had been talking about. But somehow the problems were not resolved, and the question of arms was left up in the air for many months, with periodic assurances from Washington that "we are working on it as hard as we can, but these things take time."

I will spare the reader the details of the great debate that was taking place in Washington on the question "Do we give aid to Nasser or don't we?" We in Cairo were oblivious of the fact that such a debate was taking place, and Byroade was happily proceeding on the assumption that some satisfactory package of arms would be worked out; his rather ambitious plans for Egyptian-American co-operation, which (among other things) could bring about at least a *modus vivendi* between Israel and the Arabs, thereby removing the principal source of Arab-American friction, presupposed that this would be the case. On July 16, 1955, I finished my two-year tour in Cairo and headed slowly for home, taking one month to get there. When I arrived in Washington in late August, I found waiting for me letters from both Byroade and Nasser asking me to see what I could do to break the impasse, plus copies of correspondence between my boss, Jim Allen of Booz, Allen and Hamilton, and Herbert Hoover, Jr. (then Undersecretary of State) which stated that I would be lent to the

State Department for an indeterminate period to serve on a group called "the Middle East Policy Planning Committee." The main purpose of the committee was to work out ways of taking advantage of the friendship that was developing between ourselves and Nasser.

My first official act in Washington was to take up the question of arms-to-Egypt with the man who had replaced Hank Byroade as Assistant Secretary of State for Africa and the Middle East, George Allen. George didn't appear to know much about the project except that it was held up "for administrative reasons," and he suggested that I make myself comfortable in an adjacent office and read the cable exchanges between Cairo and Washington during the month I had been out of touch. I did. I followed the messages back and forth like watching a tennis ball in a particularly active game and it soon became clear to me that the project was bogged down in pure bureaucracy, nothing else. Supplementary files did indeed contain indications of a great debate on whether or not Nasser should get the aid he wanted "without assurances that he wouldn't use them for any aggressive purposes against Israel," but these were irrelevant. They became even more irrelevant when, at lunch the next day, the Egyptian Ambassador in Washington authorized me to tell Allen that we could take the pressure off Nasser by furnishing him $2,000,000 worth of "parade items"—shiny helmets, pistols in nice leather holsters, and the like—just to "dress up the Army a bit." Whatever the administrative problems were (and I still do not understand them), they also stood in the way of parade items. So that ended that.

The last item in the file was a compelling, though undramatic, cable from Byroade stating that we had better revise our thinking on the possibility of the Russians' giving military aid to Egypt (George Allen had insisted that "Soviet aid is out of the question") and predicting that if we didn't give at least some token amount of aid quickly,

Nasser would certainly accept an offer from the Russians which the CIA had reported them to have made. He went on to predict that should this come about, the Soviets' position in the area would take the course that it has in fact subsequently taken. My "Middle East Policy Planning Committee" was duly alarmed, but still no action was taken. And in mid-September Kermit Roosevelt received a personal message from Nasser to the effect that he was about to sign an agreement with the Russians and that if he, Roosevelt, wanted to try talking him out of it he was welcome to do so. Roosevelt and I took off for Cairo the next day.

We were met at the airport by one of Nasser's aides and taken straight to Nasser's apartment at the top of the Revolutionary Command Council building. Nasser was in a teasing, "I told you so" mood, very cheerful and all set to enjoy hearing the famous Roosevelt persuasion grapple with his own unanswerable arguments. But Roosevelt surprised him. Instead of arguing that Nasser should not accept the arms (the CIA had convinced us that this would be futile, since they had been reliably informed that Nasser had *already* concluded the deal), Roosevelt said, "If the deal is as big as we hear it is, it will worry some people but in general it will make you a big hero. Why don't you take advantage of the sudden popularity to do something really statesmanlike? It won't lessen your gains if you make such an announcement as 'We are getting these arms only for defensive purposes, and if the Israelis want to join in a common effort to bring about lasting peace in the area they will find me willing.' Something like that." Nasser leapt immediately to the suggestion. "A good idea," he said.

We discussed the idea until midnight: Nasser would put his announcement of the Soviet arms deal in a noble and statesmanlike context, gaining cheers not only from the radicals but from the conservative elements of his own population and even from the East, and would then launch upon a neutralist approach to international affairs which would be acceptable to all sides, while getting on with badly needed social and economic reforms at home—with American aid. There were all sorts of possibilities. Nasser was to make a speech two evenings later to a graduating class of air cadets, and he could easily work the announcement into that speech. It was agreed that I would draft the pertinent paragraph and that Nasser and Roosevelt would edit it the next night.

A veritable platoon of kibitzers was in on the drafting— excluding Ambassador Byroade, however, who didn't even know we were in Cairo. During the day after our first meeting with Nasser, a procession of visitors arrived at our hotel suite to give us their ideas on what should and what should not go into the statement: Mustafa Amin, publisher of *Akhbar il-Yom* and a confidant of Nasser's; Mohammed Hassanein Heykel, columnist for *Akhbar il-Yom* and also a confidant of Nasser's; Hassan Touhami, Nasser's ultrapatriotic senior aide; Jim Eichelberger from the Embassy (who had heard of our arrival from Heykel and had neglected to mention it to Byroade); Ahmed Hussein, the Egyptian Ambassador in Washington; and one or two others, making a fairly large total number, but all of whom were privy to the top-secret information that an arms deal had been concluded with the Russians. For all the kibitzing, the draft came out as a short, simple statement which clearly made the point we wanted made, which wouldn't lessen the dramatic effect Nasser hoped to make on the crowd, and which would offend no one.

Kim and I presented the draft to Nasser at eight o'clock the next night, again in Nasser's apartment at the Revolutionary Command Council headquarters, just across the Nile from the British Embassy. There wasn't much to discuss. Nasser liked the draft and said that he could easily work it into his speech—the only alteration being that he couldn't bring himself to mention explicitly "peace with Israel." Instead, he would say "reduce the tensions between the Arabs and Israel"—under the circumstances a great advance and quite acceptable to Roosevelt. He had some specific ideas how this could be done, and following the Nasser speech, he was anxious to get on with them.

Nasser brought out a bottle of Scotch whisky which he kept for distinguished visitors, and just as he did so, the telephone rang; the duty officer downstairs reported that Sir Humphrey Trevelyan, the British Ambassador, urgently wanted an appointment.

"What could *he* want?" Nasser asked.

"Obviously, he wants to talk to you about the Soviet arms deal."

"But he couldn't know about that. It's secret."

"Gamal," said Roosevelt, "even if your own people haven't leaked it out the Soviets would have. It's not in their interests to keep it secret."

"Maybe you're right," said Nasser as we watched the lights of Sir Humphrey's Bentley going on in the Embassy courtyard across the river. We sat and watched the car pull out into the main street, work its way into the traffic crossing the bridge, and pull into the avenue below. Meanwhile, we discussed the line Nasser should take with the Ambassador. Sir Humphrey, like Byroade, was unaware of our presence in Cairo: true to form, Secretary Dulles' office had failed to inform the rest of the State Department, the British, or even his own Ambassador in Cairo of Nasser's invitation to Roosevelt and of the fact that we had gone out to persuade Nasser to embark upon a bold new era of friendship and economic development. What, under the circumstances, was Nasser to tell the British Ambassador? "Just to hold him until tomorrow night," said Roosevelt, "tell him the arms are coming from Czechoslovakia," the idea being that this wouldn't sound so heretical since the Czechs were also a major source of arms for the Israelis.

So Nasser went down and reported that the arms were from "Prague"—pronounced "Brag" by Nasser, in the manner of Arabs, so that Sir Humphrey failed to understand him and left the meeting thinking that Nasser had admitted to an arms deal with the Russians. We weren't able to meet Sir Humphrey and correct him on this point until he had already cabled London and the Foreign Office had released the story to the BBC.

The Nasser-Trevelyan meeting took no more than five minutes, and finally revising the draft for the speech to the air cadets took only a few minutes more. About this time Abdelhakim Amer and Zakaria Mohieddin swept into the room to take the three of us off to dinner at the house of Ambassador Ahmed Hussein. It was all very cheerful. There was some teasing from my friend Zakaria, who *also* hadn't known until a few moments ago that we were in Cairo; jokes about what would have been the look on the British Ambassador's face had Kim or I interrupted his meeting with Nasser to ask, "Excuse me, Gamal, but we're out of soda. Where do you keep the soda?"; the usual jokes about the presence of microphones in meeting places—in other words, the kind of simple, harmless banter that takes place between adults of different cultures, especially following the release of some kind of pressure.

This is relevant, because the high spirits and joking— joking of a sort that excludes anyone who comes in late to it—continued all the way to Ambassador Hussein's house and through the first part of the evening. We were more than an hour late. Already there was Ambassador Byroade, whose first knowledge of our presence in town came when we entered the party with the chief of state and his two principal deputies, all engaged in loud joking which excluded him.

For the benefit of my readers who don't know the protocol of large organizations—whether the State Department, General Motors, the Catholic Church, or the Chinese Army —let me explain that there is nothing more intolerable to a senior official than to have some Great White Father enter his domain, without his prior knowledge, and independently take actions that involve high policy. But this was the sort of thing that happened under Secretary Dulles. When a problem arose in, say, Afghanistan, the Secretary would look around the room full of Brooks Brothers suits that filled his house at a Saturday-morning staff meeting and say, "Now let's see, who's clever at Afghanistan?" choosing someone of his staff who had recently said something about Afghanistan that the Secretary considered "sound." Secretary Dulles was not the kind of man in whose presence anyone felt like saying, "But Mr. Secretary, we've got a perfectly good Ambassador in Afghanistan." Besides, the Secretary trusted—and thought about—only those who worked right under his nose.

After choosing the emissary, Secretary Dulles would then either fail to notify the appropriate embassy, or notify the embassy only in a routine way (AVERELL HARRIMAN ARRIVING ON PAN AMERICAN 100; WILL NOT WISH TO STAY AT RESIDENCE; PLEASE BOOK SUITE AT HILTON), or actually give some reason for the trip other than the real one. Throughout Secretary Dulles' time an ambassador lived with the fear that one morning, between his residence and the Chancery, he would encounter Robert Murphy or Robert Anderson or some other VIP cryptodiplomat riding by in the opposite direction, in a guest Cadillac, on his way to the palace.

Ambassador Byroade is the most easygoing, unjealous, unstuffy, unbureaucratic senior official I have ever come across, but even he was likely to be stunned at the sudden sight of Kermit Roosevelt, of all people, walking one hour late into a dinner party arm in arm with the chief of state of the country and two of his top ministers under circumstances that made it plain that they had just come from a meeting. And then there was the esoteric humor. Even under the best of circumstances it is annoying to find oneself on the fringes of a group absorbed in a private joke.

Others present were Jim Eichelberger (who had forgotten to tell Byroade that he had seen us earlier in the day), Ambassador-at-large Eric Johnston, who was in town in connection with his Jordan River plan, and the host, Ambassador Ahmed Hussein. Eichelberger and Hussein were sharing a bottle of brandy, Eric Johnston entered into the fun as best he could, and Byroade sat morosely, holding a Scotch. Except for Byroade, it was a relaxed and highly convivial evening. Ambassador Johnston launched into one of his stories, a picaresque thing which he delivered in an Irish brogue and which, among other items, had in it a pregnant nun, Moses, Jews, and a bowel movement (and no point); while Ahmed Hussein and I, with great difficulty, were trying to translate it into Arabic, Byroade cleared his throat and interrupted. "Gamal," he said, "there is a matter that I would like to bring to your attention."

The laughing stopped, everyone became silent, and Byroade launched into a tirade against the "Egyptian police state," the Revolutionary Command Council who were "behaving like a lot of juvenile delinquents," and one or two other features of Nasser's regime that had been called to mind by the rough handling, by the Alexandria police, of Byroade's Labor Attaché two days earlier. It was an eloquent performance, with every word and phrase coming out as though it had been written by a skilled playwright. But it was delivered at the wrong place at the wrong time, and to the worst conceivable audience. Nasser suddenly snuffed out his cigarette, rose, and strode out, with his ministers scurrying after him. Roosevelt followed him to the car and made some kind of apology. Byroade sat rigidly at the table, stunned not so much by Nasser's dramatic exit as because the implications (for him) of Roosevelt's and Johnston's presence at the performance had suddenly dawned on him. Johnston waited until he heard Nasser's Cadillac drive off, then tapped Byroade on the arm and said, "Time to go home, Hank." Off they went, Byroade looking like a somnambulist being led back to bed.

I understand that the system was later changed, but in those days it was possible for a visiting VIP to use an embassy's facilities to cable Washington without the Ambassador's knowing about it. As Byroade was tossing and turning through a sleepless night, he must have imagined Roosevelt and Johnston locked with the code clerk preparing a cable to Secretary Dulles which would hardly be helpful to his career. As indeed they were. Roosevelt, although contrite because he had neglected to inform Byroade, thought that "Byroade's extraordinary behavior" might jeopardize the scheme he had come to Cairo to launch; Johnston, whose business training had taught him that *nothing* justifies losing one's temper with a customer or even with an adversary, thought that Byroade was cracking up—or, as he put it in the cable, that he "needed a rest." With the seven hours' difference in time between Cairo and Washington, the cable arrived on the Secretary's desk the next morning, on the day that Nasser was to make the speech containing our carefully constructed paragraph.

At 7 A.M. Cairo time, Byroade called me from his office in the Embassy and asked me to come over. When I arrived thirty minutes later, I found him again reconstituted as Handsome Hank, the good Ambassador in *The Ugly American,* all cleaned up after an early game of tennis, wearing a beautifully tailored tweed sports jacket and a brisk, businesslike early-morning manner. His reaction to the previous night's experience was not so much worry about his own career as a statesmanlike concern that the Philistines, in the manner of the villains of Edward R. F. Sheehan's novel *Kingdom of Illusion,** were about to bring American-Egyptian relations to ruin. He threw a sheet of paper across the desk to me. "What do you think of that?"

I have forgotten the exact contents, but it said something like "Dear Gamal: I'm awfully sorry to have raised an unpleasant subject at a pleasant social gathering last evening,

---

* *Kingdom of Illusion* is a fictional treatment partly based on the Nasser-Byroade-Roosevelt relationship. See Suggested Reading List.

but I do feel strongly about having my officers beaten up—as, I am sure, you would feel in similar circumstances. Anyhow, I am truly sorry and I hope you will accept my apology. Yours, Hank." I told him I thought it was a good letter, and that I would deliver it right away.

At 9 A.M., I met Nasser just as he was getting out of his limousine to enter his ceremonial office, and he swept me along inside with him while talking volubly about what a fine party he thought it had been the evening before. "I thought Eric's story about Moses and the bowel movement was wonderful!" he said. When we got inside I gave him Byroade's letter; he read it quickly and thrust it into a drawer. "Well," he said. "I suppose I'll see you and Kim tonight." He gave no comment on the Byroade letter.

I walked to the door, but before leaving asked, "What about the letter?"

"What about it?"

"Well, what are you going to do about it?"

"Oh," he said, waving me away, "I'll just file it with the others."

"The . . . *others?*"

"Oh, Hank's always blowing up like that," he said. "I hope Kim and Eric didn't make too much of it."

Make too much of it? They had just sent a cable which would probably get Byroade transferred to Fernando Poo. I sat down again and asked Nasser exactly what he had meant by the "others." It turned out that only a week earlier Byroade had chided him about one of his pilots, a newly graduated cadet on his first official flight, who had been shot down over the Israeli border. On another occasion, Byroade had made a big issue out of some anti-American statement Nasser had made. Clearly, Byroade had established a relationship with Nasser that enabled him to speak up frankly about any of Nasser's actions he did not like; and Nasser obviously took it seriously or let Byroade's remarks go in one ear and out the other, depending on his mood of the moment, with no offense. One thing was certain: he did not want Byroade's angry remarks of the evening before, or any other such remarks, to get him into trouble. "I'll speak to Kim about it this evening," he said as I left.

There is a seven-hour difference between 9 A.M. Cairo time and 9 A.M. Washington time, but taking into account the difference in working pace, it takes only about one hour for events in Washington to catch up on the discrepancy. Thus, by 10 A.M. Washington time—5 P.M. Cairo time— several things had happened. Secretary Dulles had decided to send Assistant Secretary of State George Allen to Cairo to check on Byroade's sanity; Deputy Assistant Secretary of State William Rountree had drafted a stern letter from Dulles to Nasser pointing out the dangers of taking Russian arms; and Assistant Deputy Assistant Secretary of State Somebody had leaked enough of the story to the press to justify a news bulletin saying, "Allen to Cairo to present ultimatum to Nasser." The story was on the Associated Press ticker in Cairo by 6 P.M. local time (11 A.M. Washington time), and by 6:30, when Kim and I were to meet him, Nasser was surrounded by staff officers and was instructing one of them to take "that silly paragraph" out of his speech and to replace it with something appropriately defiant and anti-American, another to get in touch with the Foreign Office and look into the intricacies of breaking relations with a major power, and another to reserve radio time so that "an important announcement" could be made to the people at large; and, very possibly, another to pick out the shabbiest guest car available and escort Kim Roosevelt and myself to the airport in it. This, for the benefit of my non-Washingtonian readers, is what is known as a "flap"; there was a similar flap taking place in Washington.

We have Mustafa Amin to thank for getting the situation in hand and for convincing Nasser that it wouldn't do any damage if he saw Kim Roosevelt, just to hear what he had to say, before taking all these measures. Nasser eventually decided to go upstairs, where Kim was already waiting—unaware, incidentally, of the AP report because, characteristically, the Secretary's office hadn't got around to cabling the Embassy in Cairo of Allen's coming, with or without an ultimatum. Thus, when Kim found himself in front of an enraged Nasser he was totally unprepared for it.

Some months later, Nasser made a speech in which he said that "an American" had come to him to warn him of Allen's ultimatum and that he should pay no attention to it. Much fuss was subsequently made about this in the newspapers. This was Arab hyperbole. What Kim actually said was, "Why don't you get the ultimatum first and raise a row later, rather than vice versa? Associated Press is occasionally wrong, you know." Nasser didn't agree. To him, the AP was never wrong. (His censors once gave the AP's local correspondent, Wilton Wynn, a difficult time because his stories were "suspiciously accurate.") All Roosevelt could say was, "If Allen gives you an ultimatum, react to it the way you think you should. But I don't think Secretary Dulles would be sending you an ultimatum without telling *me* about it"—a totally justified but unreliable assumption. Nasser cooled down and agreed to postpone any drastic counter action until he had seen the ultimatum. But he did cut the cherished paragraph out of his speech.

The speech actually delivered was far from the statesmanlike gesture for which we had been working, but it was reasonably subdued—as subdued, that is, as was possible for a speech including such an explosive announcement. By then, both the AP and the BBC had released stories about the Soviet (or Czech) arms, so that all that was left for Nasser to announce was "Yes, I've taken Soviet (Czech) arms. What is anybody going to do about it?" But his speech left open the idea of the purchase's being a "defensive gesture," and when Kim and I met him minutes after he delivered it, he went out of his way to say, "This wasn't exactly what you wanted, but there is still time."

The next morning George Allen arrived, approximately an hour after the routine PLEASE BOOK SUITE AT HOTEL cable landed on the Embassy administrative officer's desk. Large crowd of reporters at the airport, together with Byroade and his aides; flashbulbs going off as Allen came down the ramp; pictures of Allen and Byroade shaking hands; pictures of Allen and a very junior Egyptian protocol official shaking hands; crowds on the airport observation balcony shouting anti-American slogans—the whole spectacle combined to make a very effective show to underline the Nasserist posture of defiance which the Arabs most appreciate. Before any reporters could get close enough to Allen to start asking him questions, Hassan Touhami had slipped past the cordon of American Marine guards to give him a note from Roosevelt and Johnston: "Deny ultimatum, or at least don't mention it, until we can discuss it," it said.

Half an hour later, we were meeting in Byroade's office— Allen, Byroade, Eric Johnston, Lewis Jones (Byroade's deputy), Kim Roosevelt, and myself. The idea that had prompted Dulles to send Allen to Cairo in the first place (to slip in quietly to substitute for a deranged Byroade) had become totally irrelevant. Now, Byroade was clearly in command of the situation—or, rather, as much in command as it was possible for him to be with not one but *three* Great White Fathers in his parlor. Second, the flap over the ultimatum had obscured everything else, so much so that Johnston and Roosevelt failed to perceive the real purpose of Allen's trip—and indeed, didn't learn of it until a whispered conference hours later. Third, public reaction throughout the Arab world to Nasser's arms deal had exceeded our worst fears and had become, in itself, a major problem. It was, in other words, an emergency meeting the *fact* of which was as important as its content—and it had all come about, unnecessarily, as the result of "that bloody midnight cable" as Roosevelt and Johnston both called it later.

The meeting itself was one of those games of Chinese

Checkers which, in spite of the restraint and care of those present, linger in one's memory as one confused rumble: "Driving Nasser into the arms of the Communists" . . . "If you've had as many dealings with Congress as I've had" . . . "Counterproductive" . . . "but where do *American* interests stand in all this?" . . . "At this point in time" . . . "Statesmanlike gesture." George Allen is a fine man whom I greatly respect ("Not so much intelligent as wise," his subordinates used to say of him), but I am prepared to swear under oath that he said, "Why don't we appeal to Nasser in the name of his people?" Roosevelt replied that better we should do a rain dance, and left the meeting to play tennis. Eric Johnston, who had a habit of remaining quiet until he had heard from everybody else, finally said, "The problem is the same as it was a month ago when we first heard about the Soviet arms, except that we are now contributing to its being a Big Deal—just as Nasser wants us to do. If your ultimatum has any threats in it we can carry out, by all means present it. If it doesn't, let's forget it." The meeting, with Roosevelt already gone, ended on that note.

But there *was* an ultimatum to be considered. Although it was a spur-of-the-moment concoction (as far as we could judge, the Secretary had simply said "As you are going to Cairo, you might as well take the opportunity to tell Nasser what we think of his arms deal; Bill, you go draft something"), an order from the Secretary was an order. Allen, although he approved of Roosevelt's playing it down to Nasser the evening before, had no choice but to deliver it. But the situation clearly called for playing down rather than playing up, and when Allen went to meet Nasser all he did was read parts of the letter aloud, making them sound as anticlimactic as possible, then go on to discuss more pleasant things—what Egypt was going to do with our $40,000,000, for example.

From our point of view, that was all there was to it. But Nasser was delighted with the whole thing: with the arms deal itself, with his public's reaction to it, with the talk of an "ultimatum" from us, with his own performance in response to the ultimatum, with his public's reaction to his response, and with the fact that, in the end, there was no ultimatum. Not only had he made a play that raised his standing in the Arab world (not to mention the advantages in the arms themselves), but he had managed to dramatize it in the most advantageous way possible—and with our help.

By acquiring arms from the Soviets, Nasser had achieved independence from us without paying the cost of dependence on the Soviets, thereby confronting us with these two alternatives: Let the Soviets have him, or try to woo him back. After our performance over "Allen's lost weekend," as we came to call it, it was obvious which of the alternatives we would choose. "Positive neutrality" was on its way.

8

Nasser's "Union"
of Positive Neutralists

*. . . and if a single weak player can do this
to good effect, a "union" of weak players
can do it to better effect.*

Positive neutrality—or freedom of decision, or whatever you
choose to call it—is not only Nasser's objective, it is his
strategy. In 1965, Peter Mansfield* compiled a list of Egypt's
foreign loans and credit facilities which my State Department and Foreign Office friends tell me is substantially
accurate—or, if anything, "probably on the conservative
side," as one of them said. It is given on the next page, with
the value of the Egyptian pound figured at $2.30.

Apart from money, aid from both sides included technical
assistance, gifts of industrial equipment, gifts of food—or,
what is more, "sales" of food for which the Egyptians pay
in soft currency—and some $500,000,000 worth of military
equipment from the Soviets. It is a lot more than Egypt
would have received had Nasser agreed to "stand up and
be counted" as Secretary Dulles wished. To be specific, the
"stand up and be counted" route would almost certainly
have produced no more than $40,000,000 to $50,000,000 a
year from the United States and Great Britain and *nothing*
from the Soviets, and would have meant going without

* See Suggested Reading List.

170

military aid—without which, it is important to understand, the regime would probably not have survived. The route that Nasser did take produced roughly *ten times* that amount.

As good a place as any to start in examining Nasser's use of positive neutrality to "get into the Big League aidwise," as the Embassy Economic Officer used to put it, is the time when the question of $40,000,000 in aid was first raised.

From Communist states

Soviet Union			332.5
Czechoslovakia			62.0
East Germany			45.0
Poland			24.4
Hungary			12.0
Yugoslavia			7.0
	TOTAL	£E Million	482.9

From non-Communist states

United States			535.6
West Germany			93.0
Italy			92.9
Japan			17.0
France			10.0
Britain			5.4
Netherlands			5.0
Switzerland			4.0
Sweden			3.3
Others			6.3
	TOTAL	£E Million	772.5
World Bank (IBRD)		£E Million	19.7
International Monetary Fund		£E Million	36.0
	GRAND TOTAL	£E Million	1,311.1

When Nasser and Dulles met, in May 1953, Nasser gained the impression that the order of magnitude we had in mind was $100,000,000 in economic aid and roughly the same amount in military aid, and that all that was required to get these amounts was to come to an agreement with the British over the Suez Base—and that, moreover, Nasser would not have to wait for the actual signing of the agreement so long as it became apparent that the Egyptians were negotiating in good faith and that a mutually acceptable agreement was sure to come about. It was on this understanding that Ali Sabri, then the United States' best friend on the Revolutionary Council, went to Washington to assist the Egyptian Military Attaché Abdelhamid Ghaleb, in negotiations. Today, Ali and Abdelhamid are perhaps the most anti-American of the Egyptians who advise Nasser, the reason being the runaround they think they got in connection with the $200,000,000 they believed had been promised them. Here are two of the most intelligent and competent officials in the United Arab Republic Government, one (until recently) a Vice-President, the other Deputy Foreign Minister, who have been our implacable foes over the years because of their "humiliation" which was never smoothed over.

It confused the State Department at the time, because it was clear to all those who talked to Sabri and Ghaleb that they were sincere in their belief, and that in their own minds Secretary Dulles had indeed promised Nasser the $200,000,000. Ambassador Caffery was similarly confused because Nasser's understanding or misunderstanding somehow rang true, and he wondered over the possibility that the Secretary might have said something in an unguarded moment, perhaps over lunch, that he and the various aides had missed. Consequently, late one summer afternoon Caffery requested me to visit Nasser to ask if we might borrow his memorandum of the conversation covering the meeting with Dulles. I did. It took a few minutes to explain to Nasser what we meant by "memorandum of conversation"; he had never heard of such a thing. Since then Nasser has become more sophisticated, and since about 1955 every conversation of any official importance goes straight into a tape recorder via one of the many microphones hidden in his office, his reception rooms and his dining room. At the time I asked him about the Dulles meeting, however, he thought it disingenuous of us to rush off and write down everything that was said in a "confidential" meeting. He himself had not made any such memorandum. He was surprised that Dulles had.

From this conversation, and from a subsequent one Nasser had with Ambassador Caffery, I think Nasser decided that it was all an honest mistake; he forgave us for it in a way that Ali Sabri and Abdelhamid Ghaleb could not. (As Abdelhamid told me later: "We were treated like children. One day we thought everything was cleared up; then the next day some Pentagon official would lecture to us as though we were raw recruits or some State Department official would lecture to us about peace and stability as though we were idiots.") All Nasser wanted to know was, "Well, how much *are* we going to get?"

He pressed me for an answer to this question one evening as Hassan Touhami and I were talking with him in his garden, and I didn't want to answer. It was strictly not my affair (there is a law called the Logan Act which prohibits private citizens from influencing the thinking of foreign chiefs of state so far as it affects relations with the United States Government), and I didn't want to offend Ambassador Caffery. Nevertheless, I finally said, "I would first ask for $20,000,000 and relate it to specific projects. Once the projects are on their way I would ask for more." Nasser showed no reaction, but Hassan Touhami blew up. "I'm not going to sit here and hear you insult my President," he said. "You talk to us about $200,000,000; then you offer us a handout and want us to beg for it." There was no arguing with him. Nasser went off to bed, and Hassan and I rode back to town in silence. As Hassan dropped me in front of my house his parting shot was, "Before very long *you'll* be begging *us* to accept the $200,000,000."

The next morning I hurried over to Caffery to tell him about the conversation. To my relief, he said I had done the right thing in mentioning $20,000,000 as a sensible figure— "so long," he added, "as you made it clear that you were just guessing as a private citizen." He went on to say, however, that he would press the State Department for double the $20,000,000—"or rather, for double plus ten million or so to allow for what they will knock off." This is what happened. Caffery asked for $50,000,000; the Department came back with $40,000,000.*

I did a lot of arguing in those days—my arguments all beginning with the disclaimer, "This is none of my business but . . ."—because, through circumstances, I had become a convenient unofficial middleman between Nasser and Caffery, and in the light of my own long-range interest, I wanted to avoid association with any fiasco. My own belief was that it was not the *amount* of aid that would put our relationship with Nasser on a mutually sound basis; the important thing was *how* we gave it. During a brief visit to New York in the latter part of the summer of 1953, I had given my views to Byroade (then still Assistant Secretary of State) and had ended with the suggestion that when we presented the $40,000,000 to Nasser we should make it clear to him that this was a stopgap amount, surely to be raised (or lowered) in the following year depending on how good an "investment" the amount turned out to be. I also suggested that an additional amount be given to Nasser for

* Some of my State Department friends argued at the time that considerable staff work preceded the choice of $40 million as the proper amount and that the choice was not as arbitrary as it appeared to us in Cairo. One of them added, though, "The right amount psychologically, to look right to Congress, was something under $50 million. Since $49 million would look a little like bargain-basement pricing, we latched on to Caffery's figure of $50 million when it came in and cut it a little to remove the fat we assumed he had put in."

his personal use in setting up security facilities to see him through the internal difficulties that seemed to be looming. In addition, the United States Government should send him an armor-plated Cadillac, a Secret Service man to help organize his bodyguard, a household protection and alarm system, and a lot of effective though unspectacular riot-control equipment.

These suggestions, to one looking back on them, do not now seem to make much sense, but they seemed sensible enough at the time, and Byroade, bowing to my firsthand knowledge of the situation, went along with them. He said that as much as $3,000,000 could be handed over to Nasser directly and secretly, from the President's executive budget, and that the CIA or the FBI or some other such agency could arrange for all the security items. Thus, the total amount of aid to be given the Egyptian Government in November 1953 was $43,000,000—$40,000,000 of conventional financial assistance in accordance with our laws, and $3,000,000 of unvouchered funds directly from the President's budget. The Secret Service adviser, the security items, and the riot-control equipment would come later.

The three million dollars of unvouchered funds might well have created a mystery which, were it not for this book, would puzzle archeologists of the year 5000 A.D. as much as the mysteries of the pyramids of Egypt puzzle archeologists of today. I refer to a piece of architecture, popularly known as "the Cairo Tower," which graces the landscape on Gezira island, across the Nile from the Hilton Hotel, taller than the pyramids and visible from all over Cairo and from many miles away to the giant airlines as they approach Cairo from Europe, Asia and Africa.

When Ambassador Caffery received word of the $43,000,-000—or, rather, the $40,000,000 plus $3,000,000—he thought the idea of a "personal gift" to Nasser utterly absurd, and remarked that if anybody delivered the $3,000,000 to Nasser it would have to be me. The next day, he visited Dr. Fawzi, the Foreign Minister, to inform him of the $40,000,000 in aid, but said not a word about the $3,000,000. With my confidence much shaken by Caffery's reaction, I went to see Hassan Touhami to discuss the $3,000,000—"which," I said, "the U.S. Government isn't pressing on you. I'm only telling you it's available if you want it." Hassan, who was among other things head of Nasser's bodyguard unit (it was Hassan, by the way, who fired the shot in the assassination attempt to which Nasser refers in his *Philosophy of the Revolution*), said "We can always find some use for $3,000,-000. Let's see what it looks like." After getting Nasser's personal assurance that the secret $3,000,000 was indeed acceptable, I informed Caffery—who, in exasperated tones, told me that the sum of $3,000,000 in cash had arrived that very morning by courier from Beirut. A brief consultation with various Embassy officials followed, wherein the security officer gleefully informed me that armed guards riding back with me the five miles to Hassan's house in Ma'adi would "excite suspicion"; moments later I was bumping over the country road to Ma'adi, driven by perhaps the most dishonest chauffeur in Cairo, with two suitcases containing $3,000,000 in cash jostling an order of groceries my wife had earlier ordered from Groppis.

Hassan, flanked by two Egyptian security guards, received me in his Ma'adi home with no show of enthusiam or even interest. We solemnly counted the money, twice, to find that there was only $2,999,990. Hassan's only comment was, "We won't fuss about the missing ten dollars," whereupon he and his security guards climbed into a large Mercedes and headed for Nasser's residence on the other side of Cairo.

I gather from what I heard later from Hassan that Nasser's reaction to the $3,000,000 was roughly the same mixture of annoyance and amusement as Caffery's. His first inclination was to send it back, possibly announcing the "attempted bribe" to the world in some suitable manner (as the Prime

Minister of Singapore *did* some years later when offered the same amount under similar circumstances), but this was not Nasser's style. Hassan's idea for spending the money was to build a structure, roughly modeled on the Sphinx, that would consist of two large statues on the Gezira side of the Nile, facing the site where the Hilton Hotel would one day be built: the one behind would be a large head featuring a particularly large nose; the one in front would be a hand of proportionate size with the thumb adjusted to the nose and the four fingers extending skywards. Nasser thought the idea very good but lacking in subtlety. Instead, he ordered "something unidentifiable, but very large, very conspicuous, very enduring and very expensive—costing, oh, say, something in the neighborhood of three million dollars." The result is the "Tower of Cairo" which we American friends of Egypt see across the Nile every morning as we breakfast on our balconies at the Nile Hilton.

If our Government was slow in getting the message, it was only because it takes a certain amount of time to plan and erect a large tower, even a "nonfunctional" one, as Hassan Touhami delighted in calling it. Kermit Roosevelt got the message some months before the rest of the United States Government, thanks to a report from a CIA agent on Nasser's staff alleging that Nasser's aides were referring to the Tower as *el wa'ef rusfel*—roughly translatable as "Roosevelt's erection." Roosevelt, who had taken the lead in Washington in arguing for the $3,000,000 offer (for, as we shall see later, Game-play reasons of his own), naturally found himself blamed for its backfire when news of it finally leaked out—in July 1955, eight months after Nasser had received the $2,999,990, two months after Hassan Touhami and his builders had begun construction, and three months before Allen's Lost Weekend (and, incidentally, on the same day that the CIA first got word of the impending Soviet arms deal). Those who knew about it at the State Department, on grounds that might seem obscure to the lay reader, blamed Roosevelt because they thought he had "tried to make a fool of Nasser." Hassan and Nasser's other close associates blamed him because they saw the amount as an attempted bribe—although, having parried it with a suitable riposte, they quite forgave him. Nasser blamed him because, unlike his less subtle colleagues, he had at least an inkling of what Roosevelt was *really* up to in inducing the American Government to offer such a gift. To Nasser "Roosevelt's offer" of $3,000,000 was Roosevelt's challenge. To Roosevelt, although he did not regard the offer as his own, the Tower was Nasser's formal notification that, despite public utterances to the contrary, he well understood how the Game was shaping up. Roosevelt assumed, of course, that Nasser had deliberately leaked the *wa'ef rusfel* report to him.

The whole business of aid was in fact a source of irritation to both sides. Nasser and his lieutenants (especially the latter) didn't think the amount of aid was enough; Congressmen and even some members of the State Department thought it was too much and that, besides, Nasser wasn't showing proper appreciation of it. Only Nasser and one or two diplomats on the American side understood what had *really* happened: the way the aid had been handled caused Nasser to be reminded of the old rule "The squeaky wheel gets the grease." It was only a question of time before Nasser was to learn that if a squeaky wheel is good a squeakier wheel is better.

A (then) junior State Department officer who hand-carried the project paper from office to office to get the necessary signatures for a later amount of aid to Egypt tells me that one of the State Department officials at the very top said to him, "We would have no quarrel with Nasser if he would only stick to Egypt and stop interfering in the affairs of other countries," and that he said this *as he added his signature to the document.* This was the American attitude. The more Nasser "interfered in the affairs of other countries" the more we complained about it—*but,* the more aid we gave. Even without his shrewd Oriental mind, Nasser should have been expected to conduct his own future Game play on the basis of what he saw us do rather than what he heard us say.

Whatever Secretary Dulles and others in our Government may have said about how "neutralism is immoral," we have been conspicuously more moved by neutralism than by friendship—as the Shah of Iran, President Chamaoun of Lebanon, King Hussein of Jordan and Emperor Haile Selassie of Ethiopia (to name but a few) learned to their chagrin. Nasser has been as amazed at the naïveté of these chiefs of state as the chiefs of state have been amazed at our behavior. Nasser saw our responses as clearly as Pavlov's dog heard the bell, and he reasoned that as a leader of a more widespread "union" of positive neutralists he could get even more beneficial responses. One laborer walking into a boss's office to demand higher wages for shorter hours is likely to get thrown out, but a laborer speaking for all the laborers in the plant is likely to gain a respectful audience. This, according to the rules which *we* set up, is the nature of the Game.

Or so Nasser reasoned—correctly, as American aid figures show. As Nasser saw it, his influence over the principal sources of foreign aid, the United States and the Soviet Union, went up geometrically as his "union" influence went up arithmetically. Speaking for Egypt he got X results; speaking for the Arab world he could get X^2 results; speaking for the Islamic world he could get X^3 results; speaking for the "non-Western" world he could get X^4 results— although, of course, in the latter cases he would not have to speak for the whole Islamic world or all of Afro-Asia but merely demonstrate himself to be a "key" influence, one that we and the Soviets would look to for our respective purposes instead of turning to one or another of the rival unionizers such as Sukarno and Nkrumah.

Nasser got ahead of Sukarno and Nkrumah—and, for that

matter, Nehru and Tito and all the other "positive neutrality" aspirants—because he was, as Assistant Secretary Phillips Talbot used to say, "difficult but approachable." Outside their own spheres, the other positive neutralists had almost no influence; it would never occur to our Government, for example, to consult with Sukarno about how to use his influence as a positive neutralist to bring about more truly neutral postures on the part of Communist-leaning countries of Asia, nor would it occur to the Soviets to prevail upon his Communist sympathies to help them further their aims in Asia as a whole. Nasser, however, succeeded in getting both the Americans and the Soviets to consult him over many countries in the Afro-Asian world—Vietnam, Indonesia, Syria, and even, to a limited degree, Israel. (In 1962, before supplying the Israelis with Hawk antiaircraft missiles President Kennedy "cleared" the matter with Nasser by explaining it to him and getting him to agree that, under the circumstances of the moment, we could not do otherwise.) President Johnson, in some moment of exasperation, is reported to have said, "I wish we had an ambassador in Cairo who doesn't even know where Vietnam is." Two weeks later he sent Averell Harriman to Cairo to request Nasser's help in getting the North Vietnamese to release some of our downed airmen.

When Nasser, in his *Philosophy of the Revolution,* said that Egypt was "placed at the intersection of three circles" (the Arab world, Islam, and Africa), he was merely helping to build the national myth. When he set about practicing his unionizing strategy in the Game of Nations, however, he was less interested in geography than in gaining leverage. Under some circumstances Cuba was as much of interest as a possible ally as was Pakistan, and West Africa was of more interest than parts of Africa nearer to home. Indeed, it was Nasser's supposed influence in these unlikely areas that caused some of our diplomats to start thinking of him as a "factor to be contended with" and even "a wave of the future." For the purpose of bringing about such an attitude on our part, "supposed" influence served the purpose as well as real influence. And from Nasser's own point of view it was preferable: building up a frightening appearance of influence is much easier than gaining real influence, which would necessarily involve headaches of a sort Nasser was anxious to avoid.

One headache that Nasser especially wanted to avoid was that of administrative responsibility. Responsible writers—journalists, historians, retired diplomats writing their memoirs—speak of "Nasser's dream of a North African empire" or of his "ambition to rule the Arab world." I have often heard officials of our own Government say, "If Nasser is trying to rule the Arab world he is certainly going about it the wrong way" or to observe, with considerable satisfaction, that "Nasser doesn't seem to be doing so well in his campaign to take over the Arab world." I believe it safe to say that virtually all of us who have had prolonged personal contact with Nasser (Kermit Roosevelt, Robert Anderson, Eugene Black, and Charles Cremeans, besides all our Ambassadors to Egypt) would agree that he has no such ambition. Fortunately for them Nasser has no wish to rule the Arab world—or the world of Islam or Africa or any other world—the way Hitler evidently wanted to rule Europe; he only wants to decide its foreign policy *vis à vis* the Great Powers. He wants the Westerners, when they sit down to deal with him, to be conscious of the fact that a deal with him may be a deal with a much larger segment of the world than merely Egypt, and to feel that it would be pointless to approach other governments in his sphere of influence without first consulting him. This is what the conflict, the zero-sum, part of the Game with Nasser is about. It is not a war of ideologies but, despite the high-sounding and low-sounding oratory and newspaper editorials (all part of the Game), a contest between Nasser's unionizing efforts and the deunionizing efforts, however disguised, of the other exploiters of Arab nationalism—or "Islamic unity" or "Afro-Asian unity," or whatever.

It seems odd in the light of later developments, but Nasser's first attempt at unionizing was to be through Islam, not Arabism. Islam has been the dominant Middle Eastern religion since 641 A.D. In its basic form, it was an admirably uncomplicated faith; it had a great deal of literature and tradition behind it which, with only minor adaptation, could well serve the call for unity that Nasser envisaged. Moreover, one political movement based on Islam's appeal, the infamous Moslem Brotherhood, has been at least successful enough to show that the appeal was well suited to gaining recruits, bringing them under strict discipline, and aiming them at targets similar to those which Nasser had singled out.

Another attractive feature was the possibility that the United States Government seemed ready to approve Nasser's becoming "a modernizing force in the Moslem World," as a visiting State Department official told him, and "a bulwark against Communism," as Secretary Dulles said after the Eisenhower Administration came into office—views that were especially interesting to Nasser at a time when Communist ideologues in his entourage were loudly pooh-poohing the idea that Islam was "an implacable foe of Communism" (another frequently repeated State Department view) and arguing that Nasserism joined with Communism could become a "wave of the future" in the sense in which that phrase was originally used. Until the absurdity of the arguments from both sides became apparent, Nasser was tempted: here, possibly, was a chance to "go international" wholesale, and in a manner that would provide an extremely broad base from which to goad the great powers into *real* competition for his favors.

Nasser's decision to push the Islamic circle to third place was at least partly due to Franz Buensch, a German who had come to Egypt as an expert on "Jewish atrocities"—

atrocities *by* the Jews, that is. His one book, a monumental work entitled *Sexual Habits of the Jews*, has been translated into Turkish, Persian and Arabic and was distributed widely by the Nazis during the war to prove that Jewish virility was as much a menace to Islam as Negro virility was to white Christianity in the American South. When he arrived in Egypt, Buensch settled down to more or less routine anti-Semitic writings, none of which served any particular purpose for the Egyptian Propaganda Ministry, but he did develop one project that quickly gained Egyptian interest: a plan to collect Nazi diehards from their various hiding places all over the world (Argentina, Brazil, Ireland, Spain etc.), give them Islamic names, join them to "underground assets developed in Egypt during the Second World War," build a subversive-intelligence organization combining the best in German and Egyptian talent, and "put it at the disposal of Gamal Abdelnasser for his international war against Communism and imperialism."

The plan was presented to Sa'ad Afraq, the General Intelligence Agency officer then responsible for administration and surveillance of the Germans. Sa'ad, whose genial manner covered one of the shrewdest brains in Egypt, affected great interest in the plan, but insisted that he must hear more about these German "underground assets." Buensch, who until then had been sulking at Egyptian indifference to his pet subject, began to feel that at last he was being appreciated and that perhaps he was on to something big. With Sa'ad Afraq's encouragement, he produced all the information on the subject he could remember, then pumped other members of the German colony for what they remembered. The result was enough evidence to hang half the Moslem Brotherhood, plus enough leads to keep Egyptian security officers busy for the next two years establishing the extent of influence of the organization not only in Egypt but throughout the Arab world. Information directly from the German sources showed that the Moslem Brotherhood had been virtually a German Intelligence unit; information coming later as the result of following the leads showed that the unit was still intact, as capable of working *against* Nasser as it was capable of working for him, and that it was so strong that any attempt of Nasser to work with it would result in its using Nasser rather than vice versa.

Nor was that all. Sound beatings of Moslem Brotherhood organizers who had been arrested revealed that the organization had been thoroughly penetrated, at the top, by the British, American, French and Soviet intelligence services, any one of which could either make active use of it or blow it up, whichever best suited its purpose. Important lesson: fanaticism is no insurance against corruption; indeed, the two are highly compatible. When Nasser's unionizing agents moved on to their "negative" phase, this was one lesson they kept firmly in mind.

All the same, when one proceeds against an organization that purports to be a force for the country's dominant religion, one had better do so carefully. This was soon realized by the then head of the CIA in Egypt, who was at the moment engaged in an operation to show Soviet ungodliness by circulating a lot of pre–First World War books with titles like *Mohammed Never Existed, The Harmful Consequences of Fasting During Ramadan* and *Against the Veil* while attributing the distribution to the Soviet Embassy. In October 1954, the agreement on the Suez Base was reached, at the same time when Nasser's police were at the height of their investigation of the Franz Buensch leads. Suddenly, the Soviet press launched a major attack on Nasser and his "fascist followers" while praising the Moslem Brotherhood as being the "most dependable anti-imperialist force in Egypt." The CIA chief cabled Washington to persuade the Israelis to take up the line, but to shift the emphasis to the Brotherhood's commendable capability to overthrow Nasser. Thus, both the Soviets and the Israelis had come out in favor of the Brotherhood, a situation brought about by what is known as the "praise of the enemy" technique—used in Oriental countries much in the way conservative candidates in the United States and Great Britain arrange to have themselves heckled by the most unappetizing-looking people they can gather.

The roundup of the Brotherhood took place late in 1957, but it was accompanied by vigorous propaganda on the theme, "We *need* a good Moslem organization, and an international one; what a shame that the Moslem Brotherhood isn't it." Emphasis on the evidence produced against the Brotherhood was not so much for the purpose of proving that it was against the State as to show that its members were enemies of their own religion, *perverters* of their own religion. At the same time, apparently sincere efforts were made to establish a *good* Moslem organization, although by this time Nasser's heart wasn't in it; he had seen that any serious Islamic union would soon begin to look like the old caliphate and become resistant to political control; that it would awaken and give voice to antimodernist forces; that it would accentuate differences, rather than mitigate the differences, between the various Moslem sects and their offshoots—Sunnis, Shiites, Druses, Assassins, Yazidis; that it would breed leaders who would become as irritatingly pious as those of the Brotherhood. Just the same, Anwar Sadat and Hassan Touhami talked him into giving them free rein to form an Islamic Congress and make of it whatever they could.

The Islamic Congress was founded in 1954 with Anwar Sadat as its head, Hassan Touhami becoming his deputy a year or so later. It sent Koranic literature to Africa, and it held conferences on such subjects as Islamic law, Islamic art and Islamic archeology. Religious attachés were sent to various Egyptian missions abroad and assigned the task of watching for opportunities to use common religious interests to achieve at least tactical "union" against one or another of the Great Powers on some specific issue. The

American Government at first gave limited encouragement to the program, on the theory that the Egyptians could help persuade some of the countries of Africa (northern Nigeria, for example) that progress wasn't inconsistent with the teachings of Islam. The encouragement was discontinued in the early 1960s when it became apparent that the religious attachés were less concerned with progress than with developing ties that would be helpful in "the struggle against our common enemy, imperialism."

The next "circle" to concern Nasser, in order of ascending importance, was Africa—or rather, Afro-Asia; as events worked out, the "colored nations of the world" were showing awareness of his movement on a much broader geographical scale than he had imagined possible. His defiance of the Western world, "the colored man standing up to the white man," was being applauded in editorials and cartoons from Senegal to North Korea. Obviously, he could not aspire to the formation of a great Afro-Asian empire (or perhaps it was not so obvious—many Western commentators seemed to believe that he hoped for just that); he could, however, make himself such a figure in the eyes of the non-Western world that he could bring about "union" conditions on many specific issues and, on an *ad hoc* basis, team up with this or that African or Asian country to achieve some tactical advantage in the Game of Nations. The latter would help the former: the more he got in the newspapers in association with the Congolese, the Guineans, and others, the more he would be taken seriously as a figure of possibly genuine influence and as a "factor to be contended with" on a wide international scale.

In February 1955 he met Nehru and ten days later Tito, disliking the former and liking the latter. Nehru preached to him, while Tito talked to him as a younger equal, but they both made it clear that they took him seriously. To start with, *they* took the initiative in arranging the meetings and called on him on his home ground, Cairo. In the second place, they both appealed to him to take certain initiatives in the upcoming Afro-Asian conference in Bandung, Indonesia, that could be effective only when coming from a leader of recognized stature. Thanks to these two, he had a feeling of being in the Big League long before he reached Bandung.

Prior to Nasser's departure for Bandung, his American friends were delighted. They too were encouraging him to believe that here was a chance to get himself into the Big League: specialists from Washington came out to write State Department–style "position papers" and had them translated into Arabic by Ali Sabri, minister without portfolio at the Presidency, in the hope that he would borrow some of the ideas. Members of Nasser's entourage were briefed on what to expect from Chou En-lai and the Communists, and a mass of information was passed on to Nasser on the current state of Indonesian politics, a subject that was of great concern to the United States Government and of at least surface concern to Nasser, since Sukarno was sure to be one of his rivals at the conference. Since the specialists who came out from Washington reported, in the Embassy, only to Ambassador Byroade, the results of Ali Sabri's translations of their material added to our enthusiasm. Written on Presidency stationery, with no indication that they were simply translations of American papers, they appeared to represent positions that Nasser actually intended to take. Peter Chase, the Embassy's political officer, when presenting Byroade with his English translations of the papers, commented that the views expressed in them were the most intelligent he had seen expressed by any government in the Middle East and that the United States Government might have, in Nasser, a formidable asset for influencing the nations of Africa and Asia to be truly neutral rather than "neutral on the side of the Communists," as "positive neutrality" had begun to seem.

By this time, however, the Soviets had come around to

favoring Nasser's increasing influence in Africa and Asia. From their anti-Nasser attitude at the time of the Suez Base agreement, they had swung over to the belief that Nasser could be a major asset in the war against "Western imperialism," which, in place of "bourgeois nationalists" in Afro-Asian countries, had become the main enemy. Thus, the prospect of Nasser's playing a leading role at Bandung was even more welcome to the Soviets than it was to the Americans. And Nasser, at Bandung, did not disappoint them. While he later convinced Western governments that he had succeeded in diluting the "anti-imperialist" line of the conference, and had brought it around to comparatively moderate anti-Westernism, the results were nevertheless welcomed by the Soviets.

Thus Nasser had managed to please both sides, but there was a difference: the Soviets were unrestrained in their praise of Nasser's behavior, while our side had reservations. Nasser had indeed shown up as an impressive figure. Beside such midgets as Sukarno and Nkrumah, Nasser loomed as a statesman on a par with Nehru and Chou En-lai. These two, of course, deferred to him at every turn: at one point, Chou En-lai was so insistent that they have at least one meal together that he arranged a midnight dinner at which they both appeared after attending other functions. Nasser, without being particularly susceptible to flattery, could see that he had arrived. At the first opportunity after Bandung the Soviets let him know that they too thought he had arrived. We, however, didn't.

By a medley of mishaps, our lack of enthusiasm was brought home to Nasser in the most irritating way possible. To start with, Ambassador Byroade failed to place himself at the foot of the ramp when Nasser, aglow with his new prestige, descended from the presidential plane upon returning to Cairo. And when Nasser arrived home after a ride through cheering crowds, the first report to reach him claimed that not only had Byroade stayed away, he had advised all other Western Ambassadors to snub the triumphal entry. The truth is that Byroade called the British Ambassador to inquire about the proper protocol, and the British Ambassador had advised him, in effect, to let the Afro-Asian Embassies have their day. Subsequently various Western Ambassadors called Byroade to ask, "Are you going?" and he replied that he thought Nasser's arrival should be strictly an Afro-Asian show and that he thought Nasser would appreciate it if "we white folks sat this one out." His intentions were good, but the security-service telephone tappers' summary of them, losing their friendly tone in translation, gave the impression that Byroade talked as though he were a member of the Ku Klux Klan. A separate report informed Nasser that members of the American Embassy were referring to the Bandung conference as "the Darktown Strutters' Ball." Nasser's reaction is easy to imagine.

Following his Bandung success. Nasser systematically set about cultivating African leaders and developing the machinery to make the most of his new prestige. As he did so, many of our diplomats greatly misunderstood his goals and rejoiced at his failure to achieve goals he had never possessed—in particular, for his failure to bring about African unity and for failing to have Egypt accepted as an African state. But, as with his other two "circles," he sought only to bring about a degree of general coordination in policies, *vis-à-vis* the Great Powers, in support of his positive neutrality and to spot tactical allies with whom to join from time to time in order to get himself courted by one or another of the Great Powers on some specific issue. It was all worth the trouble so long as he was able occasionally to speak for Nkrumah of Ghana, Touré of Guinea and Keita of Mali in international councils. (Incidentally, the first two of these admitted to me personally that they often saw fit to have Nasser speak up in their behalf when it would have been awkward for them to speak up for themselves. They gained the "third-party advantage," a standard Game of Nations gambit, while Nasser got the advantage of showing himself to the Great Powers as a man of wide Afro-Asian influence.)

Nasser's administrative machinery for developing his "second-circle" capability was similar to that which he had created to gain influence in the world of Islam—except that he took seriously the development of a capability in Africa and Asia but had lost any serious interest in making much of a "first-circle" capability. A unit of the General Intelligence Agency was given the task of spotting likely areas on which to concentrate. The Foreign Office was required to set up a special office to devise policies with that peculiar kind of flexibility which is required in dealing with nations south of the Sahara. A small unit was established at the Presidency itself to coordinate policy and actions in Africa, and this unit was eventually given precedence over the other two units and status comparable to a ministry. With all this organizational emphasis, it is understandable that the zeal of Nasser's experts on Africa got out of hand and that projects got launched which indicated unrealistic ambitions.

The fact is that Nasser's ambitions in Africa and Asia were modest. Cario became a haven for anyone from Africa who was in trouble with a colonial government. Radio Cairo became one of the most persistent supporters of independence movements throughout Africa. Nasser's championing of the Mau Mau in Kenya infuriated the British, but the policy, in the eyes of much of the world, was justified when Jomo Kenyatta emerged from prison to become Kenya's first independent Prime Minister. All these activities might prompt an uninformed observer to infer inordinate ambitions, especially since they occurred at the same time as the series of whirlwind visits Nasser was making to Brioni, Monrovia, Tunis, Accra, Addis Ababa, Casablanca, and Belgrade, to dramatize Egypt's common cause with other nations in similar situations. The fact is, however, that the splash made by such activities in the world press, with the consequent attention of the Great Powers, was out of all proportion to their small cost. And they enabled Nasser to gain numerous tactical advantages, while appearing to fail in reaching his (erroneously) supposed major objectives. To give specific examples, Nasser failed to turn the African countries against Israel (not a serious objective), but he did succeed in gaining widespread Afro-Asian support for resolutions, in the United Nations and elsewhere, condemning colonialism and imperialism, while supporting self-determination and an increased role in the world for Afro-Asian states and, as the result, in causing the British, French and Americans to adopt policies more favorable to Egypt in attempts to buy him off.

Nasser's best chance of building an effective union lay in his Arab circle; and this was a circle that *had* to be successfully unionized. Also, here was a part of the game that was genuinely zero-sum from the point of view of *both* sides. And there is probably less understanding about the terms of the conflict than there is about any other conflict of major concern in the world today.

Here again, it is Nasser's objectives that are misunderstood. As I have said, Nasser is not an Arab; he didn't, until recently, know very much about Arabs; he has no particular affection for Arabs as such; he has no ambition to saddle himself with the headaches of "ruling the Arab world." "Arab nationalism" is an extremely important force in Nasser's scheme of things, but its importance is as a myth, not as a reality.

Consider the following:

Language: Among the various answers to the question "What is an Arab?" perhaps the most common is "Anybody who speaks Arabic as his native tongue." The fact is, however, that Arabs have a common language only in the way in which Medieval Europe had Latin as a common language. Classical Arabic, the *written* Arabic which is understood by the literate minority from Morocco to Iraq, bears the same relation to the various dialects of spoken Arabic that Latin had to Medieval Italian, Portuguese, Spanish and Rumanian. A taxi driver from Baghdad cannot carry on an intelligible conversation with a taxi driver from, say, Tunis—or even Cairo. If an educated Baghdadi can converse with an educated Tunisian, it is only because they know enough of each other's dialect, plus classical Arabic, to make sense of one another.

Culture: A broadened definition of "Arab" might include some reference to a common culture. There are, of course, similarities in the cultures of the various Arab countries which result from the prevalent religion, Islam, but these similarities are shared with the millions of Moslems living outside the Arab world. There are also superficial similarities in preferences for music, restaurant foods (not home-cooked foods), and various "pop" pursuits. These arise, however, from the influence of the Egyptian cinema and the enterprise of Lebanese restaurateurs spread all over the Middle East and Africa. Except for these similarities, there is as much difference between the cultures of Iraqi villagers, Bedouin tribesmen, Lebanese townspeople, Egyptian *fellahin* and all the other categories of Arabs as between the various societies of the Far East—more, probably. Moreover, there is tremendous mutual hostility between the various societies which makes cultural fusion virtually impossible. The Druses, the Alawites, the Metawalis, the Kurds, the Assyrians, the various Christian sects, the Jews, the Armenians, the Shi'as, the various cultural divisions of the Sunnis—these groups tend to despise one another and to defend their local customs of dress, marriage, family relations, and so on with a fierceness that stands up to everything except Egyptian films and Um Kalthoum (the Egyptian folk singer).

Race: One has only to look at a very black Sudanese standing beside a very light Lebanese, a swarthy-looking Iraqi, a "true Arab" Saudi tribesman, and a Greek-looking Syrian to see that the idea of an "Arab race" is as spurious as is the idea of a "Jewish race." The majority of the inhabitants of the Arabian Peninsula are racially Arab, but the Egyptians, the "leaders of the Arab world," have virtually *no* Arab blood in them, nor do the Sudanese, the Lebanese, and the "Arabs" of North Africa. Turks, Kurds and Circassians have provided the dominant ingredients for the Syrian mixture—as for the Iraqi mixture, with a little Indian added. Anyhow, the idea of *racial* Arabs is abhorrent to Nasser, so this is one facet of Arabism that need not concern us.

Political aspirations: "Whenever any of us is doing something constructive," said a famous "Arab" friend of mine, "like building a bridge, or mending a shoe, or baking bread, or filling a tooth, he is at that moment a Syrian or an Egyptian or a Lebanese engineer, cobbler, baker or dentist. When he is doing something *destructive* he is an Arab." In the pursuit of his normal, everyday economic interests he is moved by *wataniya*—patriotism, loyalty to his particular state; when he complains about Israel or "imperialism," or when he joins a mob burning down a foreign embassy, he is moved by *qawmia arabiya,* the "consciousness of being an Arab." American diplomats newly assigned to an Arab country are particularly confused by this. Everywhere he hears talk of "Arab aspirations" and references to "Arab unity" and "our Arab brothers," yet nowhere does he see any genuine enthusiasm for an Arab customs union, an Arab common market, or a unified Arab state or even a federation of states.

Then, as we said in an earlier chapter, Nasser's understanding of the Arab world was very limited when he tackled this particular circle. But for his purposes this was unimportant. He merely wanted to persuade leaders of the various Arab countries that they would get a better deal from the Great Powers if they could coordinate their foreign policies and not make individual agreements with any of the Great Powers in a way that would weaken the common front. In addition, he wanted to strengthen the Arab myth to such an extent that any leader breaking the common front would appear to be a dangerous heretic. It should be easy enough for anyone to understand how Nasser can be uncompromisingly determined to accomplish these two objectives without having a profound understanding of the various Arab countries or any particular sympathy for them. He adopted the objectives for the benefit of Egypt. Any benefit to the other countries would be, so far as he was concerned, strictly incidental.

When I arrived in Egypt in July 1953, I did not come across one of Nasser's associates—and I met most of them— who had any interest in Egypt's potential as a leader of an Arab union or of any other kind of union. Nasser himself was intrigued at my knowledge of other Arab countries, particularly Syria. In fact, I think that my store of anecdotes about Syrian coups and coup attempts was what made me *persona grata* in Nasser's household. For example, Nasser was greatly amused at my account of how Husni Za'im had failed in his first coup attempt (one that he had tried on his own, before the one reported on pages 50–54). Za'im attempted to enlist the assistance of Ahmed Sherabati, the Defense Minister, and Fawzi Qawuqji, leader of the "Free Palestine Warriors"; after secretly meeting late one night to plot the coup, each of the three, including Za'im himself, went straight to President Quwwatli to inform on the other two. This and other stories indicating Syrian untrustworthiness caused Nasser to chuckle appreciatively, but he always

showed signs of bewilderment. He was even more be-
wildered at the way our Government seemed to be interested in bringing about some kind of Arab economic union,
apropos of which he told an American management consultant: "We Egyptians think more or less alike and we can
throw ourselves together behind the same cause, but we
resist efforts to make us work with outsiders in any orderly
way. We might get other Arab countries to agree with us
on common objectives, but for us to work together in reaching those objectives would be nearly impossible." The coup
had been strictly Egyptian, and none of its leaders, least of
all Nasser, thought of it as anything else.

By the end of that year, however, the idea of a union—
some kind of union—to gain more leverage with the Major
Powers was coming to the fore. Perhaps Nasser had had it in
his mind all along, I do not know, but in December of 1953
he called home his leading Ambassadors, sat them down
with the Revolutionary Command Council, and told them to
hammer out a foreign policy that would be divided into two
parts: a policy toward those countries which were in the
same circumstances and which shared the same objectives,
and a policy toward those countries which would be common "targets" of these countries—the United States, Great
Britain, France, the Soviet Union, Japan, and the countries
of Western Europe. Toward the former, the emphasis would
be on gaining cooperation; toward the latter there would be
conflict—although, it was hoped, not unfriendly conflict.

It was at these meetings, which continued into January,
that the policy of an "Arab bloc" was first discussed—*but*
for the purpose of "protecting the interests of Islamic, Asi-
atic and African peoples." Nasser's attitude on the subject is
revealed by his reply to someone at one of the meetings who
asked, "Why not a North African union—Egypt, Libya,
Algeria, Tunis, and Morocco?" Nasser replied that if it was
mere geography which concerned him, the *maghreb* might
be of interest, "but what new strength would we gain from

it? The eastern Arabs have oil, transportation routes, and a Palestine problem"—all concerns of both the Western powers and the Soviets.

Patrick Seale regards July 23, 1954, as the day when Nasser *officially* designated Egypt as "Arab," and I am inclined to agree. On this date, the second anniversary of the coup, Nasser announced (in his anniversary speech):

> Compatriots, Egypt has started a new era of relations with the Arabs—an era based on true and frank fraternity, facing up to and thinking out problems and endeavoring to solve them. The aim of the Revolutionary Government is for the Arabs to become one nation with all its sons collaborating for the common welfare. . . . The revolution also believes that the weight of the defense of the Arab states falls first and foremost on the Arabs and that they are worthy of undertaking it.

This was one week after Nasser, through General Naguib, received assurances from President Eisenhower that an Anglo-Egyptian agreement on the Suez Base would open the way for large-scale American financial aid, together with off-the-record assurances by members of the American Embassy that the amount of such aid would be affected by the extent to which Nasser managed to "become a moderating influence" in Arab affairs. Nasser told me at about this time that "before you become a moderating influence you've got to become an influence," but, without knowing what we meant by "moderating," he saw no problem.

Specifically, the Arab countries over which Nasser sought influence were: Iraq, Saudi Arabia, Syria, Lebanon, Jordan, Kuwait, and Libya—whose leaders were, respectively, Nuri Said, King Saud, Adib Shishakli, Kamil Chamaoun, King Hussein, Salim Sabah (known simply as "the Ruler"), and King Idris al Senussi. Of these, only one, by the wildest stretch of the imagination, was at all likely to show enthusiasm for the idea of letting Nasser make foreign policy for all the Arabs. But Nasser believed he had some good arguments—after all, he was saying "*Whatever* it is we all individually want from the Great Powers, we have more chance of getting what we want if we face up to them together," and he was talking principle, not specific issues. Besides, the only specific issues that could conceivably come up would not, Nasser believed, be ones on which disagreement was likely. He certainly had no plans for making himself *personally* the leader of any Arab-union movement—not, anyhow, plans that would be apparent to the other leaders, because, after all, Naguib was still ostensibly chief of state in Egypt. And Naguib, Nasser believed, could become sort of a "chairman" of the movement—appropriate enough, because whatever feelings the other chiefs of state might have about active Egyptian political leadership, they must certainly accept Cairo, the cultural center of Arabism, as the logical headquarters.

When he began to feel out the various Arab leaders, however, he found that the problem wasn't all that simple. For example, the team he sent to Baghdad (in August 1954) to talk to the King, the Regent and Nuri found that the Iraqi leaders were in no mood to be neutral because they were actively afraid of the Soviets and the Communists and had much to gain, with nothing to pay, from close association with Britain and the United States. Nuri did, however, agree to continue discussions on the subject, and one month later he came to Cairo for the purpose. Here it became apparent to Nasser that the Egyptians who had gone to Iraq had done a poor job of representing Nasser's arguments and that, besides, Nuri had conducted the Baghdad discussions with full knowledge of the foibles of the principal Egyptian negotiator, Salah Salem—knowledge which, Nasser firmly believed, could only have come from the CIA. Having concluded that the CIA was responsible for Nuri's gaining an advantage over Salem, Nasser then found it easy to believe that the CIA had framed Salem by arranging a loaded press conference, where skilled questioners had tricked Salem into a public statement that infuriated Arab leaders everywhere, especially in Syria and Saudi Arabia.

The statement was in answer to a question about Egypt's attitude toward bipartite unions between Arab states—a clear reference to the possibility of a Syro-Iraqi union which Egypt had long opposed. Salem's answer, as anyone knowing Salem could have predicted was, "If two or more Arab peoples wish to unite in some form, Egypt does not object." The Syrians knew that Nuri would not have discussed such a union with the Egyptians, but they could easily imagine the upstart Egyptian revolutionaries taking it upon themselves to offer Nuri their backing should he decide to annex Syria. The Saudis assumed that the Syrians knew about the talks and that it was they who had been left out. Even the Lebanese showed some concern, since Salem's statement caused them to suspect that the new Egyptian Government was setting out to reorganize the Arab world, the talk of "united front" being only a cover. Important lesson: in the Arab world, even the most innocent, high-sounding statement (and Salem's statement was just that) is examined microscopically for hidden meanings and can be given the most sinister implications by a clever opponent bent on doing so. Nasser learned the lesson well, and since then he is never deliberately ambiguous unless he has control over the way in which the ambiguities will be interpreted.

Contacts with other Arab leaders—through their ambassadors in Cairo, through Egyptian ambassadors in the respective capitals, and through visits back and forth by teams of various composition—were similarly unsuccessful. In December, Nasser invited foreign ministers to Cairo to attend a meeting at which he hoped to make clear his ideas on a united "positive-neutrality" front, but the meeting became bogged down on specific issues and nothing was accomplished—although Nasser did make some gains for his cause simply by staying out of the discussions of particular issues and arguing instead, "Whatever the issues, let's make up our minds that they *must* be resolved" and by showing that Egypt considered no single issue important enough to jeopardize overall unity.

By the end of the year, Nasser had given up his attempt to re-educate the Arab leaders—at least, the ones then in power. Already, he had instituted a propaganda program directed to the Arab world; he now issued orders that gave Radio Cairo's "Voice of the Arabs" sufficient kilowattage to reach Arabs everywhere, with more clarity than the Voice of America, the BBC, or any of the stations of the various Arab countries, and loaded it with a content to attract and hold the listeners—news broadcasts and propaganda dramas, many of which were in local dialects, being so interspersed with music and light entertainment that even listeners in the middle of the Arabian desert would find it convenient to tune their stations to Radio Cairo and leave them there.

The themes were as follows:

We Arabs must unite to protect ourselves from imperialist exploitation: The principal "imperialist" villains were the British, but the Americans and the Russians were also included. Stories were presented of the British—or the Americans, or the Soviets—coming to an Arab country with tempting offers of help, then exploiting the country and making it dependent on that help. There were no attacks on individual leaders, but those leaders who had openly advocated or condoned relationships with the Great Powers suddenly found that they were on the defensive, explaining their reasons.

We are an Arab people: The myth, in other words. There was no advocacy of Arab political union, or of cooperation at the administrative level—no talk of customs unions, eliminating the requirement for visas for Arabs traveling to other Arab states or even settling the various disputes that plagued the Arab world. Under this heading, the material was largely cultural—historical plays, philosophical talks, and all kinds of more down-to-earth ways of encouraging listeners to start thinking in terms of an Arab identity.

Nasser standing up to the Great Powers: After the removal of Naguib, and after an example or two of Nasser's appearing as the first Egyptian leader in hundreds of years to drop his subservience to the Europeans and get away with it, programs began to appear that played up this facet of his "image." Radio plays had Nasser maintaining icy calm before desk-pounding British colonels, then ending the exchange with some devastating punch line delivered in a firm, unemotional voice; there were readings by actors of poeticized excerpts of Nasser's speeches; there were news stories of poor Africans, Asians and Arabs enduring various kinds of humiliation at the hands of Europeans, then intoning "but Nasser will save us"—all pretty corny, but effective with unsophisticated audiences. Every possible means of building Nasser's personal image was used—including such wide distribution of his photograph that even in Kuwait, by no means a Nasserist stronghold, hardly a shop in town was without a photograph prominently displayed.

Nasser in the Big League: When Nasser brought his leadership into the open, following the removal of Naguib, leaders of other Arab countries considered him a *parvenu* not to be taken seriously by experienced old-time politicians. But when they began to see frequent newsreels showing Nasser hobnobbing with the great figures of the world and holding his own with them, they began to think of him with respect. In one month alone (February 1955) Nasser received in Cairo Tito, Nehru, Anthony Eden, and King Hussein—these in addition to a flow of Congressmen, MPs, and internationally famous correspondents who from this month onward poured in in droves. The reaction of the Arab people can be compared to that of the inhabitants of a country town when they see one of its sons consorting with important people on some TV show. They shared his triumphs. He was theirs. He was theirs *as an Arab.* "Since Nasser," an Iraqi editor wrote—and he was speaking for

people of all levels of education throughout the Arab world—
"I feel as an Arab, no longer as an Iraqi."

Thus, Nasser created his myth: Arab nationalism led by *a*
Nasser, a hero figure, not necessarily *the* Nasser. The *reality*
of Arab nationalism remained nonexistent: it still took two
hours to cross the border between Lebanon and Syria, and
about as long to cross the Syria-Jordan border (the latter
crossing involving a physical search and other indignities);
Arab governments were still on bad terms with each other,
and cultural hostilities between Syrians, Lebanese, Iraqis,
Egyptians and the others remained the same; Palestinian
refugees, while "our Arab brothers" according to the myth,
were treated as foreigners by all the Arab countries. But the
myth grew into what informed observers could call "the
dominant force in Arab world politics today." It is as real to
Arab leaders as is Santa Claus to Macy's.

But not dominant enough. Nasser had succeeded in putting before the leaders of the Arab countries the line of least
resistance, the line of Arab nationalism as defined in Cairo,
but there were still those leaders who were strong enough—
or resentful enough of Cairo—to go it alone, and to "scab"
on Nasser's union. Thus, Nasser had to move on to the "negative" phase of his unionizing.

9

Nasserism and Terrorism

*If you're going to have a union, you've got
to make life intolerable for the scabs . . .*

I spent a good part of late 1956 and early 1957 giving talks
to groups of American Government officials in which I
would take the part of Nasser, seeing his problems as he saw
them and explaining the actions he took to solve the problems. I was also often called to Secretary Dulles' or Undersecretary Herbert Hoover, Jr.'s office to help predict Nasser's
reaction to some action our Government was contemplating.
Making Nasser's behavior understandable, and even deserving of our sympathy, was normally not difficult. But
there was one aspect of it which I found difficult to put
across and which only ruffled my colleagues and superiors
whenever I tried. I have been told that shortly after I left
one of the more important conferences where I had to "do
the Nasser act," as Foster Dulles used to say, a senior State
Department official turned to his neighbor and said, "I don't
trust that guy; he talks more like Nasser than Nasser himself." On another occasion, kindly Allen Dulles turned to me
with real anger and said, "If that colonel of yours pushes us
too far we will break him in half!" If anybody in the world
understands—and habitually uses—the put-yourself-in-the-
other-fellow's-place approach to political analysis, it is Allen

Dulles. The fact that even he could work himself into a rage over Nasser's behavior illustrates what a sore subject it was.

The aspect of "Nasserism" that was (and is) beyond our understanding was its synonymity with terrorism. The Americans don't like terrorism. Although it sometimes plays an essential part in the West's own operations against recalcitrant Afro-Asian leaders, we conceal this fact. Nasser, on the other hand, publicly endorses terrorist actions. While his own country is a model of law and order, his Radio Cairo has loudly called for civil disorders in those countries whose leaders oppose him—or even, in some cases, for assassination of the leaders. American politicians have been horrified at these incitements, and diplomats and intelligence operators disturbed by the indiscretions.

It happens that there is some intelligent reasoning behind Nasser's use of terrorism. In a general way, as a "union" leader he has no choice but to combat "scabs"—and, like leaders of labor unions or other kindred unions, to go to any extreme in doing so. Unions are effective only when there is unanimity of action; scabs puncture this effectiveness to an extent out of all proportion to their strength or number. If, in dealing with his own scabs, Nasser uses methods more violent than, say, those of our labor-union leaders in the United States (and there are some grounds for questioning this), the difference can be explained by the difference between our societies.

It is perhaps harder for us to accept a related point: that violence is best conducted by terrorists, rather than by ordinary people turned violent by circumstances. The participants of even our worst riots could hardly be called terrorists; Nasser-inspired riots in scab countries, however, get most of their force from terrorists—or, as they are called by Nasser's political activists, "fanatics."

A "fanatic," in Nasserist political jargon, is anyone who abnegates self and who will go to any lengths, regardless of harm to self, in the interests of a cause. He is a loser by definition, but he is an important weapon in the hands of the determined nonfanatic—one who intends to *live* for the cause, in other words. Nasser can count on him to go on losing and losing so long as he prevents the enemy—the scab—from achieving his purposes. The fanatic's game, in others words, is similar to the game of "Chicken"; it is as though he were saying to himself, "I know *I'm* not going to win; I'm probably going to die, but I'll bring you down with me."

A player of limited popular resources such as Nasser is understandably tempted to use fanatics, whereby, as has been proved time and again in history, small minorities can cause majorities to make concessions to them out of all proportion to their numbers or the strength of their arguments —if, indeed, they have any clear arguments at all. When entirely on their own (and this is rare), fanatics sooner or later make such nuisances of themselves that the majority clamps down on them, paying whatever price it takes. In the hands of nonfanatical leadership, however, they can become a weapon of flexibility and finesse. They can be brought to a halt just short of suicide, while their willingness to go to suicidal lengths is so manifestly genuine that the opponent cannot know *where* they will halt—or even be sure that they *will* halt. The nonsense they talk can be polished up so that it not only makes a modicum of sense, but seems to be on a high moral plane. So long as the more vocal members keep their mouths shut (or can be kept away from direct contact with journalists), a fanatical movement can be excellent public relations material. They are "a valiant body of men fighting for their beliefs against overwhelming odds." They are sometimes as valuable dead as they are alive. They are beautifully expendable.

There is also the advantage of easy availability. In any country where frustration is general there are bound to be fanatics, or latent fanatics, just waiting to be awakened by the right Messiah. Young men are educated to use their brains (and to abhor physical work), and are made aware of the comforts the twentieth century has to offer—an awareness that is heightened by Western films and television; but they soon learn that there is no need for their brains—or that even if they find employment in some intellectual pursuit, their pay will be no more than a fraction of what it would take to live the way films and television have taught them that Westerners live. In our own culture, we are brought up to believe that anyone, even somebody possessing only mediocre intelligence, can rise from a sharecropper's cabin to the presidency of General Motors, provided he has the ability to work out a sensible career for himself and the determination to stick to it. After arguing this belief with dozens of young Middle Easterners, however, I am convinced that except for a lucky few the majority are doomed to lifetimes of being without what they are taught to want. The *only* way open to most of them is to sacrifice their own interests and attach themselves to a holy cause—particularly one that is *against* something and so best gives vent to feelings of frustration, which are by nature negative feelings.

The fact that fanatical movements are usually *against* something makes them undesirable in one's own country— except, as was the case during the early days of Nasser's rule, when they can usefully be set against some force other than the Government itself—but it makes them extremely useful when the purpose is to bring pressure on the leader of some other country. It takes very little ingenuity to convince fanatics of *any* country of the wickedness of their government, whatever its complexion. To frustrated people, things are not as they should be; the government is the most convenient target. In this case Nasser found it easy to point out flaws in the Governments of the scab leaders whom he hoped to bring around; it was not even necessary to suggest specific remedies, only general ones ("get rid of imperialism," for example) which not only have the greatest appeal to fanatics, but are the least vulnerable to intelligent criticism.

But finally—and here we come to the essence of Nasserist scab-fighting technique—fanatics need no specific direction, only a general "go" sign. The Americans and the British—and, to some extent, the Russians—normally go into elaborate detail when they plan the overthrow of some government, and their coup d'etat operations (or most of them) are organized as carefully as straight military operations. (The operation against Mossadegh, for example, required two to three hours of classroom explanation—complete with maps, details of power stations, disposition of forces, etc.) In using fanatical movements in the way Nasser does, however, all one has to do is set the stage internationally, attack the target leader by Radio Cairo, single out the fanatical movements that seem most incited by the attack, furnish them with arms and whatever else they need, and leave them to it. If one takes any interest in their plans at all, it is only because one wants to know their chances of success and a basis on which to make follow-up plans—without which the local fanatical group wouldn't be able to consolidate its initial victory.

To summarize the Standard Operating Procedure in bringing about the overthrow of a scab government: first, attack the government on Radio Cairo, making accusations against it that are most likely to incite fanatical groups while refraining from specific accusations which might be embarrassing to Nasser should the coup succeed; second, study the reactions to the propaganda so as to identify fanatics and fanatical groups that may be counted on for action; third, approach the fanatics (sometimes more than one group, even groups that are rivals to one another), arm them, and learn what can be learned about *their* plans; fourth, identify suitable *non*fanatics who might take over the leadership at the right strategic moment (sometimes before the government is overthrown, sometimes after) and consolidate the gain, and make such agreements with them as will ensure that whatever objectives are accomplished the Egyptian "union" objective will be among them; guarantee recognition of the new government once the coup succeeds, plus continued support of Radio Cairo.

This approach has two important shortcomings: first, setting off such an operation is like starting a forest fire; it is easy to start but difficult to stop; second, the nonfanatics in the operation, who are likely to be as Machiavellian as Nasser, cannot be counted on to stick to their bargain. Nasser's recurrent feud with Jordan's King makes a good example to illustrate the first flaw: when Hussein had once told Nasser, in effect, "All right, I give up," Nasser had no way of unscrambling the eggs. The Iraqi coup of 1958 is an example illustrating the second: although its leaders would almost certainly not have launched their coup without Egyptian encouragement and assurances that after the coup they would receive "union" applause from all directions, they nevertheless turned out to have minds of their own and to show tendencies toward independent action which were as intolerable as those of their predecessors.

All the same, Nasser's war against the blacklegs *did* eventually make it virtually unthinkable for any Arab leader to make an agreement with a Major Power, Eastern or Western, without considering the "union," and even Nasser's personal wish. At least, this was for a while the case. If there has been an increasing number of breaks in the common front, it has not been because the strategy wasn't basically sound at the time it was conceived, but only because international circumstances have changed.

I have been very frank in pointing out to my Egyptian friends, and on occasion to Nasser himself, that Nasserism's known association with fanatics of neighboring countries brings such discredit on it in the eyes of the Western world that it offsets the advantages of the "union." They well appreciate this. But they argue that our "strike breaking" is supported by power and wealth which they could not hope to match; they must use what is available to them. Use of terrorism is consistent with the whole strategy by which a weaker nation, with virtually no power assets at all, holds its own in the Game of Nations against the major powers.

To follow this argument, we must have an understanding of the "strikebreaking" strategy that Nasserist leaders see, or think they see, on our side. The strategy has been confusing to them because we seemed to employ it while simultaneously trying to *use* Nasser's "union," his area-wide influence, to advance one project or another of interest to us—as, for example, Eric Johnston's Jordan River scheme which, Johnston admitted, could be put across only as the result of such influence. Another example is our repeated attempts to get Nasser to take the leadership in "reducing the tensions between the Arabs and Israel"; our Government has launched at least one operation that involved our supporting Nasser's "union" so that he would be able to bring about this result.

All very confusing. We have, on balance, worked harder at undermining Nasser's influence than we have at building it—and we have done so more openly.

First, there was the Baghdad Pact. Patrick Seale* says it "had a profound effect on every level of Arab politics"; P. J. Vatikiotis* says it was a "traumatic experience" for Syria. These are understatements. The Baghdad Pact so shook the Arab world that, for a while, it seemed beyond our competence, for all the economic aid at our disposal, to save any sort of position for the West in the Middle East. And virtually every British and American official *directly* concerned with the Arab world knew about it. But at the time I would have defied Seale or Vatikiotis or anybody else to march into one of these meetings in Secretary Dulles' office and announce this to be the case.

* See Suggested Reading List.

In April 1954, Turkey and Pakistan signed a "treaty of friendship and cooperation for security." It was not, strictly speaking, a military pact, and ostensibly it was instigated by the Turks and the Pakistanis themselves without any prodding from the United States or Britain. Nasser's security police at the airport, however, photocopied the pages of the passports of all significant Americans, British and others passing through emigration, and it was easy enough to establish that before the signing of the agreement at least three Americans who would logically be associated with it had passed through Cairo bearing canceled Turkish and Pakistani visas. That same month the United States formally agreed to give military assistance to Iraq, under circumstances that made Nasser strongly suspect, although Iraq had made no formal commitments such as Gerhardt and Eveland had asked him to make, that Nuri had made some kind of off-the-record concessions. Nine months later—in January 1955—Iraq and Turkey jointly announced that they were going to conclude a pact, which they did the following month—with Great Britain to sign three months later.

At the time, I was living in Cairo, but making frequent visits to Syria and to the United States, where I always found time to visit my former colleagues in Washington. Bill Eveland, during his visit to Cairo with Al Gerhardt, had told me in November 1954 of the probable chain of events, and he had hinted strongly to Nasser that Egypt might find itself left behind, but neither of us believed him—nor did Ambassador Caffery and Jim Eichelberger. On the day in January when the Turks and the Iraqis made their announcement, Eichelberger read about it on the Embassy news ticker, not a word about it having appeared in telegrams from the State Department. He suggested that the two of us proceed immediately to Nasser's house to tell him about it. We did. Nasser sat absolutely still for a moment; then in an ominously quiet voice he reminded us that whatever hints Eveland and Gerhardt might have dropped, all the

Americans in contact with him, including Ambassador Caffery himself, had led him to believe that we would give him time to build an Arab regional organization, not linked openly with the West but so constructed that it could quickly fall in line with Western plans should a common danger arise. Hassan Touhami, also present, started to lose his temper, but Nasser quieted him. The two of them sat silent as Eichelberger and I left.

A day or so later I went to Damascus, on an unrelated business matter, and my old friend Mejdeddin Jabri, then Minister of Public Works, took me to see the Foreign Minister, Feidi el-Atassi, who treated me to a lecture which was so full of childish suspicions and superstitions that it could not have been repeated in Washington without making him appear a lunatic (which he certainly was not) but which gave an eye-opening exposé of how our side looked to the Arabs: "Imperialism" . . . "trying to keep the Arabs weak" . . . "you aren't happy unless we are your slaves" . . . "you prefer us when we are backward and romantic" . . . "CIA" . . . "Fadhil Jamali an American agent" . . . "The Regent hopes to become King of Syria" and so on. The next day, I spent six hours fighting my way through the snows and custom officials of Mount Lebanon to get to Beirut and spent an evening with various pro-Nasser Lebanese who gave me much the same treatment. I got a very different kind of treatment from a lot of anti-Nasser Lebanese, but in terms which confirmed much of what the others had said. The same day, in the men's room at the American Embassy I ran into an acquaintance who was on a visit from Washington; he grabbed me by the arm and said, "I think we've finally got you Nasser lovers on the run."

By the time I got back to Cairo, preparations were under way for a meeting of Foreign Ministers of Arab states. My Egyptian friends concerned with the meeting would barely speak to me, except to pour forth abusive opinions about Secretary Dulles, and when the Foreign Ministers actually arrived (I knew about half of them, and managed at least short talks with most of these), they expressed a range of views which suggested that while they were far from agreement among themselves, their differences over the new "Baghdad-Cairo polarization" might escalate into a split which would suit the Soviets much better than the West.

Meanwhile, Byroade arrived to take up his post as Ambassador, and he, Nasser and I—along with Abdelhakim Amer and Hassan Touhami—had the dinner at my house already reported. Earlier, Eichelberger and I had briefed Byroade on our negative views of the Baghdad Pact, and Byroade, away from the atmosphere of Washington, more or less came round to our view, at least to the extent that at dinner he urged Nasser to reserve judgment and to consider the possibility that things might not be as bad as they looked, at least as far as American and British support to the Baghdad Pact was concerned.

In March, however, we learned that Britain was going to sign the treaty, and that pressures were on the United States to follow. By this time, Byroade had the "field perspective" as much as any of us, and he suggested that I concoct some business reason for going to the United States, and while there manage to drop in on friends in the State Department and the CIA to tell them orally what he and Eichelberger had been trying to convey in the very circumspect cables and memoranda they had been sending since Byroade's arrival—*necessarily* circumspect, I hasten to add, because for Byroade to have shown an abrupt change from the views he had held in Washington to the views he almost immediately gained on arrival in Cairo would have been not courageous, but foolish. In any bureaucracy, modification of a once strongly held position must be done smoothly, so as not to shake confidence.

When I arrived in Washington I visited Kermit Roosevelt at the CIA and gave him my views on the Baghdad Pact, which were roughly the same as those in the Seale and

Vatikiotis books. Although Kim did not entirely agree with me, there was enough "field perspective" mixed into his "Washington perspective" to make him appreciate what I was saying and to encourage me to be completely outspoken. With a telephone call or two, he arranged for me to drop in for a few minutes on a State-CIA meeting which was to take place that afternoon in Secretary Dulles' office. It is the atmosphere of that meeting which makes me confident that not one of the many writers who saw so clearly what was wrong with the Baghdad Pact would have been able to shake the views of Washington policy makers of that time, even if they had had the temerity to present their views with the same conviction evident in their written words.

Present at this particular meeting were the Secretary himself, Bill Rountree (who had just replaced Byroade as Assistant Secretary of State for NEA), Kermit Roosevelt of the CIA, and four or five of what Kim used to call "the Department's professional Bright Young Men," who had virtually memorized all the facts about the various countries of the Middle East, their natural resources, and all other strategic data. Possibly Bill Eveland was also present, I do not remember, but there was certainly a representative from the Pentagon. At any rate, they comprised most of the top planners of our Middle East strategy, and they had available to them all Washington's and London's information on Soviet strategy and military strength, the current state of nuclear armament, projections of petroleum production to the year 1970, the state of European industrial development, the various NATO issues, and so on. They were very polite and ready to give me their full attention. But somehow, in their presence, I could not bring myself to launch into a detailed explanation of the ins and outs of Ba'athist politics, Arab sensitivities to such questions as Nuri Sa'id's Fertile Crescent scheme, and local protocol taboos, our violation of which looked heavy-handed in the area itself, but which seemed too silly to make a fuss about when viewed from

Washington. Here were gentlemen who saw world affairs in the perspective of the atom bomb, the East-West cold war, NATO and the Warsaw Pact; their thinking about the Middle East was in terms of its economic problems and resources—apart from the question of Israel, that is, which, for reasons of domestic politics in the United States, demanded an awareness out of all proportion to its strategic importance.

To them, Syria was a country of less than six million people, about a quarter the size of Greater New York. I had once had the experience of having the consul of some such place as Ruanda Urundi explain to me how the Heebie Jeebies were at odds with the Mumbo Jumbos, and how "World War III is being brewed right here in Ruanda Urundi"; I knew how childish "localists" (General Bedell Smith's word) could sound.

Anyhow, I did not put on much of a performance. On the way out, Kim Roosevelt said he had enjoyed hearing me "roar like a kitten," and when I got back to Cairo both Byroade and Eichelberger felt that I had let them down. But then, that is the sort of thing that happens. There are indeed a "field perspective" and a "Washington perspective," and except for brief lightning flashes every now and then, the two remain utterly incommunicable.

But Washington *did* agree that our government should stay out of the Baghdad Pact, thereby ensuring that we got the worst of both worlds. The pact was all the weaker for our absence, while the signatory powers were annoyed with us for letting them down. At the same time, the Egyptians and everyone else knew very well that the pact was Secretary Dulles' brainchild, so we got the blame from that side as well. However, although Nasser could hardly thank us formally for taking such a position, any more than we could thank the Soviets for sending troops into Czechoslovakia in August 1968, he warmed to Byroade perceptibly.

The Baghdad Pact provided Nasser with an excellent

basis for attacks on the scabs, especially after one of its principal signatories (Britain) joined the Israelis and the French in the famous Suez assault in October 1956. It was, however, necessary for Nasser to make the attacks. However unpopular the Pact, however much a public relations liability to the Iraqi leaders who had signed it, it was nevertheless a means whereby one country which was essential to the union could act independently of it. The same might be said of the second major "strikebreaking" operation, the Eisenhower Doctrine.

The Eisenhower Doctrine (see pages 215–16) was an outcome of the Anglo-French-Israeli fiasco at Suez. The Game of Nations possibilities, and dangers, which this afforded Nasser were awesome. The most interesting possibility, of course, was that the Soviets and the Americans, with the British out of the picture, would embark on a campaign of competition for Egypt's favors. Nasser's Ambassador in Washington cabled that we recognized that a "vacuum" had been left by the British as a result of their Suez action, and that State Department planners were sitting up late trying to think of something. Nasser hates that word "vacuum," implying as it does that if one Great Power is essential to the scene, and if that one Great Power leaves, then of absolute necessity another Great Power must step in. But what bothered him more was that we dragged our feet in releasing Egyptian funds which we had frozen pending the outcome of negotiations over settlement of Suez Canal Company claims. When we gave only vague answers to his urgent request for wheat and pharmaceuticals, and the Soviets responded almost immediately to the same requests when made to them, Nasser concluded that our idea of "filling the vacuum" was going to be something other than a courtship of him and acquiescence to his union of positive neutralists.

He had every reason to be apprehensive. The scabs, with fingers crossed behind their backs, had jumped to his side at the time of Suez and made a great show of solidarity. But now the crisis was over. Nasser knew that they had been greatly shaken by the crisis and were most uneasy at the loss of influence of the British—and that consequently they must be hopeful of some kind of support from the United States. One of his senior officials told me at the time that the Egyptian Ambassadors in Beirut, Baghdad, Amman and Jidda either were getting cool treatment from the Foreign Offices of the respective countries, or were received with "such effusive and strained politeness that we know something is up." When the Egyptian Ambassador in Washington cabled on January 1, 1957, that he believed the United States Government was about to launch a program to bring Nasser down, Nasser could only hope that we would come up with something as embarrassing to the blacklegs as the Baghdad Pact had been.

We did. I was in Washington at the time, working on a committee that was supposed to be responsible for all the what-to-do-about-Nasser staff work, and I remember coming to the office early one morning in January to learn that a new "doctrine" had been concocted which was sure to pose highly embarrassing stand-up-and-be-counted problems to Nasser's enemies without giving them what they *really* needed to withstand the assault on them Nasser was sure to make. The general idea, which came to be known as the "Eisenhower Doctrine," was proposed to Congress by the President on January 5, 1957, and it became a reality in the form of a Joint Congressional Resolution in March of the same year. The resolution authorized President Eisenhower to commit American troops to the defense of any Middle Eastern government endangered by "overt armed aggression from any nation controlled by International Communism" and, in circumstances short of overt military danger, to give any economic and military aid that these governments might require to build up their own defenses. To this day, I do not know who originated the idea—perhaps it was Secretary Dulles, or it could have been Bill Rountree. All I remember, clearly, is that neither the "Middle East Policy Planning Committee" (State, Defense, and CIA) nor the regular staff of the Bureau of Near Eastern and African Affairs had anything to do with it. All of us were quite prepared to believe that the plan might have made sense in some subtle and delicate domestic political context beyond the ken of us "field" people, but in the light of extant intelligence on the Arab world it made no sense at all. As I remember, the Middle East hands were fairly unanimous about this. When the CIA representative on the MEPPC was asked, "Would you fellows like to send someone along on the mission that's going out to explain it to Arab chiefs of state?" he replied, "We can't afford to associate ourselves with every lunatic scheme that comes along."

Nasser wasn't exactly pleased at the news, even after a moment's reflection brought to him the realization that when President Eisenhower referred to "any nation controlled by International Communism" he probably had Egypt in mind. But he did have the satisfaction any player has when he sees his opponent make a wrong move. As he told me later, the only aspect of the Eisenhower Doctrine that gave him pause was the assignment of Congressman James P. Richards to take the happy news to President Chamaoun, King Hussein and the others. The choice of an emissary who could be presumed to have about as much comprehension of Arab affairs as Nasser had of pop art greatly puzzled Nasser, and made him suspect that the project had some Machiavellian twist that was going over his head. "The genius of you Americans," he once told me, "is that you never make clear-cut stupid moves, only *complicated* stupid moves which make us wonder at the possibility that there may be something to them we are missing." The Eisenhower Doctrine, which he assumed to be entirely Secretary Dulles' brainchild, was to his mind one of the shrewdest mistakes ever made by a Great Power diplomat.

A zero-sum game was on. Soviet propaganda suggested that the Americans had been a part of the British-French-Israeli plot, their role being that of the Good Policeman who comforts the prisoner after he has been given a good going over by the Bad Policeman. Radio Cairo propagandists added twists of their own and passed it on, together with "proof," which it claimed to have received from a variety of secret sources all over the Middle East, that the United States was launching a campaign to "split and enslave the Arabs" and that we were counting heavily on our "agents" in the various Arab governments to put the campaign over.

In the early days of Nasser's war on the scabs, his actions were directed not so much at individuals as at ideas: his objective was to create public attitudes—"emotional environments," as his propagandists called them—in which potential scabs would be frightened into acquiescence. The actions were not completely successful, but they went a long way toward success; at least, they taught the Arab peoples to recognize a scab when they saw one and to regard Nuri of Iraq, Chamaoun of Lebanon, and King Hussein of Jordan as scabs long before they actually rose (successfully in the first two cases) against them. Increasingly, however, Nasser felt it necessary to step up the level of activity and to direct them at specific targets.

Scab Number One on Nasser's list was, of course, Prime Minister Nuri Sa'id of Iraq. But bringing down Nuri would take time, and it would be a much easier job if he could be isolated. Thus, before the announcement of the Eisenhower Doctrine, priority had been given to King Hussein, Scab Number Two. Although less important than Nuri, Hussein was in many ways as much of a nuisance. When, in January 1956, the British Government sent Sir Gerald Templer to Amman to persuade King Hussein to join the Baghdad Pact, a simple call from Radio Cairo, backed by more direct encouragement delivered through Egypt's headquarters for subversive activities, brought about countrywide rioting and the fall of the cabinet. In the months that followed, Egyptian-trained Palestinian commandos stepped up their raids into Israel from Jordanian bases, thus bringing Israeli reprisals against Jordan which further embarrassed King Hussein. All this activity put Hussein in a much more co-operative frame of mind. He announced that he had no intention of joining the Baghdad Pact, and two months later he dismissed General John Bagot Glubb, the British commander-in-chief of the Jordanian army, to replace him with the pro-Nasser General Abu Nawar. In June, Parliament was dissolved, and in October there were elections which were a landslide victory for pro-Nasser candidates.

Egyptian officials insist to this day that they did not send a single one of their specialists at troublemaking to Jordan during this critical period; if this is true, as it probably is, Nasser's handling of this particular scab was first-class. His fanatics, of course, were the most irreconcilable elements among the Palestinian refugees; his nonfanatics were Jordanian Army officers and opportunist politicians. His means of reaching these were indirect: General Abu Nawar, ostensibly on his own initiative, came to Cairo to learn whether or not he could depend on Nasser's support on the international front once the coup he was plotting had succeeded —support that he hoped would be rather more effective than the NATO allies had given the Hungarian rebels whom they had encouraged to revolt in 1956. Abu Nawar was authorized to tell Suleiman Nabulsi, the pro-Nasser prime minister who had come into the Jordanian Government in June, that Radio Cairo would present him to the Arab world as a hero. In another move, which was completely consistent with the Nasser technique, Nasser so played on King Saud's age-old family rivalry with the Jordan royal family as to induce him to give financial support to anti-Hussein factions.

Thus, King Hussein bowed to the pressures—the Palestinian refugees, the Israelis, the Saudis, and Radio Cairo—

and left for Cairo to meet Nasser, King Saud, and the Syrian Prime Minister, Sabri Assali, to agree on joint defense arrangements, to make it possible for Jordan to forgo Anglo-American financial aid, and thereby to remain gracefully outside the Baghdad Pact. The King had joined the "union."

Meanwhile, the Syrian Government was presenting a new kind of blackleg problem: not making independent deals with western countries, but gaining a special position *vis-à-vis* the Soviets. Syria was co-operative enough in joining Nasser's common front in dealing with the West, but this was hardly enough. Nasser's "union" strategy required that the Arabs maintain a common front against both sides—the whole idea, after all, being to play one side off against the other.

In 1954 two Syrian political parties of compatibly vague ideologies had joined together to form what we know today as the "Ba'athist" ("resurrectionist," in English) Party. While certainly not Communist, nor ideologically much of anything, the party's prejudices made it a congenial framework for the development of Communism in Syria. When the Ba'athists came into prominence in the elections of 1954, the Communists gained a seat or two as well—including one for Khalid Bagdash, the Syrian communist leader since the mid-1940s who had been run out of the country by Husni Za'im. Khalid, an extremely likable and comparatively honest Syrian politician, owed much of his support to ordinary personal popularity which, at the time, was enhanced by the absence of any real differences with Syria's leading politicians of the day, Ba'athist and other. "We're all against the same things," he once told me: namely Zionism, imperialism, the Turks (who had been holding on to the Sanjak of Alexandretta), and the Hashemites (King Feisal of Iraq and King Hussein of Jordan). Their arguing about the nicer ideological distinctions, as one of our diplomats in Syria put it, "would make as much sense as a lot of whores arguing about virtue."

At any rate, at the time of the Eisenhower Doctrine announcement, Syrian policy was increasingly friendly toward, while increasingly independent of, Cairo. But since Nasser required adherence to the union rather than friendship, such an attitude was unacceptable. Thus, when, in mid-1955, Russia publicly guaranteed support for Syria against any aggression from the Baghdad Pact signatories, Nasser was beside himself. When, in March 1955, Foreign Minister Molotov said, "The U.S.S.R. supports Syria's attitude and is willing to extend to it aid in any form whatsoever," Cairo's newspapers and radio launched attacks on the Soviets which were as bitter as those against the members of the Baghdad Pact. The Game of Nations situation in the Middle East in 1955 was thus an odd mixture of triangles: the Egyptians trying to play off the Soviets and the Americans against one another; the Americans trying to play off Nasserist Arabs (the "Progressives") and the anti-Nasser Arabs (the "Reactionaries") against one another; the Soviets trying to play off the Syrians against the Egyptians, and the Syrians trying to play off the Egyptians against the Russians. Except for Egypt, the purposes of all of these were tactical, merely squeezing out an advantage here and there. Egypt's objective, however, was fundamental and strategic. It was a situation that Nasser had to go to any lengths to remedy.

Throughout 1956 the Syrians and the Soviets came closer and closer together, to such an extent that healing the breach in the united front *vis-à-vis* the Soviets was becoming as much a problem to Nasser as that posed by the pro-Western scabs, Nuri and Hussein—and *more* of a problem as Hussein moved increasingly into line. As is possible under the Nasser style of game play, Nasser consulted with American friends about cooperation in plugging the hole in his eastern front while consulting with the Soviets on the problem of plugging up his western front, which was becoming as leaky as a sieve. As is possible under *our* style of game play, we were able to exchange ideas with Nasser on the problem of Syria while continuing to weaken his union hold on the other Arab countries. Nasser, I must hasten to add, would not discuss with us the possibility of joint action against Syria, but he thought it important that we know the extent of the deterioration there, the extent to which the Soviets were exploiting it, and the absolute necessity, therefore, for us to refrain from launching a coup operation which, he believed, was sure to fail and sure to make the situation even worse. Nasser's American friends responded by assuring him that, given our experience at getting our fingers burned in Syria, we had no intention of meddling in the affairs of that country. We added, however, that we had information of an extremely reliable quality (as I recall, it came from a Russian defector) to the effect that the Soviets intended, first, to get a pro-Soviet government into power, then to provoke a situation that would cause this government to invite them in to restore and maintain order—an operation much like the one that the United States Government did, in fact, launch in Lebanon a few years later.

Nasser believed what we told him about the Soviets' intentions, but he didn't believe what we told him about our own intentions. There was a lot of coming and going to excite his suspicions: Loy Henderson, then Deputy Undersecretary of State and previously Ambassador to Iran at the time of "Ajax," ostentatiously visited Ankara for a Baghdad Pact meeting, then "secretly" visited Beirut to pay "purely personal visits, nothing official" to Syrian friends. Dulles made a public announcement expressing anxiety about Syria, and President Eisenhower warned that Syria, influenced by the Communists, might attack her neighbors—an assertion so absurd, in the light of the well-known Syrian military strength, that it could be interpreted only as mood music of a kind with which Nasser was eminently familiar. There were troop movements in Turkey, on the Syrian border, and the Iraqis and Jordanians, who had suddenly reverted to their earlier behavior, began making obvious military preparations. It was in such an atmosphere that the Roosevelt cousins, Kim and Archie, visited Beirut and held court for distinguished Syrian, Iraqi, Jordanian and Saudi visitors. Abdelhamid Ghaleb, Egyptian Ambassador in Beirut, cabled Cairo that "the Americans are plotting something" but that it was the most unsecret operation he had ever seen. When I met him by chance one day in the St. George Hotel lobby he asked puckishly, "When the day of your coup comes, are you going to sell tickets?"

Nasser's first reaction to all this was to do nothing, since it looked as though his kind of operation, the only kind he knew how to run, would only add to the confusion, make a bigger failure out of the supposed American operation than he already thought it would be, and in the end give the Soviets the final advantage. Nasser has that kind of mind, however, which is incapable of accepting appearances at their face value, and he was personally acquainted with enough American cryptodiplomats, including Kim and Archie Roosevelt, to be suspicious of surface indications that they were about to bumble into an unsecret secret operation. Ambassador Raymond Hare, who had replaced Byroade in Cairo, told Nasser that our Government was "much concerned" about Syria, but planned no subversive operations against it, and I later told him the same thing—at the request of the CIA chief of station in Beirut, who said it might uncomplicate things a little if I would take the opportunity, on my next visit to Cairo, to "tell Nasser that we aren't planning anything at all like what he suspects we are" and that he had better worry about Soviet subversive activity in Syria, not American. Nasser seemed to accept these assurances.

My impression at the time was that although we officially pined for a Syria that would be independent of Nasser's union, our anxieties about the Soviets would have enabled Nasser to drive a bargain with us: certainly, even with his union of positive neutralists, what he had to offer was preferable to the Arab world we saw shaping up. Nuri was in a highly exposed position; Hussein was at last playing along with Nasser, while continuing to suffer the insecurity that joining the union was supposed to free him of; King Saud was an old fool whose behavior in moments of friendliness to us was as unsettling as his behavior in moments of co-operation with Nasser; Lebanon, divided about fifty-fifty between the Christians and the Moslems, could explode under any pressures that upset the balance. We and Nasser were in agreement in deploring the situation—at least so long as it was apparent that the Soviets were about to make dramatic capital out of it. The idea of a deal was tempting to both sides.

I do not think anybody really knows what undermined this possibility. Perhaps it was simply that Abu Nawar, the pro-Nasser Chief of Staff of the Jordanian Army, decided quite on his own that he could get away with a coup against King Hussein. After all, the Egyptians had planted the idea in him and the Prime Minister, Nabulsi, before King Hussein's joining the union had rendered the move, in Nasser's planning, unnecessary. At any rate, Abu Nawar planned and actually attempted a coup which held the prize for the clumsiest in modern history until the cup was passed on to King Constantine of Greece in 1968. King Hussein, with a minimum of reorganization, re-established the loyalty of the Army, instituted martial law, and waited with some eagerness for the Syrians to try to do something about it. They did not, of course, but the United States Government moved the Sixth Fleet to Beirut and put itself in precisely the same relationship with Syria that the Soviets had enjoyed a month earlier. King Saud, who had announced that he would help Syria against any aggression—*American* aggression he meant—was bought off by means which I am not at liberty to divulge, but which anyone acquainted with his tastes and foibles can easily imagine. Nuri was reassured, and both American and British intelligence services brightened up enough to report that "possibly" the unrest against him would simmer down to controllable proportions. President Chamaoun of Lebanon, in some ways the most anti-Nasser chief of state in the Arab world, embarked on security measures to bring under control all Nasserist and Communist activity in Lebanon and to disrupt Beirut's position as command post for movements against Nuri, Hussein, and other blacklegs. By the end of 1957 the only member of Nasser's "union" was Egypt.

One member does not make much of a union. And since the union was still an essential part of Nasser's strategy, he had no choice but to begin the long uphill climb toward getting the Arab world into the shape he wanted. The only resolution to the Syria problem, which Nasser saw as being at the heart of the whole problem, was to break one of his cardinal rules: take authority wherever you can get it, but avoid responsibility like the plague. He had set out to gain control over Syria's foreign policy, but wound up with control over Syria's domestic policy (from which, after all, foreign policy stems) with all its administrative headaches. In January 1958 he agreed to the union of Syria and Egypt into one state, the "United Arab Republic," thereby becoming president not only of Egypt but of a country he had never set foot in.

If I were to write an account of this tragicomic episode in our game with Nasser I would only repeat what Malcolm Kerr said in *The Arab Cold War 1958–1964,* so I refer the reader with an eagerness for detail to that excellent little book.* I can only add that no matter how one sees the ins and outs of this mutually unsatisfactory experience, the lesson Nasser brought out of it was this: stick to appeals at the grass-roots level which will cause pressures on the leaders to stay away from independent deals with the Great Powers, and make such appeals exclusively by Radio Cairo or by other means, if any can be found, that do not involve personal contact between Egyptian officials of the target countries. If fanatics of these countries provide the best material for operations built on such appeals, so be it.

* See Suggested Reading List.

10

The Showdown of 1958: Crisis in Lebanon

... and run the risk of pushing their powerful opponents too far ...

A review of official American reporting on what happened, in early 1957, to be the peak of our "game of conflict" with Nasser reveals considerable understanding of Nasser's behavior and little animosity toward it. Other than Secretary Dulles himself, and perhaps one or two officials who worked directly with him, there was not much enthusiasm in the Department of State for the Eisenhower Doctrine, and when Nasser reacted strongly to it there was little surprise. When Nasser released campaigns of scurrilous propaganda against the "scabs" who accepted it—President Chamaoun of Lebanon and Prime Minister Nuri Sa'id of Iraq—the prevailing reaction at the State Department was "What else could we expect?" A report from one of our embassies in the Middle East contained the sentence "We can hardly blame Nasser for using methods which have proven their effectiveness," and the desk officer in Washington who received it wrote in the margin, "The shame is that we have *allowed* them to work." There was, then, an element of self-criticism at the passiveness of our reaction, but most of our officials concerned with policy toward the Middle East seemed to believe that once Nasser *had* become the wave of the future, by whatever method, we had no choice but to deal with him as such.

The attitude of the CIA, an organization whose officers are somewhat more cold-blooded than those of the State Department, was also far from hostile. Nasser's first "anti-scab" move to counter our "strikebreaking" move (i.e., the Eisenhower Doctrine) was an attempt to encourage the formation, in Lebanon, of a "United National Front" composed of anti-Chamaoun Moslems and Christians who felt that Lebanon should play a larger part in Arab affairs and not, as President Chamaoun apparently wished, withdraw from them altogether. Our countermove to Nasser's countermove, administered by the highly competent CIA team then in Beirut, was to leak information about the "Front" to fence-straddling Lebanese politicians which would scare them away from it and toward supporting Chamaoun. Afterwards, our Embassy in Beirut (not the CIA) gave modest "campaign contributions" to a few pro-Western candidates in the June 1957 elections (modest in the sense that they were of about the same amounts that the British, French, Soviet and Egyptian embassies were contributing to their respective candidates) and the Egyptian General Intelligence Agency team in Beirut somehow managed to parlay the information it had acquired on our contributions into convincing "evidence" that the CIA had rigged the elections. But to both sides, this was all fair game. Although it is hardly general information, the great intelligence services of the world have a kind of professional respect for one another and even engage in a degree of official liaison—although, of course, between "unfriendly" services it is very limited. In Beirut, relations between the various intelligence chiefs were especially close—something like what existed in Tangier during the Second World War. The American CIA chief and the Egyptian GIA chief enjoyed friendly social relations which their bitter professional conflict affected very little. The CIA's "proof" of Egyptian support to the "United

National Front" and the GIA's "proof" that CIA had rigged the elections provided a basis for mutual admiration, not hostility.

But pro-Western, anti-Egyptian candidates *did* come out on top in the elections, and such an outcome was hardly a fit subject for good-natured Egyptian-American conversation over after-dinner coffee. Following these elections, beginning in late 1957, Egyptian subversive activities in Lebanon began in earnest. It became clear to observers in Beirut—or, for that matter, to audiences of Cairo's "Voice of the Arabs" broadcasts—that Nasser was ready to go to any lengths to bring down Chamaoun. When I visited Cairo in August 1957, my Egyptian friends confidently predicted that during 1958 "Chamaoun, Hussein and Nuri will fall—and in that order." As it turned out, their chronology was wrong and their prediction only two-thirds correct, but there was no mistaking their determination. And they seemed oblivious to the possibility that the fall of these leaders would lift the struggle from the GIA-versus-CIA level and escalate it to proportions beyond their capacity to handle.

The Egyptians—and, to a certain extent, our own State Department—overlooked the extent to which Lebanon had become a country of importance to Western commercial interests. Before the 1950s, Americans who knew the Arab world were mostly missionaries, educators, archeologists and miscellaneous romantics; the leading influence in the area —and the leading influence on our own Government on Middle East questions—was the American University of Beirut and its sister institutions in Istanbul (Robert College), Cairo (American University of Cairo) and elsewhere. Increasingly, during the 1950s, big oil companies were in evidence—and naturally, they were followed by sellers of engineering equipment, by investors who foresaw the possibilities offered by the growing communities of American oil-company families, and, finally, by representatives of companies selling a wide variety of consumer products. And when oil production finally got into full swing, newly rich Kuwaitis and Saudi Arabians began to spend vast sums of money in Lebanon, causing a boom-town prosperity which drew more and more investors and sales representatives into the area—with their families, of course, thereby enlarging the American and European communities, with consequent further increase in the business possibilities. By the mid-1950s our commercial interest in the area, almost non-existent ten years earlier, was tremendous. Beirut was the business world's "New York" in the Middle East.

The American commercial presence in the area became especially conspicuous during the Suez crisis when the United States Government sought the advice of business leaders through a number of committees that it sponsored, mainly committees of oil-company executives. Oil-company lobbies, which had until that time been largely on the defensive ("antitycoon" feeling in Washington had been strong throughout the administrations of Presidents Roosevelt and Truman), began to exert some influence on our foreign policy. Although the companies lost enthusiasm for the committee approach after the Justice Department threatened one committee with antitrust proceedings (despite the fact that it had been formed at the request of the State Department), their new boldness on Middle East policy questions survived. By the time of the Lebanese crisis of 1958 they had become a major influence.

Communist and other anti-Western newspapers like to depict American oil-company executives as power-mad, profit-mad, unscrupulous individuals who care little for "the good of the people" and who will stoop to anything to achieve their ends—backing their own candidates in elections, bribing and otherwise corrupting officials who are already in office, and bringing about the overthrow of governments whose key officials resist their influence. Whatever the character of these "tycoons" as individuals, the fact is that they are backed by the most highly sophisticated expertise on economics, sociology, anthropology, and political science and not merely by lawyers and accountants. Thus, for totally practical reasons, they know that stable governments and happy social environments are essential to the continued success of their operations. They spend millions of dollars on projects that even their bitterest critics must admit are "for the good of the people," and they disapprove strongly of influences that might weaken the integrity of any of the Governments with which they deal— and this includes the influence of our various intelligence agencies and the negative influence (or lack of influence) of Embassy officials who subscribe to the view, expressed by one of our Ambassadors, "I can't get too excited about the way Arabs persist in behaving like Arabs."

By the mid-1950s, Beirut had a large Western-oriented commercial community to share this view: builders, bankers, shipping companies, suppliers of building and oil-well equipment, field offices of companies selling consumer products, and a large number of consulting firms specializing in various aspects of the oil companies' (and other large companies') adjustment to the environment. The net result was a new attitude toward the West's game with Nasser. While the tendency of the State Department was to remain "soft on Nasser," this tendency was more than offset by the opposition of the commercial community to such an attitude. Everyone knew that "Whether we like it or not, Nasser is a factor to be contended with" but whether the proper solution was resistance or appeasement was another question. Before the growth of these commercial interests, the West, or at least the Americans, leaned toward appeasement. By late 1957, when the Egyptians were stepping up their subversive activity in Lebanon, they were beginning to lean the other way.

From this time onward, those of us in touch with the situation expected a blowup at any minute. I resigned from the State Department in May 1957 and set up my government-relations-consulting office (for an oil company, an airline and a bank) in Beirut in July. At about this time the other major oil companies were establishing special "government-relations offices" to keep in touch with the increasingly explosive situation—backing up the Trans-Arabian Pipeline's highly competent government-relations office under "Sandy" Campbell and David Dodge (the latter the son of Bayard Dodge, former President of the American University of Beirut, and one of the most fluent Arabic speakers in the Western community). Harry Kern and Samir Souki, at about this time, wrote the first of their "Foreign Reports," the confidential newsletter which is perhaps the most influential —and certainly the most expensive—circulating among the major oil companies. Shortly afterwards, Fuad Itayim began his "Middle East Economic Survey" series, and a dozen imitators followed. For some years, Beirut has had more banks than New York City and more newspapers than London. By the middle of 1958 it had more confidential newsletters than New York, London and Paris put together. From then on, the covert Game of Nations between Nasserists and the West was like one of those nighttime shows in an African game reserve where the animals think they are unseen but are actually being flooded with infrared light rays and keenly observed by spectators equipped with special glasses. In Lebanon in late 1957 and early 1958, it was perhaps clearer to the spectators than to the participants that an explosion was inevitable.

For official observers, we had not only the American Ambassador—Donald Heath until late 1957, to be replaced by Robert McClintock early in 1958—but a number of high-ranking official and semiofficial observers who were only loosely under the Ambassador, or independent of him altogether. First, there was Wilbur ("Bill") Eveland, who had been sent out as a special White House emissary to keep in touch with President Chamaoun in following up the Eisenhower Doctrine agreement—and, as a friend at the State

Department told me, "to act as sort of a balance to Ambassador McClintock." Then there was a CIA station chief of extraordinarily high rank. Although he had been instructed to act only as "coordinator of information sources" and to stay out of clandestine operations, his rank, the importance of his position as "coordinator," and his standing in Washington (especially with the Dulles brothers) gave him virtual independence from McClintock. Complementing him closely was the ordinary CIA chief, the "resident," who actually controlled secret operations. Although he was not an American citizen, his tremendous intelligence and persuasive power gave him a great amount of influence not only among insiders (including the intelligence community —it was he who had held up the American side in the election duel with the Egyptian GIA) but with Washington intelligence analysts, who treated his reports and recommendations on a par with those of the Ambassador. Finally, there was the flow of high-ranking "visiting firemen" who plague Beirut even in normal times (Beirut is an ideal spot for a junket) but who became overpowering while the crisis was on. "With all these high-powered kibitzers around," an Embassy officer told me, "Ambassador McClintock has the most thankless job in the Diplomatic Service."

The spark that ignited the blowup finally came on May 8, 1958, when unknown persons shot and killed one Nesib Metni, a pro-Nasser journalist whom Chamaoun's enemies believed to be so irritatingly anti-Chamaoun that Chamaoun's guilt for the murder could, in accordance with the Lebanese sense of justice, be assumed. In the preceding few weeks some twenty-odd lives had been lost in incidents of violence at various places in Lebanon, but this particular murder fitted perfectly the specifications of drama and timing that the anti-Chamaounists' outburst required. Chamaoun—and Bill Eveland—argued convincingly that the reaction of anti-Chamaounists was so immediate and so well organized that it could only have been awaiting some such signal as the Metni murder and that anti-Chamaounists were therefore at least as suspect as pro-Chamaounists. This opinion was widely shared, and when the anti-Chamounists threw up barricades at strategic points throughout the city, blocked main transportation routes, closed down shops, dug trenches around defensible areas, and otherwise tried to bring the commercial and social life of the country to a halt, pro-Chamaounists quickly replied in kind. Within two or three days, Lebanon was in a state of civil war—a stalemate civil war, but nevertheless one that paralyzed the country.

The anti-Chamaounists—"the rebels," it is fair to call them, since they were against the established Government —were of two categories: leaders of whole communities that were anti-Chamaounist, who therefore came to be regarded as bona fide leaders of segments of the population, and leaders who had only followings characteristic of city (that is, Beirut) political life (members of "machines," beneficiaries of patronage, paid political hacks, and so on). The former—Sabri Hamadi of the Bigqaa Valley, Rashid Karami of Tripoli, and Kamal Jumblatt of the Druses—requested from the Egyptians, and got, military supplies with which to defend their positions, but it was soon found that with the exception of Jumblatt they could hold on easily enough with very little aid. The Lebanese army, under General Fuad Shehab, refused to support Chamaoun's position beyond keeping the combatants apart, and there were no armed civilian supporters of Chamaoun to challenge Hamadi and Karami. Jumblatt, however, found himself fighting members of the well-armed "Parti Populaire Syrien" (PPS), a right-wing group which had little use for Chamaoun but was violently anti-Nasser.

The latter category—the "Beirut Four": Sa'eb Salaam, Abdallah Yafi, Adnan Hakim, and Abdallah Mashnuq— depended entirely on aid from the Egyptians, not only in weapons but in funds with which to buy support. While the Egyptians gave Kamal Jumblatt the material aid he desperately needed, their strategy was built around massive support to the "Beirut Four," who, they believed, could eventually call out "the street" (the city mob) and gain control of the key area, Beirut itself. The Egyptian GIA chief assigned to Beirut was an intelligence officer who would do credit to any intelligence service, and his "staff" team were all high-quality officers. His "field" team were Syrian desperadoes, sent over the mountains by the Syrian intelligence chief. Abdelhamid Serraj, who provided an ideal link between the Egyptian professions and the Lebanese "street." It was a formidable capability that confronted Chamaoun and his western supporters by June 1958, one month after the civil war had started.

But the Western side was not similarly clear with respect to its strategy, nor so well coordinated in its efforts. There were "too much disagreement over how to interpret what's happening, too much conflict in sympathies, and too many prima donnas to influence events," as one of the confidential newsletters put it. Ambassador McClintock at first leaned to the view that President Chamaoun should succeed himself in office (and so expressed himself to President Chamaoun), but later switched to the opposite view—leaving Bill Eveland, the CIA, and much of the business community with his original position. The rest of the business community, especially the government-relations offices of the major oil companies, saw the real issue as one of law and order versus the mob and believed that "Whatever happens," as one oil-company official said, "terrorism must not be shown to pay." At least one company actively tried to get the "bona fide resistance leaders" (that is, all of them excluding the Beirut Four) to agree with "moderate Chamaounists" that "the most important thing is to stop destroying our lovely country, and to agree to settle our dispute by peaceful means" and to enlist the backing of the American Embassy for the move.

The series of disputes between influential Americans

over what our Government's policy and strategy should be is worth reporting, because it to some extent explains the new attitude that since about 1958 has been the dominant factor in our Government's game not only with Nasser but with other national leaders who imitate his style. Immediately after the Lebanese crisis, it was far from apparent that such an attitude existed (indeed, two of our Ambassadors to Cairo since then seemed to be unaware of it), but by the early 1960s it had begun to dawn on all observers of the game, and finally on the Egyptians themselves, that the new factor had become sufficiently important to have changed the whole nature of the game—with even the players themselves not quite realizing it.

The most forceful current in the American attitude was the distaste for violence as a means of attaining objectives, even worthy objectives. To give force to this current was the belief, held by our conservative diplomats and virtually all our businessmen, that the way to forestall violence was to ensure that it did not pay. The current was further enforced by a conviction, held by the same people, that those who resort to violence, however "right" their cause, cannot be trusted in *any* circumstances. They disliked the method; they disliked those who used it. Anybody who used it was to be resisted; anybody against whom it was used had at least a right to a fair hearing, a right to defend his case on a rational basis. Among the Americans concerned with the crisis in Lebanon, official and unofficial, there was no quarrel over this belief. The diplomats and the businessmen differed only in their degree of cynicism as to its relevance.

The attitude of our diplomats, as it appeared to the businessmen, was exemplified by what an Embassy officer said to Sandy Campbell of Tapline: "What else can we expect? To hope that the Lebanese won't resort to violence is like hoping dogs won't chase cats." Diplomats and cryptodiplomats hardened by a Game of Nations in which all sides used bribery, terrorism and appeals to man's lower instincts—

and in which such means were unquestionably successful—
thought such behavior a normal feature of the Lebanese
scenery. The businessmen, who had seen their Lebanese
friends only in sensible pursuit of business profits, did not
agree. Their letters to Congressmen, which were routed to
the State Department along with blasts from the Congressmen themselves, reflected their disagreement.

The principal Lebanese advocates of the law-and-order
theme in whom Western businessmen had confidence were
Emile Bustani, a Christian millionaire contractor, and Fawzi
el-Hoss, a Moslem millionaire contractor. Both had discussed
with me the possibility of using my friendship with President Nasser as a channel through which to discuss the
possibilities of a solution to the Lebanese crisis that would
enable both the Egyptians and the Americans to withdraw
their support of the Beirut Four and the Chamaoun Government respectively and would leave the way open for a
compromise between anti-Chamaoun and pro-Chamaoun
factions who had in common a desire to stop the destruction
of their country. I had been in touch with both Presidents
before the Lebanese crisis came to the boil, and when, in
early June, one of the major oil companies endorsed the idea,
I agreed to talk first to Chamaoun, then to Nasser, not to
sell the idea but to test its chances of acceptance.

Kamil Chamaoun, a handsome gray-haired man with a
startling physical resemblance to Yugoslavia's Tito, had
been an "Arab" long before Nasser ever heard the word: at
the American University of Beirut, where intellectual Arab
nationalism was born, Chamaoun had been an ardent advocate of Arab unity and united Arab resistance to the rise
of Zionism. In more recent years, however, he had become
disenchanted with Arab nationalism as a practical political
proposition and had come to believe that it was more and
more a tool of Moslem politicians of the worst type, some
of whom he knew to be in the pay of Cairo. He had an
incurable fear that should Arab nationalist politicians bring

about the kind of Arab unity they had in mind, the Christians of Lebanon would become a persecuted minority in a sea of resentful Moslems.

Nasser appreciated Chamaoun's concern; he might even have sympathized with it, because his own deliberate association of Arab nationalism with Islam was a convenience, not the result of any ideological conviction. He did, however, object to Chamaoun's attempts to remain neutral in the struggle between the "progressive" Arabs and the "reactionary" Arabs—on grounds, incidentally, that were much the same as those on which Secretary Dulles had said that neutralism in the East-West struggle was "immoral." Also, Nasser was uneasy at the apparent fact that Lebanon was increasingly being used as a base for operations against the newly formed U.A.R.: Abdelhamid Serraj, Chief of Intelligence and Security in the Northern Region (Syria), during his first briefing session with Nasser, had convinced him that this was the case. Finally, and worst, Chamaoun was a scab. Although he had not joined the Baghdad Pact (this would not have made any sense anyhow), he had welcomed the Eisenhower Doctrine.

On June 20, Fawzi el-Hoss and I called on President Chamaoun to get his authorization for me to quote him to President Nasser as agreeing to meet with Rashid Karami, Sabri Hamadi and Kamal Jumblatt and to make an honest effort to obtain a truce with them in exchange for Nasser's agreeing to discontinue support of the Beirut Four. Chamaoun was not receptive to the idea. Clearly, behind his reaction to it was the assumption that American intervention, under the terms of the Eisenhower Doctrine, would be forthcoming on demand. Silenced by such a reception, Fawzi and I sat quietly as he told us he had no confidence in the American Ambassador, whose fault it was in the first place that the re-election issue had become so important, and that Bill Eveland, in whom he *did* have confidence, was advising him to stand firm.

Upon the urging of Emile Bustani and Fawzi el-Hoss I went to Cairo anyhow and, after a talk with Ambassador Raymond Hare, went along for a meeting with Nasser. From these two I learned that the idea of Emile Bustani and Fawzi el-Hoss had already occurred to Nasser and that he had suggested something like it to Hare. "Since the United States and the United Arab Republic are the two outside parties interested in the Lebanese crisis," he had said, "representatives of the two should sit down to work out a compromise and impose it on the Lebanese." Hare, after exchanging opinions with Washington on the suggestion, had returned to Nasser with a reply that deliberately misinterpreted his suggestion. "Our Government would be happy to arbitrate the dispute between you and President Chamaoun," he said. Nasser, who was used to having American Ambassadors walk uncomplainingly into his traps, was extremely put out. When I got to him he was still smarting from Hare's ploy, but he did hold forth on his opinions about the Lebanese crisis long enough to make one point: if the solution were entirely up to him, he would make General Shehab President and Rashid Karami Prime Minister, and he would happily scuttle the Beirut Four—with whom, he admitted, Ambassador Abdelhamid Ghaleb had been having more than his share of troubles. "As things now stand, though," he concluded, "we'll have to see it all through to its end, with you backing your side and with us backing ours."

I told Hare that I thought my friends in Beirut, both American and Lebanese, were going to be disappointed and would possibly think that his reply to Nasser had undermined the only kind of agreement that could end the conflict. He replied that he had been greatly tempted by Nasser's suggestion, but that from his exchanges with Washington he had received the impression that the business community in Lebanon would have objected strongly to a favorable reply. "All along," he said, "you have argued that nobody, not Nasser or anybody else, should be allowed to bomb his way to the conference table and that if Nasser wants to negotiate at the U.A.R.-to-U.S. level, instead of the Nasser-Chamaoun level, he'd better prepare himself to talk in more constructive terms." Ambassador Hare was quoting almost verbatim from a report written by a senior American oil executive in Beirut—a report that had also included the observation, "This has turned into a battle between Nasser's goons on one side and Chamaoun's goons on the other, but Chamaoun's goons have the advantage of official status." Hare was only partly in agreement with this outlook, but he said that it was the New Look in Washington— thanks largely to the new influence of unofficial reports of businessmen in Beirut which, by the time they got to the State Department, had strong endorsements from parent companies, from Congressmen to whom the companies had forwarded copies, and perhaps from influential persons who were on the boards of directors of the companies. As for Nasser's suggestion that General Shehab should be made President and Rashid Karami Prime Minister, the State Department as well as the business community would regard the ascendancy of these two to office as the final evidence that law and order in Lebanon were no more.

When I returned to Lebanon, I found a huge operation under way—or, rather, a number of small operations loosely coordinated so that they would not work at cross purposes— whereby wealthy Lebanese Moslems, under the chairmanship of Fawzi el-Hoss, would pool their resources to buy off supporters of the Beirut Four (supposedly not too expensive a project, since Egyptian financial aid had been suspended pending investigation into the alleged peculation of one of the Four), and the highly respected speaker of the house, Adil Osseiran, would arbitrate an agreement between moderate anti-Chamaounists and moderate pro-Chamaounists. During my absence, I learned, the American Ambassador had told President Chamaoun that evidence of

U.A.R. interference was far from conclusive—the United Nations observers on the scene had found *no* proof of it— and that invoking the Eisenhower Doctrine to the extent of bringing in the U.S. Marines was out of the question. With Chamaoun thus "deactivated," as Fawzi el-Hoss gleefully put it, a compromise settlement was possible whether Chamaoun liked it or not.

There is reason to believe that the operation would have succeeded, but the coup d'etat in Iraq on July 14, 1958, changed the situation. The CIA had information to the effect that a major three-pronged operation against Nuri Pasha and the royal family in Iraq, President Chamaoun in Lebanon, and King Hussein in Jordan, had finally been launched (with U.A.R. backing if not U.A.R. instigation), and the American Ambassador decided that President Chamaoun was therefore entitled to United States military aid under the terms of the Eisenhower Doctrine. Chamaoun made the formal request, and Ambassador McClintock promised that assistance would arrive within forty-eight hours—not realizing that the fleet was only a day away. The fleet arrived in less than twenty-four hours, to unload wave after wave of grim-faced Marines, rifles poised for action, to be greeted by startled bathers sunning themselves on Beirut's beautiful beaches and hordes of little boys selling chewing gum. Adil Osseiran saw it all from the back seat of his air-conditioned Cadillac as he was on his way up the Phoenician Coast to Tripoli to get Rashid Karami's agreement to the arbitration plan.

There followed an exchange of invective, by radio, between the American Ambassador and the Naval captain in charge of the Marine landing party, mostly about who takes orders from whom, the upshot of which was the arrival of the Naval captain in the Ambassador's residence announcing, "We have prevented an economic depression in the United States!" More exchanges, more insults, the to-be-expected mutual contempt between "cocktail-pushing diplomats" and "brassbound military"—with President Chamaoun and his cabinet, most of the Christian Lebanese, the American business community and the CIA all rooting for the military. The Ambassador wanted the Marines to make the point that the United States Government had unhesitatingly lived up to its commitments under the Eisenhower Doctrine, that no "imperialism" had followed, and that once the mission had been accomplished the move was over—with as few casualties as possible. President Chamaoun wanted the Marines to move in on the Moslem quarter, the "Basta," and clean up the opposition (not trying to make too fine a distinction between "loyal" opposition and the other kind) and block off aid coming across the Syrian border. The American business community, shaken by the horrifying reports coming to Beirut on the Iraqi coup, were more or less in agreement with Chamaoun as to what should be done, except that their reasons were different. The virtually unanimous view of businessmen was: Decide anything you want, but don't make any concessions to the Beirut terrorists.

The Ambassador's view prevailed. By highly commendable fast footwork, he managed to get the Marines into place all over Beirut without any resistance from either the terrorists or the Lebanese Army—in fact, he secured the cooperation of the Lebanese Army. The Marines stayed in Lebanon for three months, spending large amounts of money and mixing easily with the Lebanese, and departed without, as Ambassador McClintock said, "a single shot having been fired in anger." Most people who had any knowledge at all of the more complicated aspects of the situation appreciated the operation as a brilliant feat of the Ambassador. Washington, however, was getting reports from sources other than the Embassy. Although many of these reports were based on only a partial understanding of the problems, some of them were extremely convincing—especially the ones that were written in practical, businesslike language, in contrast to the Ambassador's somewhat literary style. When some of the more influential journalists began to write stories which, like these reports, implied that the Ambassador was not entirely on top of his job, Secretary Dulles decided upon the standard solution: send out a Great White Father.

The Great White Father in this instance was Robert Murphy, a man of such long-established reputation that, by the time he was sent to Lebanon, he had fallen into the habit of neglecting his homework and relying on his experience and sagacity to make the right decision on what is euphemistically described as a "fresh look" at the situation. When ordered by Dulles to Beirut, Mr. Murphy was working a twelve-hour day on a wide miscellany of problems, none of which had any connection with the Middle East. Nominally, he was to be political adviser to the Commander in Chief of the military forces that had just been landed in Lebanon. Actually, he was to use his senior rank, prestige, and long background as a "diplomat among warriors" (the title of his autobiography) to knock heads together and do whatever was necessary "to promote the best interests of the United States incident to the arrival of our forces in the Lebanon," as he puts it in his account of the mission. Wits in the business community were saying, "Mr. Murphy has been sent out to prevent a coup d'etat in the American Embassy." At any rate, since he did not really understand much about the situation or the controversies over the proper interpretation of it, it can at least be said that he approached it with an entirely open mind.

It is pointless, in this book which is concerned with cryptodiplomacy rather than the *ad hoc* statesmanship of Great White Fathers, to go into the details of Mr. Murphy's mission, except to say that his actions were guided by that ancient piece of wisdom, "I listen to the extreme views of both sides, and in the end I usually find that the truth is somewhere in the middle," and to comment that the "two sides" in this particular case were considered to be President Chamaoun and the Beiruit Four, the first being the duly

elected President of the country and the second being leaders of terrorist gangs supported by the U.A.R. Embassy. In
the thirty minutes allowed me, I pleaded with Mr. Murphy
that on the anti-Government side he should confine his
dealings to those who were clearly representative of their
constituencies and stay away from those whose status was in
doubt, especially those who were known to be in the pay of
the U.A.R. He listened politely, and less than an hour later
he was on his way to meet with the leading U.A.R. agent in
Lebanon, in this way reviving his influence, which had
been falling since the arbitration effort. The meeting was
supposed to be secret, Mr. Murphy later explained, but it
was hardly in the interests of this particular politician to
keep them secret. Photographs of the two shaking hands
were widely distributed under the caption "President Eisenhower's representative sympathizes with the Revolution."

Most writers commenting on the Lebanese *évènements*
agree that the Marine landing was a remarkable feat of
diplomacy. On the world stage, perhaps it was. It certainly
proved that we live up to our commitments and that we are
prepared to act in a way that the Soviets have not proved
themselves prepared to act in aid of *their* friends. But the
outcome was exactly what Gamal Abdelnasser was seeking.
It was as though the Marines had been brought in to
achieve Nasser's objective for him. First, the President and
the Prime Minister who came into office were the two whom
Nasser wanted to see in office, Shebab and Karami. Second,
terrorism had been established as an effective—even respectable—weapon. Within days of the end of the crisis,
groups of *all* religions and political color were arming themselves, with the idea that "We must fight for what is ours,
because the Government isn't going to help us." There were
those in our Embassy who argued that "The Lebanese are a
lot of gangsters anyhow" and that it was silly to expect anything better of them. But there was at least a chance to
establish new ground rules and make them stick, and our

dealing with a terrorist leader on an equal basis with the President of the country contributed at least a little bit to ruining that chance. Third, the Eisenhower Doctrine was dead. Nasser had one less blackleg to worry about. For years to come, no Lebanese Government was likely to make a deal with the West that would offend the following that Nasser could activate in Lebanon whenever he wished.

Thus, toward the end of 1958 Nasser was in many ways at the peak of his power—that is, as "power" is meant in this book: having the maximum leverage *vis-à-vis* the Great Powers to the benefit of Egypt. According to some observers, he had "failed to bring Lebanon into the U.A.R."; he had similarly failed in Jordan, where, after the departure of British troops (which had landed there when the American Marines landed in Lebanon) he had reportedly attempted another coup d'etat and had failed; a coup in the Sudan, which appears to have taken his CIA team there by surprise, had brought in a new government which was going to be "independent" of Cairo; he was being attacked by President Bourguiba of Tunisia. To anyone who assumed that his ambition was to take over the Arab world, he appeared to be in difficulties. But anyone reading State Department cables at that time, in which he was referred to as the "wave of the future," or counting up the financial and technical aid he was by then getting from both the United States and the Soviets would have to conclude that his failures, if that was what they were, were extremely profitable. During the next four years, despite ups and downs in his political relations first with the Soviets and then with the United States, he received well over £1,000,000,000 in foreign aid from the United States and the Communist states alone. His success was admitted, at least in Washington, to be because of his being a "factor to be contended with," a phrase which was used just as much by those who argued that he had "failed" in the Cold War of 1957–58 as by those who thought him "the wave of the future."

All the same, Nasser's known involvement in the Lebanese crisis provoked the undying hostility of Western business organizations, some of which will "do business with the devil when there is certain profit to be had" but all of which are, *au fond*, moved by a practical realization of the devil's long-range dangers. Many business concerns, seeing short-term advantages, have done business in Egypt since 1958. At the same time, the great Washington lobbies of the business world have hammered hard on anti-Nasser themes and have harassed and denounced "pro-Nasser" officers in the State Department (including even those who insist mildly that Nasser "is not *all* bad") into silence or into asking for transfers. Because of important global considerations not known or appreciated by the businessmen, our Government held off from a conspicuously anti-Nasser policy for the next four years—and, as we shall see, Nasser occasionally performed some act outside the Game of Nations which eased the anti-Nasser pressures on our Government. Nevertheless the pressures remained—and grew—in such a way that it nullified Nasser's strength in the Game of Nations which was built on his ability to play us off against the Soviets.

11

The Home-Front
Costs to Egypt of
Nasserist Foreign Policy

*... and push upward, beyond what you can afford,
the costs of maintaining the façade
required of an international power ...*

While it was Egypt's part in the Lebanese crisis of 1958
that aroused the Western business community against Nasser, to Western diplomats and to Nasserists this crisis was
only a segment of a broad front. As we said earlier, Nasser
had responded to the Baghdad Pact by starting campaigns
to bring down Nuri Sa'id of Iraq, King Hussein of Jordan,
and Kamil Chamaoun of Lebanon. Long before the outbreak of troubles in Lebanon, his agents had stirred up
Palestinian refugees in Jordan against King Hussein, and he
had managed to induce King Saud of Saudi Arabia to support the campaign financially. Our Government, believing
Nuri and Chamaoun to be the most secure of Nasser's three
targets, sent Kermit Roosevelt to Saudi Arabia to persuade
King Saud to withdraw his support and to Jordan to see
what could be done to reinforce Hussein's resistance. Roosevelt easily proved to Saud that Nasser had tricked him into
opposition to Hussein and into subsidizing Communist newspapers in Beirut and Damascus. Moreover, he convinced
Saud he should attend a summit meeting in Cairo, which
Nasser had called for January 1957; get Nasser and the
Syrian Prime Minister, Sabri el-Assali, to agree to subsidize

Jordan to make up for the British subsidy which Hussein lost when (under pressure from Nasser) he denounced the Baghdad Pact; then judge the reliability of his partners on a basis of whether they did or did not come through with their contributions. Saud blew the game by falling too easily for blandishments offered him by the United States Government when he went on to Washington from Cairo, thereby giving Nasser an excuse to withdraw his offer of a contribution. No matter: the Saudi-Egyptian split was effected. The same in Jordan. Nasser got Hussein in his union; Roosevelt got him out again—according to Nasser, by passing "disinformation" to Abu Nawar and Nabulsi to delude them into thinking they could effect a coup against Hussein, thereby pushing them into Hussein's trap.

In 1953, Nasser had launched Radio Cairo's "Voice of the Arabs" as a means of building the myth of Arab nationalism, to designate the foreign enemies to it, and to establish the criteria by which the people would identify "imperialist enemies in our midst," leaving it to them to decide whether or not Nuri, Hussein and Chamaoun fitted the criteria. Immediately after the signing of the Baghdad Pact, the Voice of the Arabs added two more hours to its daily broadcasts and shifted the emphasis from the building of the myth to warning against its enemies. From then onward, Cairo's broadcasts increased in time, power, and intensity of content. By 1957, it was explicitly calling for uprisings and assassinations. Of Nuri, one broadcast announced that "a traitor has been found" and suggested that the Iraqis, if they had any human decency in them at all, would "kill him and throw his carcass to the jackals."

Broadcasts of this sort come to the attention of American and British intelligence agencies by means of an organization known as FBIS—Foreign Broadcast Information Service. FBIS receivers in Cyprus tape every broadcast emanating from the Middle East, most of Africa and parts of the Soviet Union which come in clearly at this listening post.

When the Voice of the Arabs announcer called for the assassination of Nuri, analysts in Washington and London—and, no doubt, Moscow, Paris, Peking and half a dozen other capitals—began as intensive a study of Radio Cairo's broadcasts as has ever been made of propaganda of any kind since Hitler. Retroactively, these broadcasts were sifted and re-sifted for evidence of outside influence, for indications of the general strategy behind them, and for material that could be thrown back at the Egyptians as counterpropaganda. Item by item, the broadcasts had sounded like nonsense. Taken as a whole, however, they shaped up as a highly skilled, well-integrated campaign. Early in 1956, the CIA sponsored a survey of Radio Cairo's reception in all parts of the Arab world, from Iraq to Morocco, and found that it was being widely heard, even in the middle of the desert, and that its prolonged effect was a conditioning of Arab attitudes much as is achieved under hypnosis. Even listeners too educated to accept the content of the broadcasts intellectually were beginning to *assume* certain attitudes without consciously knowing why. One of the analysts told me at the time, "Even a Western-oriented tradesman who leaves the radio on out of habit, consciously hearing but a little of the broadcasts, will eventually find his suspicions of the West growing, also his susceptibility to Nasser's arguments." The appeal, as our motivational researchers would say, was "subliminal." And it was unquestionably effective.

Nuri was relatively unconcerned. His idea of answering the Voice of the Arabs was to have Radio Baghdad play over and over again a humorous song about a postman—intended to ridicule Nasser because his father had been a postman, but actually gaining as much sympathy for Nasser as Nasser's own broadcasts. The Voice of the Arabs replayed Radio Baghdad's Song of the Postman to show to what depths Radio Baghdad had sunk. Radio Baghdad replayed the Voice of the Arabs' calls for the assassination of Nuri to show to what depths Radio Cairo had sunk. Given the

Manchurian Candidate treatment which the Iraqis had been undergoing until Western analysts caught up to it, it is easy to imagine the net result of the exchange.

The United States Government experimented with a wide variety of projects to counter Radio Cairo, which, by early 1956, was trying to extend its coverage into Africa. Use of Radio Liban facilities was considered, but when American propagandists sat down with Lebanese planners, it quickly became apparent to both sides that any really effective propaganda would run the risk of exacerbating Lebanon's Christian-Moslem frictions and that Lebanon would do well to stay out of this aspect of the Cold War. Then there was some talk of setting up a new station in Adana, Turkey, or helping the British to expand their facilities in Cyprus—and, as a matter of fact, some progress was made in this latter idea. It soon became apparent, however, that building a broadcast capability to match that of Cairo would be like trying to transplant Hollywood to Des Moines, Iowa. Cairo had a community of actors, singers, directors, writers and technicians that could not be matched in any other city in the Arab world for many years and then only by an impractical amount of effort. The final idea was to await an opportunity to bomb Cairo's transmitters out of existence. The opportunity came. At the time of the Suez crisis in October 1956, an RAF pilot dropped a cluster of bombs on them. He missed.

Whatever its effectiveness, by 1957 Radio Cairo had become an extremely expensive operation. Moreover, the intelligence and political-action follow-up was also expensive. There is no way of calculating the total costs of Egyptian operations in Lebanon in 1958, but Western penetrations of these operations revealed specific expenditures that were in millions of dollars, and the Lebanese Government, after the crisis, uncovered convincing indications that one of the Beirut Four had received as much as $7,000,000. By putting together such information as this and adding to it what was known about the GIA and related organizations in Cairo,

Western intelligence services concluded that Egypt's budget for intelligence and political action must greatly exceed their own budgets—which, in 1957–58, were by no means small.

But the direct costs of political action were only part of the total costs. The real cost was in keeping up the front at home. One of Nasser's top lieutenants once said to me, "If some catastrophe were to separate Egypt from the rest of the world, float us like an island in some great ocean but leaving us our Nile, our soil and all our other resources, we would make out very well. Some of us would grow cotton; others would make it into textiles; some would grow rice and corn; others would process it; some would fill teeth, some make shoes, some teach school and all the rest. But when we've got to be an international power, most of our people are at work on jobs that contribute nothing to our welfare." People thrown on a desert island somehow make out, so long as they are unaware of neighbors—no "international relations," in other words, no keeping up with the Joneses.

But there seemed to be no way for Egypt to isolate herself from the rest of the world. Even should Egyptians become isolationist and seek to withdraw into the "Egypt first" kind of marginal self-sufficiency which some of Nasser's lieutenants have advocated, the outside world would continue to press in. After all, even the United States Government, which has from time to time encouraged a reversion to "Egypt first" isolationism, gave its original support to Nasser on the theory that he would set an example to the rest of the Arab world.

"Leadership by example": that is what the Americans had in mind. If the United States Government jumped with delight every time Zakaria Mohieddin came back into prominence—as Prime Minister, as Vice President, as head of some special commission or other—it was not because he was pro-American (he was not, and is not) but because he advocated and, within Nasser's entourage, represented the constructive approach of gaining leadership over the Arabs by setting a good example for them to follow rather than by setting terrorists against their chiefs of state.

Economically, the Americans had in mind a situation that was roughly what Egypt had before Nasser's coup, but modernized and improved. They wanted Egypt to play Nebraska to Europe's New York. Features of the economy would have been as follows:

Export of raw materials: The Americans believed that the Egyptians, like others who were late in industrializing, would never be able to manufacture radios, automobiles, and other such products as cheaply as they could buy them from countries with long industrial experience. There was, they believed, no question of "catching up"; while the Egyptians were improving themselves, with no particular native talent for sophisticated manufacture to begin with, the Italians, Germans and French—not to mention the Japanese—would be improving themselves that much faster. No matter how determined the Egyptians, the gap would become wider, not narrower. Let the Egyptians stick to development of their natural resources. They would sell them to the Americans for hard currency, and with the hard currency buy what finished products they needed.

Modest industrial projects: It was believed that the Egyptians should industrialize, but that they should stick to simple manufactures which were within their capabilities, which were based on their agriculture, and which would save them in hard currency. We were against industry for the sake of industry—"prestige projects," in other words, like steel mills and automobile factories, which the simplest arithmetic revealed to be uneconomical.

Free enterprise: Western management consultants who worked in Egypt during the early days of Nasser's regime were appalled at the size and clumsiness of the bureaucracy.

It seemed obvious to them that the only way new industry and new hard-currency-earning projects could be started would be by giving the maximum incentive to individuals and relying on that old magic, human ingenuity. The *most* important contribution the Government could make, these experts believed, was to leave such individuals alone. If any thought at all was to be given to their activities, it should be to the end of helping them be more productive, not to the end of seeing that they did not get away with anything.

Foreign investors, foreign experts: Also, the Americans saw a possibility of Egypt's capitalizing on the willingness of Western manufacturers, many of whom were seeking tax havens, to enter Egypt, to set up joint enterprises with Egyptians, to make licensing agreements, or even establish their own plants (although employing Egyptians). Here, it was thought, was an opportunity for Egypt to gain hard currency, employment for many Egyptians, experience, and markets—markets not merely for the products manufactured by the foreign companies in Egypt, but for products manufactured by the Egyptians themselves which could be distributed through the same channels.

A civilian society, a small army: The State Department appreciated the necessity for Nasser to maintain a strong army for his internal-security, "repressive-base" purposes—and even, to a degree, the necessity to use army officers in nonmilitary jobs where the civilian administration had been particularly corrupt. Westerners who were concerned only with the economy of the country, however, saw the need of a strong regime only to keep order, and the army that would be required for this simple purpose would be numerically smaller than the "military class" which Nasser required for the kind of "repressive base" he had in mind. Western businessmen and economists were brought up to think of the Government as something that changes naturally from time to time—by elections, that is—while it was Nasser's intention to stay in power.

Memoranda of conversations between various Westerners, both official and unofficial, and Egyptian officials during the early years of Nasser's rule reveal an assumption that there was no conflict between Nasser's philosophy and the ideas listed above and that if they were not being put into effect it was only because Nasser, in his inexperience, did not really appreciate their importance. After the troubles in Lebanon, however, it became very clear that Nasser had ideas of his own which did not support these assumptions at all. These troubles, remember, were the first to hit the Western business community so generally. Up to then only the oil companies had taken a close look at the revolution that was taking place. But the Lebanese crisis roused the direct interest of at least one hundred and twenty American companies, besides the British and European companies, who had been using Beirut as a base for their Middle Eastern operations and who suddenly had to re-evaluate their respective positions. And considering the outcome of the Lebanese crisis, the first question they wanted an answer to was "What are Nasser's ideas on the economics of the area that he hopes to dominate, and how will such ideas affect us?"

In June 1958 my partner and I had three clients: an oil company, a bank, and an airline. By September of that year we had received dozens of requests from American companies in the Middle East for studies of trends we could expect after Nasser's "victory" (no businessman saw it any other way) of that summer. Other consulting firms in our line of work had the same experience, and we were in a position to know that virtually all American companies which had major investments in the area, or which were considering making any, were making studies of their own back in their home offices and were badgering the State Department for relevant information.

It was after the Lebanese crisis that the State Department and American business interests in the Middle East, the oil companies included, began to go their separate ways—although the fact that they had done so did not become apparent until the Kennedy Administration came into office and Nasser went into Yemen. The prevailing view at the State Department was that Nasser had not really "won" anything in Lebanon, that the Government which had come into power there was basically neutral, and that the Eisenhower Doctrine, while dead, had served a worthwhile purpose. As for Nasser's future behavior, he should be regarded as preferable to any alternative leaders who might take his place should he be overthrown—and, anyway, he was preferable to the other Arab leaders of the time, certainly Qassim of Iraq (with whom Nasser was beginning to fight because he was scabbing Eastwards, instead of Westwards as had Nuri), anachronistic old King Saud, and even President Shehab of Lebanon—whom, incidentally, some of our diplomats regarded as a "Naguib without a Nasser." Moreover, despite the odd catastrophe every three or four years, he was going strong. He was "there."

Here, it finally dawned on us, was what Nasser saw wrong in the idea of his playing Nebraska to our New York: First, the kind of government that is natural to such an arrangement would not be strong enough for the purposes of his first objective, merely to stay in power. The bureaucracy, as he saw it, was not only an organization of civil servants concerned with the duties of public administration, but a power structure. Those in it were not only civil servants, they were people. All one million of them, most of whom were resident in Cairo, comprised a *class* which was an important element in his following. They provided the membership for his political party. A mere 180,000 "civil servants" (this number being the *maximum* that Nasser's American consulting firm said could be efficiently employed in the government) would hardly serve the purpose. Neither would an army of a mere 50,000, the number that would be required to deal with civil disorders inside Egypt. As Nasser saw it, he needed a military "class" of at least 600,000.

Second, an economy that has as its principal feature the export of raw materials and the import of finished goods somehow means that those who live under that economy are second-class citizens, "the natives" of British colonial days, and so think of themselves as such that they can never have the pride in themselves that Nasser believes to be essential. Coupled with this feeling, there is the belief that such an economy is unduly dependent on factors that are almost entirely under the control of the customers. The ups and downs of the cotton market, for example, shake the Egyptian economy out of all proportion to their importance in the countries where the markets exist. Moreover, Nasser has had experience with outside powers' exploiting his disadvantage in this respect. For example, during one prolonged period, the Soviets jumped in to take up the slack left by a fall in the cotton market in the West, bought all they could get, continued to pay prices above the world-market price so as to gain a greater and greater percentage of Egypt's total exports, then began to sell it throughout the world at prices below the market. This kind of cryptoeconomics brings home to Nasser the realization that depending on the sale of raw materials is practically dangerous, as well as socially debasing.

Third, Nasser believes that the society of a nation which only furnishes raw materials to industrialized nations, and whose own "capitalists" are largely traders (as opposed to manufacturers and investors, as are most capitalists in Western countries), shortly has on its hands an unpatriotic, corrupted wealthy class which contributes nothing substantial to the product of the country and which is inclined to export its profits to Switzerland. Unlike the all-for-one-and-one-for-all society which might exist on the theoretical "island" or in Nasser's socialist society, the society growing out of the kind of economy we advocated would have a wealthy and influential element which would tend to think in terms of French perfumes, imported sports cars, and vacations on the Riviera. In fact, this is the kind of upper crust which Egypt *did* have before Nasser's coup. Nasser was as anxious to eliminate the wealthy merchant class as he was to create the civil-servant and military classes—and, of course, a class of laborers, an industrial proletariat.

Which brings us to the fourth point. When International Monetary Fund experts were advising Nasser to concentrate on stabilizing his currency and to eliminate plants whose products cost the customers more than competitive products that could be brought in from abroad, he replied, "But industrializing is an objective in itself, not just a means of getting products." A self-respecting well-rounded national community is made up of civil servants, soldiers and officers, intellectuals, entertainers, professional people, managers, and laborers in certain proportions suitable to the overall health of the society. "If somebody invented a means of manufacturing food industrially so that you wouldn't need farmers any more," Nasser once told an American visitor, "I think you would resist it simply for the reason that you don't want to eliminate farmers. In the same way, we want to gain laborers—even if we have to build plants we don't really need to get them."

Just as important, Nasser wants a managerial class. He would, in fact, like to have a "managerial revolution" like that of the James Burnham book.* Egypt has the only management school in the Middle East of any standing, using as it does materials (and occasionally instructors) from the Harvard School of Business Administration and other such reputable institutions. And his professors, all of them Western-trained, visit Baghdad, Khartoum, Tripoli, and even Beirut to give courses. Although Nasser denies it, there is reason to suspect that at least a few of his industrial estab-

* See Suggested Reading List.

lishments were set up for no other purpose than to enlarge his corps of managers. I asked the head of the management school (National Institute of Management Development) why one of these marginal factories was being kept going, and he replied "Oh, we need it as a sort of a laboratory in which to try different managerial techniques." Also, I know of others which were to be closed, but which were allowed to remain open as the result of vigorous pleas from this school.

Finally, and most important from our point of view, there is the fact that a Big Show gets more attention than a Little Show—and, it certainly has been proved, gets more foreign aid. It gets it either because, directly, it attracts more interest and attention on the part of those giving the aid, or because, indirectly, it makes for more influence in the "neutralist union" and therefore moves the donors of aid on political grounds. Many of our economists argued energetically that Egypt could settle down to a basically agricultural economy, although shifting from cotton to food so that her dependence on the cotton market would be reduced, and could move carefully and systematically into a program of industrialization that would benefit the country much more than the sprawling mess of factories it in fact did create. But these same economists were talking about small amounts of outside aid in connection with the modest and sensible approach, and large amounts of aid in connection with the Big Show approach—because, as an AID official explained to me, "Although we don't like the more ambitious approach as much as the modest one, in granting aid we have to consider that it's on a larger order of magnitude." Since Nasser preferred large amounts of aid to small amounts of aid, such an observation would go in at one ear and out the other except for the reference to "order of magnitude."

But when Western investors and potential investors looked at the whole Middle East following the confused summer of 1958, they saw Nasser's Big Show at home as "imperial economics"—to borrow a phrase from a *Fortune* article that appeared in October 1958 and that was read by practically every American businessman with any kind of interest at all in the Middle East. This article, by Gilbert Burck, explains that Nasser's "efforts to bring one Arab national after another under the political hegemony of Cairo are only one part of his grand design," and the other part was to make of Egypt "the industrial mecca of a modern Arab empire." According to this article, and according to a dozen or so confidential studies circulated among leading oil executives, bankers, and other categories of businessmen, Nasser's plans for industrialization, his vast schemes of socialization, his outsized civil service and military, and all the rest could not possibly be justified in terms of purely Egyptian interest. Assuming it to be the part of the iceberg above water, the part below the water necessarily included economic domination of the whole Arab world, with all its resources including its petroleum resources—or so observers of the business community thought.

The few professional Nasser watchers who were without either political or business bias did not see it quite that way, but in a way that was just as alarming. First, they could appreciate that Nasser was determined to be independent, not our pro-Western tool, and they understood that no leader of any other country who is truly independent will behave entirely to our liking. Second, they understood (as the businessmen did not) that remaining in power would have to be his primary objective and that a strong government, with its repressive base, was necessary. Third, they understood that gaining popular support, to add to his repressive base, would require actions that we find distasteful —Egyptians having political tastes which are different from our own. Fourth, they even understood the necessity for Nasser's positive neutrality and, in the light of the results obtained, for his using it as an ideological cover for playing the West and the Soviets off against each other. Fifth, although they strongly disapproved, it came as no surprise to them when he tried to get other nations to join with him in a "union" of positive neutralists so as to gain greater leverage —and even when he resorted to terrorism to bring the scabs into line. The reader who doubts that we were as understanding as this might take note of the fact that *after* Nasser's behavior according to this pattern had become clear, we gave him more aid during the following two years than we had given in any two years before. What *did* seriously disturb our Government, as well as many of Nasser's own friends and supporters, was that he had caught himself in a vicious circle. He needed the Big Show in order to get recognition and aid from the outside world, and then needed more aid and recognition than the outside world could give just to keep the Big Show going.

And Big Shows don't go. They bog down.

12

The Bipolar World Becomes a Multipolar World

. . . and the game board may change on you, making your role irrelevant . . .

At the end of the crisis in Lebanon, pressures against United States Government aid to Nasser began to build up in Washington. About the same time, our diplomats in Arab countries, bitter about the Eisenhower Doctrine (which they had almost unanimously opposed), began advocating "facing the fact of Nasser" and realizing that the "Arab world of 1959 is not that of Lawrence of Arabia," to quote one much-quoted dispatch of that period. My impression, shared with most of the diplomats with whom I have discussed this point, is that the anti-Nasser lobby would have carried the day had it not been for one thing: Nasser's reasonableness, and constructive help in the settlement of the dispute between the "Northern Region" of the U.A.R. (Syria, that is) and Tapline, the pipeline company owned by the same four majors who owned the Arabian American Oil Company (ARAMCO) in Saudi Arabia (Standard of New Jersey, Mobil, Texaco and Standard Oil of California), which has been followed up, to this very day, by impeccable conduct in dealing with oil companies active in his own country. Even at a time when lobbies of the majors were most actively buttonholing Congressmen with complaints against our diplomats who were "soft on Nasser," the executives of oil companies who were directly in touch with Nasser were proclaiming in private that they would prefer to deal with top-level Egyptians even when they were in a hostile frame of mind than with any other Arab leaders when they were friendly. While this hardly became the prevalent attitude of executives at home headquarters (oil companies have a headquarters-versus-field phenomenon like that of the State Department), the manifest competence of the Egyptians, contrasted with the unreasonableness and downright dishonesty of the Syrian officials, caused an important segment of the American business community to relax its hostility to Nasser.

Then came President Kennedy. A month or so after his inauguration, apparently in response to some routine greetings he had sent out to all Arab chiefs of state, he received a letter "from the oldest but poorest country of the world to the President of the youngest but richest country of the world." The letter, which State Department analysts who were skilled at this sort of thing believe could have been written only by Nasser himself, commented on similarities of age, family and so on between the two Presidents and ended with the suggestion that it might be worth President Kennedy's while to see the difference between running a country like Egypt and running a country like the United States and that if President Kennedy would like to send along someone he especially trusted, President Nasser would see to it that he got a firsthand view.

President Kennedy, greatly moved by the letter, answered it promptly, and the Nasser-Kennedy dialogue was under way. It was many months, however, before Kennedy could take Nasser up on his offer to give some trusted friend a close-up view of the difficulties of running Egypt. Finally, however, in May 1962, Kennedy decided to send his old friend and teacher Edward Mason to Cairo. Mason, who had been Kennedy's economics professor at Harvard, had

written books and articles about the economics of underdeveloped countries which were thoroughly in accord with
Kennedy's own views, and Kennedy knew him to have no
prejudices on the subject of socialism that would color his
judgment of Nasser's program, then in progress, to nationalize cotton-exporting firms, banks, insurance companies and
some two hundred or more trading and industrial companies.

So Professor Mason went to Cairo. From the day of
Mason's arrival, Nasser made it clear that he was to be
given every opportunity to "see this country as I see it, to
feel its difficulties as I feel them, and to be with me every
step of the way as I try to solve my problems." Nasser gave
Mason the run of the house, seeing to it that he got full
briefings from his Vice Presidents, Ministers and other key
officials. In his own meetings with Mason, Nasser would ask,
"Are we doing anything differently than you would do it
if you were running the country?" The answer, more often
than not, was "No, Mr. President."

In July 1962, Mason returned to Washington to tell President Kennedy that he could not conscientiously find fault
with any of Nasser's major actions. Nasser had forced him
to admit that those actions which the United States Government found so objectionable—nationalization of large
segments of the Egyptian economy, various totalitarian
measures such as censorship of the press and arrest of dissident politicians, and even the propaganda assaults on other
Arab leaders whom Nasser believed to be friendly to the
West—were actions that Nasser could logically be expected
to take given his circumstances. "Nasser is constantly called
upon to choose the least unsatisfactory of a number of alternatives," said Mason, "all of which are unsatisfactory."

But that wasn't all. In a debriefing session at the State
Department, Mason refused to allow his understanding of
Nasser and of Nasser's way of solving his problems to be
interpreted as a recommendation for greater support. "The
question of whether or not Nasser's behavior coincides with

American interests is another matter altogether," he said. The officials who debriefed Mason and summarized his findings concluded that although Nasser's actions might be justified on the grounds that he was only doing what he had to do under the circumstances, these actions were nonetheless highly inimical to the interests of the United States. We must either: (1) change the circumstances, (2) change our interests, (3) bring about Nasser's replacement by someone who will react differently, however illogically, to the circumstances, or (4) conduct our own future actions with respect to the area on the assumption that Nasser, however understandable his actions may be in the light of his own interests, is an enemy of the United States, to be dealt with as such.

By this time, all but one or two of the State Department officials who had played the Game of Nations with Nasser Dulles-style had been transferred. Among the new lot, high morality was the In Thing. The new crowd found it embarrassing to have to admit that another government can become its enemy simply by doing what it has to do in its own interests, particularly when the other government was of an underdeveloped country whose desire to be "free of imperialism" had the announced sympathy of President Kennedy. Some of the officers refused to accept the possibility that such a situation could exist. Others, more realistic if less "in," were happy to have support for the argument that Nasser was a menace and should be dealt with as such, although they would have liked grounds for believing that Nasser was bad not only for the West but for his own country as well—grounds that were not to be found in Professor Mason's report.

On balance, the thinking of White House and State Department Middle East specialists throughout the Kennedy Administration remained sympathetic to Nasser—as sympathetic, anyhow, as they dared considering that American business organizations and, in turn, their Congressmen, were constantly complaining about Nasser's anti-American and

pro-Soviet utterances in public and his foreign adventures
of which, since Lebanon, businessmen were becoming increasingly aware. When Syria broke away from the United
Arab Republic, in the autumn of 1961, Nasser's reasonableness toward Tapline, which had taken the steam out of the
oil companies' opposition, became irrelevant. Nasser understood all this, and he had hoped that the Mason visit would
result in a practical kind of sympathy which would produce
more concrete results for Egypt, but at the same time would
be less embarrassing to the executive branch of our Government *vis-à-vis* Congress.

For some weeks after Mason returned to Washington,
Nasser told me repeatedly how pleased he was with the
visit, not only because of what he thought he had been able
to convey to President Kennedy about his own problems but
because of the understanding he had gained from Mason of
the problems of the United States Government. In September, however, he received a visit from the American Ambassador, John Badeau, who frankly admitted the dilemma
that Mason's report of his visit had caused in Washington
and said that our Government was "undergoing considerable
soul-searching" in an attempt to arrive at a position on
Egyptian-American differences that would be "morally defensible." The Ambassador, an academician whose ways of
thinking and talking were virtually the opposite of Nasser's,
delivered the message along with the usual friendly assurances that our Government had no aims for the area other
than peace and stability and that we were being guided
by the great sense of moral responsibility that characterized
policy making of the Kennedy Administration.

Nasser was so appalled that he couldn't think of a reply.
When I saw him the next day, he was beside himself. He
wasn't bothered by our unremarkable discovery that Egyptian and American interests were not always one hundred
percent in accord. After all, he had cut his teeth on Secretary Dulles' conviction that what was good for the United

States was good for the world. He was most upset, however, to learn that despite President Kennedy our State Department still believed it was engaged in a war of good versus evil and that we could not arrive at a decision on a basis of pure self-interest without feeling afterwards that we had to concoct some high-sounding moral position to justify it. "So long as you delude yourselves with so much moral rationalizing," he said, "I am just as uneasy when you are with me as when you are against me. If you would only just play the game."

In his relations with the Eisenhower Government, Nasser saw the game as a strictly amoral affair in which we were out for our own interests and he for his. As Zakaria had said in one of his lectures: "The Game of Nations is what happens when all the nations, in their respective self-interest, pursue their national goals by means—*any* means—short of war. It presupposes the existence of conflicting interests even between the friendliest nations, and it assumes that many of the gains of any one nation will be at some cost to the others. A skillful player will get all he can for his own side, he will form tactical coalitions with other players in the pursuit of mutual advantages, and he will distribute the cost among the losers in such a way that no one of them will be moved to drastic counter action or to drop out of the game altogether—that is, resort to war." This kind of thing Nasser understood, and while he wasn't entirely happy in his game during the Eisenhower-Dulles era, he at least knew what was going on. Now, with Kennedy in the White House, he had a new kind of "moral considerations" to contend with.

From the opening days of the Kennedy Administration down to the present, Nasser has been puzzled at the way our moves seemed both *im*moral (as opposed to *a*moral) and irrelevant to the objective of making gains, yet were almost aways favorably responsive to his own game-play moves to gain advantages for Egypt. Our Government allowed him to "win" his game yet had no discernible game of its own. Nasser insists that a political analyst visiting Earth from Mars, and examining American and Egyptian moves solely according to criteria of self-interest, would be similarly puzzled.

Nasser's puzzlement started to turn into worry in late 1962, by which time the Game of Nations had changed into a new kind of conflict and the interests of Egypt and the United States were beginning to clash in a manner that might force the United States Government to oppose him actively. The way in which we sometimes opposed him and sometimes sided with him, in a manner unrelated to our interests as he understood them, put Nasser under an apprehension which lasted through the Arab-Israeli war of June 1967. A review of the events beginning in September 1962, one month after Nasser's talk with Ambassador Badeau, will illustrate.

In this month, the Imam of Yemen died, to be succeeded by his son the Crown Prince. A week later, a group of Yemeni Army officers took control of the Government, seized the radio station, and announced that the Crown Prince had been executed. Egypt, along with all the Arab states except Saudi Arabia and Jordan, recognized the new "Republic of Yemen." So did the Soviet Union and Communist China, thereby giving the coup the appearance of Communist orientation and a threat to Western interests in the oil-rich Arabian Peninsula. Shortly thereafter, it turned out that the new Imam had not been executed at all, but was still very much alive, busily organizing tribal support with which to stage a countercoup. Nasser dispatched military advisers to bolster up the republican regime, then small numbers of troops, then large numbers of troops. The United States Government began vacillating between withholding recognition of the new Government, as the British and the Pentagon were urging, and recognizing the regime "as a means of curtailing the growth of Egyptian, Soviet and Chinese influence over it," as a State Department spokesman explained.

During the time we were vacillating, Nasser was kept on edge not so much because of doubts as to what our final decision would be as because of the reasoning that apparently lay behind our deliberations—as he was able to surmise it from his talks with Ambassador Badeau, from reports of his own Ambassador in Washington, and from current newspaper accounts. Reasons which, to his way of thinking, should have militated against our recognizing the republican regime were being advanced in *support* of recognition, and vice versa. In December 1962, Badeau called on Nasser to seek his assurances that Yemen would not be used as a base for military attack on Saudi Arabia and for harassment of British positions in South Arabia. Nasser, amazed, promptly gave the assurances; the United States Government recognized the Republic of Yemen on December 19, 1962.

It should be recorded that Nasser's view of Yemen, in itself, was similar to our own—to wit, the human race would not be seriously inconvenienced if the whole country were to slide quietly into the Indian Ocean. On the other hand, he knew what anyone using the subversive approach knows: that you cannot make effective gains in an area by means of local uprisings and guerrilla activity unless you have a *presence* near by. Fanatics are no good, and they eventually go out like Roman candles unless there are nonfanatics ready to step in at the right moment. Nasser was not interested in Yemen, he was interested in the whole Arabian Peninsula. Yemen was only a foothold. Similarly, the United States Government was not interested in Yemen—or shouldn't have been—but in having an orderly situation in Aden and in eliminating any "wave of the future" that might prematurely overrun King Feisal, the ruling family of Kuwait, and the other Gulf sheikhdoms. Nasser saw this clearly, and it was inconceivable to him that we could not— that instead, we were talking about avoiding a "Communist orientation" of the new Yemeni government.

For the next few years, Egyptian-American relations fluctuated between moderately good and moderately bad, the ups and downs having no more apparent relation to Egypt's actions than they had had in the previous years. Nasser's "dialogue" with Badeau, established as part of his friendly relationship with President Kennedy, deteriorated into a periodic exchange of banalities and would have been discontinued altogether had not Nasser held Badeau in such high esteem personally. In August 1964, Badeau was replaced by one Lucius Battle, a career Foreign Service officer of considerable bureaucratic skill but whose understanding of the Game of Nations consisted of an almost superstitious conviction that the CIA was conducting subversive operations all over the place and was out to get him. A week or so after Battle's arrival, a mob of students burned down the Kennedy Memorial Library in Cairo; the Egyptian Air Force shot down an airplane belonging to Texas oilman John Mecom, a close friend of President Johnson; and Nasser, in an extremely vitriolic speech, announced that if the new American Ambassador did not like his behavior he could lump it ("Go drink the Mediterranean," in Arabic). The United States House of Representatives was sufficiently moved by all this to pass a resolution discontinuing aid to Egypt, but this seeming setback to Egyptian-American relations was rectified by a reversal of the bill in the Senate.

That American actions concerning Egypt related to Egyptian actions only in some mysterious, unfathomable way, if at all, was demonstrated conclusively to Nasser's satisfaction in the following month when Egypt, along with other African nations, broke off relations with Britain, an action that Nasser believed would be as severe a jolt to the United States Government as any direct affront. Two days later President Johnson's personal envoy, Averell Harriman, arrived in Cairo to seek Egyptian aid in gaining the release of American prisoners in Vietnam, and three days later the American Ambassador announced that American wheat shipments to Egypt were to be continued. The United

States Government was seemingly oblivious to the fact that Nasser had just broken off relations with its closest ally.

Nasser told me in the summer of 1964 that he had given up trying to understand American actions, and his closest friend, Mohammed Hassanein Heykel, wrote an article in his newspaper, *el Ahram,* opining that Egypt's foreign policy (that is, its adventures in Arabia, its attacks over Radio Cairo on King Feisal and King Hussein, and its harassment of American and British positions in international affairs) was a "sound investment because it brings practical as well as political benefits to Egypt—economic aid from the United States and military aid from the Soviet Union." Nasser said that he appreciated our dissociating the question of aid from political considerations, if that is what we were doing, but that he would be more comfortable in his relationship with us if he had a clearer understanding of what it was we really wanted. On the matter of Egypt's foreign policy being an "investment," as Heykel had said, Nasser told me and others that he agreed with Heykel in general (although I learned later that he had given Heykel a thorough scolding for the article), but that he doubted it could be all that simple. He suspected that there were hidden complications in his relations with the United States which he was somehow missing.

In September 1965, Zakaria Mohieddin and other lieutenants of Nasser convinced him that there *must* be some deeper interaction between Egyptian positions and American positions and that the Egyptian Government would do well to identify them. At the time, over 80 percent of the bread consumed in Egypt's urban centers came from American wheat, and the $100,000,000 of hard currency that Egypt required for its development program could come only from financial institutions of which the United States Government was the principal shareholder. Also, the Egyptian Ambassador in Washington, Mustafa Kamel, was reporting that opposition in America to Nasser was growing, as was opposition to "pro-Nasser elements" in the State Department. According to Kamel, "the Pentagon is under the influence of the British, the CIA believes that Nasser is a Soviet agent, and the State Department's Bureau of Near Eastern Affairs is manned by a lot of tired Arabists who have long ago lost what little influence they ever had." Zakaria believed that the only way of establishing constructive mutual understanding with the United States was by reaching President Johnson himself, and this should be done by some means similar to the Kennedy-Mason channel. From what he knew of Johnson, he believed that those most likely to influence him constructively were his "Texas oil millionaire friends." From what he knew of Texas oil millionaires, he believed that they could be moved only by criteria of "bankability," the favorite word of Zakaria's favorite Texas millionaire, former Secretary of the Treasury Robert Anderson.

In other words, Zakaria believed that if Egypt would only cut out the Game of Nations nonsense and settle itself down to building the country economically, renouncing for a while all its Arab-world and Afro-Asian interests, it might impress President Johnson's millionaire friends, and as a result soon begin to enjoy good relations with the United States and Western Governments and financial institutions in general, while not necessarily jeopardizing its relations with the Soviets.

Nasser, having no better ideas at the time, decided in October 1965 to appoint Zakaria Prime Minister and to leave the running of the country pretty much to him. Zakaria settled down to a policy of "Egypt first," announcing that if Egypt was to have leadership of the Arab world it should be by example—i.e., by having a more efficient government, by making more of its economic resources, and by generally obtaining more benefits for the people—rather than by exerting sheer political influence. He admitted publicly that Egypt was in a bad way economically, while

instituting rigid austerity measures, and, to Nasser's surprise, actually gained popularity for the Government by so
doing. He revised the Government's agreements with the
Western oil companies so as to get better terms for Egypt
but, at the same time, to encourage the companies to step
up their operations. He entered into negotiations with the
World Bank, with the International Monetary Fund, with
the Kuwaiti Fund for the Development of the Arab World,
and with major private banks that were possible sources of
hard-currency financing, and he tried to gain financial assistance from them on a basis of bankability rather than because of political considerations. Having persuaded Nasser
to come to an agreement with King Feisal over Yemen a few
months before he took office, he pressed Field Marshal
Amer to hasten the withdrawal of troops from that country
—his only venture into Arab affairs during his tenure as
Prime Minister. His actions would not have been different
had he been checking them off according to a list provided
by the American Embassy. He ran a serious risk, in fact, of
getting himself labeled an American agent.

As for the American reaction to Zakaria's model behavior:
Ambassador Battle paid a courtesy call on Zakaria when he
first became Prime Minister, another to accompany David
Rockefeller, and one or two others under formal circumstances when only routine exchanges were possible. That
was it. Zakaria saw nothing of the American Ambassador
from this routine call right up to the routine call he paid
upon finishing his assignment in Cairo. Meanwhile, senior
officers of the American Embassy held lively discussions on
international affairs—Vietnam, Yemen, African and Asian
politics—with Egyptian Foreign Office members and with
political advisers at the Presidency, thereby exploding any
notion that our Government was interested in Egypt for
Egypt's sake and re-establishing Nasser's conviction that the
United States Government was interested in Egypt exactly
to the extent that Egypt cuts a figure in international affairs.

—i.e., the conviction expressed in Heykel's "our foreign policy is an investment" article.

Zakaria was by now flooded with indications that the "deeper interaction" that he had set out to discover was something other than what he had hoped. King Feisal's advisers, observing the withdrawal of fifteen thousand Egyptian troops from Yemen and fearing a cooling of the anti-Nasser feeling that had been building up in Washington, prompted the King to launch a drive for an Islamic Alliance to "stop Communism" (and, of course, to "stop Nasser"), with the predictable result that Nasser promptly sent the troops back to Yemen and reopened the conflict. At the same time, the international bankers whom Zakaria hoped to impress decided that unless the Government would devalue its currency (unacceptable to bloc creditors) and discontinue its prestige industrial projects (unthinkable in the light of domestic politics) Egypt was much less bankable than other countries where they could put their money. "It is not enough for Egypt to be favorable," one banker told Zakaria; "it's got to be more favorable than all the other places open to us."

In other words, the Game of Nations was still on, even with the United States—"*especially* with the United States," Zakaria told me. He was kicking himself for ever having doubted it. It all made no sense to him, but he thought there must be some way of simply "finding the pattern," as he put it, and adjusting to it without the frustrations of trying to figure out "why." Thus, in October 1966, he and other Vice Presidents, Ali Sabri and Abdelhakim Amer, sat down with Nasser for a *tafsir il aam.*

Tafsir il aam has been loosely translated into English as "agonizing reappraisal," the translators having been influenced by Secretary of State Dulles' phrase. Actually, it is something quite different. An "agonizing reappraisal" *à la* Dulles is a moral thing, a struggle of conscience, whereas a *tafsir il aam*—literally "general clarification"—is cold-blooded and amoral, the kind of review made by a military commander or football captain who sees that his past strategy has not been working and that he must call time out in the game to redefine his objectives, re-examine obstacles and aids (which may have reversed their places), and devise new strategies. While Nasser and his Vice Presidents were undergoing their *tafsir il aam,* so were the American banks, airlines, oil companies and other kinds of companies which felt that they could protect their interests only by strategies that were to a degree independent of Egyptian-American diplomatic relations. So were parts of the United States Government which, in spite of the limitations imposed by international moral and legal considerations (the United Nations treaties and ordinary diplomatic practice), somehow had to look after American interests. A "new game" was on the board, and ordinary diplomacy could not play it.

As I said earlier in the chapter, this was hardly the first time that either side of the Egyptian-American "game" had sat down for a general stocktaking, nor was it the first time that unofficial and unconventional diplomacy was called upon to take over, behind the scenes, from ordinary diplomacy, leaving our regular diplomats the task of seeing that the openly known actions of our Government suited the moral criteria of public opinion both at home and abroad. This particular "general clarification" is important, however, because it took place in the face of four new features of the Game of Nations, the advancement of which took us into the Arab-Israeli war of June 1967, which are still with us to exacerbate the aftermath, and which increasingly pose similar problems elsewhere. They are: (1) the change of a bipolar world (in which Nasser, Nkrumah, Sukarno, and others could play one side off against the other) into a multipolar world; (2) the deterioration of order and security throughout the Arab world, with the consequent disappearance of "Arab unity" in *any* form; (3) the approach of Israeli patience to the breaking point (with the Israelis feeling, in early 1967, "We can't go on like this indefinitely; we must make the break sooner or later, so we'd better grab the first opportunity"); (4) the Soviets' giving up any idea of there being an advantage in remaining neutral in the Arab-Israeli struggle, and therefore becoming ready to cooperate fully with any Arab government that would meet them halfway. These changes in the game board obviously required new strategies for all concerned, the Egyptians in particular. When a respected American journalist told an Egyptian diplomat, in late 1966, that "We don't even consider Nasser a nuisance any more," it was a signal that an *entirely* new strategy might be needed.

13

The Climax:
The Arab-Israeli War
of June 1967,
and Its Aftermath

. . . and you are likely to come to a Sad End.

On the new game board, what kind of strategy is there for a leader like Nasser? Let us assume that you accept:

- —that Nasser *had* to be the sort of person to whom personal power was important, else he would not have been able to seize power and hold it;
- —that it was logical for such a leader to require a "repressive base" and that such a base, of necessity, would involve a bureaucracy and an army of sizes beyond what Egypt could normally afford;
- —that gaining popular support from a frustrated people, which inevitably exists in a country like Egypt, required the taking of positions that were counterproductive if viewed in any rational light;
- —that Nasser's popular support depended on his being "neutralist" and that it was inevitable that, once neutralist, he would begin to regard neutralism not only as an objective but as a strategy *vis-à-vis* the Great Powers;
- —that once such a strategy started to work (and it was the West, not Nasser, that made it work), he could be expected to maximize its effectiveness by getting other powers to join in with him so as to face the Great Powers as a united bloc;

—that once the "union" strategy began to show results (as it, in fact, did) he was bound to employ strong-arm methods against the blacklegs—just as any kind of union organizer does;

—that, in the end, while sophisticated analysts in Washington, London and Moscow might have understood all this behavior as logical, the rest of the world eventually got so sick of it that at least one of the competing Great Powers had to stop the courtship and say, "The others can have him!" thereby making it possible for the other side to get him cheaply.

The answer, to anyone who has not traveled down this road, is simple enough. It is the same as the answer to the problem of the man who has been earning $50,000 a year and who suddenly goes down to $12,000 a year: trim your ambitions down to reasonable dimensions, and be as happy as you can be within your new income. This is exactly what some of us, mainly Robert Anderson, former Secretary of the Treasury and a close friend of President Johnson, proposed to Nasser. In January 1967, Anderson and Mohammed Habib of the U.A.R. Embassy drew up a list of highly influential financiers and businessmen, all personal friends of President Johnson, and Habib arranged for Nasser to invite them to Cairo. They came in February and were duly impressed, not only with the economic prospects for Egypt but with President Nasser personally. When they returned home they conveyed their favorable impression to President Johnson. It looked for a while as though it would be possible for the United States Government and Nasser to start off, from scratch, a new relationship by which Nasser would drop his unionizing (although with the new game board he could be as neutralist as he liked), cut his ambitions down to reasonable dimensions, and concentrate on building Egypt; and we—the United States Government and private business interests—would back him financially so that he could do so.

But such optimism did not take into account the tremendous momentum that a movement like Nasser's builds up and the extent to which, like a large airplane, it thenceforth depends on that momentum. Cut the army down to 50,000 men? Cut the bureaucracy down to 180,000? Denationalize the nationalized industries? Disband the Arab Socialist Union, and leave to chance what would take its place? Such actions, when you get right down to executing them, suddenly become unthinkable. That Nasser found it so is no indication that he had become "power-crazy" or that he had lost his reason.

Then, there was the Soviet influence. The Soviets had an advantage over us, because they could refrain from putting on any pressure. Nasser's behavior throughout the area suited their purposes just as it was. As Nasser told our Ambassador, "What I am doing in Yemen and elsewhere I would be doing even if the U.S.S.R. didn't exist." On the other hand, with our responsibility toward Israel and King Feisal, we could hardly back Nasser on a basis of "Anything you do is all right by us."

And almost immediately after the departure of the wealthy Americans, the area situation so occupied Nasser's attention that any thought of reverting to an "Egypt first" kind of program was put right out of his mind.

The events from that moment up to the outbreak of war with Israel in June 1967 are brilliantly explained by Walter Laqueur in his *The Road to War 1967*—a book which, incidentally, I consider to be worth all the other books on the subject put together. Speaking from a background of many years' study of Soviet interests in the Middle East, Professor Laqueur is able, as I am not, to explain how the "Soviets wanted an Egyptian show of strength," but only one that would be a "limited exercise in brinkmanship, not war." In the light of what I have heard from my Egyptian friends, this makes sense to me. Also, I tend to agree with Professor Laqueur's simple explanation of how the war started—"that Nasser stumbled into it, that Israel was unprepared and confused, that Russian intelligence was incompetent and Russian judgment poor, that America was powerless to do anything"—except that I would add that Nasser did not exactly stumble, and that Israel was not exactly unprepared. Nasser planned his operation in detail right up to the moment Vice President Zakaria Mohieddin, in Nasser's name, was to back down magnanimously (over the Straits of Tiran issue) in response to appeals from the United Nations; the Israelis had no wish to let Nasser get away with such a prestige-building gesture. Despite their promise to President Johnson that they would hold off until Zakaria got to New York, the Israelis struck on the very morning Zakaria was supposed to depart. After all, they had been rehearsing their assault for years, and never again would they get such favorable circumstances in which to launch it.

Not knowing what went on in Tel Aviv and Washington, and knowing only so much of what went on in Moscow as my Egyptian friends knew and cared to tell me, I can only contribute what I saw firsthand in Cairo, which is as follows:

1. The basic worry of Nasser and his lieutenants two months before the war was the economy of the country. Early in that year, a team of researchers working for my firm totted up most authoritative figures to be found on Egypt's hard currency and gold on hand in July 1952, the time of Nasser's coup; added to this amount the total foreign aid (loans and grants) that the Government had received; added to these two amounts the total in export earnings between the middle of 1952 and the end of 1966; and from the total thus obtained subtracted all the expenditures. The result showed that Egypt's trade deficit, at an average of almost $400,000,000 a year, had just about exhausted all these resources, including borrowings which the Government was unable to pay back. According to Professor Laqueur, Egypt's reserves were down to $40,000,000 in gold and $46,000,000 in hard currency, but anyone chasing around Cairo in March of 1967 trying to locate this

$46,000,000 would have been hard pressed to find more than $2 or $3 million with which to pay for even emergency purchases. Factories were closed down for want of spare parts costing no more than a few thousand dollars. The United Arab Airlines, for want of spare parts, at one time had four of its seven Comets out of action—and the UAA is a hard-currency earner. Even had the Government sold all its remaining gold, proceeds would have paid for only a little more than one month's normal imports. The American Embassy's quarterly economic reports had been suggesting for as long as a year that the U.A.R. was virtually bankrupt, and hardened old cynics among the foreign observers were saying, "We've been hearing that old story for years, but somehow Egypt always gets along." This time, though, it was clear that the U.A.R. *had* hit bottom and that, with no more help coming from the West, the Soviets, observing the competition finally ended, were going to mete out small amounts piecemeal as *they* saw fit.

2. For years, I had considered Nasser's regime to be the most coup-proof in the Arab world. I still think it is. But in March and April of 1967 it certainly looked as though Nasser had reached the end of the line, and that he knew it—and that his lieutenants knew it. The Big Show, it seemed, was over. Our own Government, which had put over $500,-000,000 into Egypt since the crisis in Lebanon, was finally insisting that sensible use of our aid, rather than political pressure, was the criterion. And Egypt, by the wildest stretch of the imagination, did not meet the criterion. Ward Elliott, a Washington lawyer writing in Harvard University's *Public Policy,* spoke what was on the mind of practically all Western aid officials and bankers when he said, "Nasser's insistence on posturing on the stage of world politics cost the Egyptians precious resources which might better be invested elsewhere, and the country that aids Egypt must realize that it thereby frees resources to gratify Nasser's

extraterritorial ambitions—in effect, helping him to 'piece his opulent throne with kingdoms.'"

The point is that key people in the U.A.R. power structure had finally come to realize that this was our attitude. Although I did not think there would be a coup against Nasser, it certainly appeared possible that his best friends, conceivably with his reluctant agreement, would "Sukarno-ize" him, as Cy Sulzberger would say. Indonesia had been in a similar predicament; the answer had been to elevate Sukarno up to the chairman of the board level, turn the affairs of the country over to respected trustees, and start rebuilding the country from a state of bankruptcy. I am reliably informed that this way out of the mess was seriously discussed by key individuals of the U.A.R. Government whose loyalty to Nasser was above question, and I can believe that one or another of them had the temerity to mention the idea to Nasser. Knowing Nasser, however, it is no suprise to me that it didn't get anywhere. When Nasser goes out it will not be with a whimper but with a bang—*Götterdämmerung,* even.

3. Nasser's lieutenants were caring less and less about what other Arabs thought of their regime—while becoming increasingly annoyed at the way, to the civilized world, Egypt was coming to look like the Azania of Evelyn Waugh's *Black Mischief*—but it remained very important to Nasser that he not lose face *vis-à-vis* the Arabs. Just a few days before fleeing Cairo in the face of the oncoming catastrophe, I asked one of Nasser's staunchest followers, "Why is it so important to Gamal to appear a Big Wheel to a lot of losers?" and he could only answer, "I wish we knew."

But it *was* important to Nasser, and when the Saudis and the Jordanians began taunting him about his having shown no sign of reaction to the crescendo of Israeli raids into Syria and Jordan, he neglected really important economic problems to preoccupy himself with launching propaganda counterattacks. It was specifically the Jordanian charge of cowardice and accusation that he was hiding behind the UNEF, I believe, that goaded him into closing the Straits of Tiran. Professor Laqueur says, "The Syrians and Nasser should have known that making threats from a position of weakness is a dangerous policy," but I think that this is exactly what the Syrians and Nasser do *not* know—inasmuch as, after all, they have been doing this effectively for years. (I might add that even with their critically weakened position since June 1967, their bargaining has been as forceful as if they had won the war—and rightly so, since their forcefulness seems to be accepted as normal and is, in a way, effective.)

4. Finally, there was the factor of Syria. On April 7 some Syrian planes, flying over the demilitarized zone, found a group of Israeli tractors as an easy target. This being the only kind they can hit, the temptation was irresistible and they blasted away, killing a number of farmers. No sooner had the raid been accomplished than a number of Israeli Mirages appeared out of nowhere, chased the Syrian MIGs to Damascus, and shot down six of them almost within the city limits. The howls that went up from the Syrian Government and newspapers were agonized even by Syrian standards. For the following weeks, Radio Damascus openly called for war, and preparations of the Syrian Government and Army were such as to give perfectly clear indications, to anyone not knowing the Syrians, that they actually intended to attack Israel. No doubt emboldened by their recently signed treaty with Egypt (November 1966), they gave the Israelis all the evidence they needed to present themselves as being on the defensive.

The Soviets and the Egyptians had apparently thought that the treaty would restrain the Syrians, but it had the opposite effect. Under the umbrella of the treaty, with (as they thought) the Egyptian Army at their beck and call, they could roar and posture in a manner that would otherwise have been too rash even for Syrians. It was clear by early May that they, not Nasser, had the initiative.

Although I had no contact with the Syrians, Egyptian friends who met with Syrian leaders during the buildup period have assured me that the Syrians really wanted war and that they were confident that they would win it—with the help of the Egyptians, of course. At the same time, I disagree with the numerous writers who say that the Egyptians also estimated themselves strong enough to defeat the Israelis. Nasser told me himself of a conversation with Field Marshal Amer, only a week before the war started, in which he berated Amer for being "ten years behind the times" and for the Egyptian Army's not being capable of defeating a lot of Yemeni hopheads, let alone a modern, well-trained Army like the Israelis'. And Nasser was not the only one. His principal lieutenants were very concerned about the state of readiness of the Egyptian Army. One of them told me, only days before the outbreak of war, that if Egypt got out of the crisis with a diplomatic victory she would leave the Syrians to go it alone—if they were still so inclined.

Nasser's lieutenants; the Americans in Cairo, including myself, and just about all other informed observers in the area thought that Nasser had as much as a fifty-fifty chance of pulling off an impressive diplomatic victory—although many of us were unnerved by his speech of May 29 in which he said, "Preparations have already been made. We are now ready to confront Israel. . . . Now we are ready to deal with the entire Palestine question. . . ." And, "We will decide the time and place and not let them decide." Such a statement, although Israel's Prime Minister Eshkol had said much the same kind of thing on May 11, not only gave the Israelis further excuse to strike the first blow (in addition to what excuse the Syrians had already obligingly given them), but virtually made it imperative that they do so. When I left Cairo for London at about this time, I told my Egyptian friends that I would bet my last dollar that Nasser had let himself in for a Pearl Harbor, although Zakaria's mission to Washington had been planned and President Johnson had received the Israelis' assurances that they would not attack until the world saw what he had to say in New York. As I said, the chances looked about fifty-fifty. Nasser gambled, and in a sense, he lost.

According to the great French strategist, André Beaufre, to "win" a war is either to destroy the enemy completely or to get yourself into a position to dictate the terms of surrender to him. According to such a definition, anyone observing the postwar dispute between the Arabs and Israelis would have to agree that the Israelis did not "win" the Six-Day War. And after it was all over, Nasser emerged with his position as ruler of Egypt stronger, much stronger, than it would have been had the crisis been averted. This is the answer to the question, If Nasser were confronted with a similar situation in the future, what would he do? My answer to this question should be clear enough to anyone who has read this book carefully.

Where do we go from here in our relations with Gamal Abdelnasser? Throughout this exercise I have tried to make the point that, given the circumstances which have surrounded him, Nasser's conduct has been almost entirely normal and predictable. I believe that he has behaved in a manner in which anyone else with his mental and cultural equipment—the mental and cultural equipment he *had* to have if he were to rise to power in the first place—would have behaved. I like him personally; I know of no one with whom I would rather spend a long evening of conversation and joking. He is one of the most courageous, most incorruptible, most unprincipled, and, in his way, most humanitarian national leaders I have ever had the pleasure to meet. He has a sense of humor. He does not, as many think, act out of pique, whim or any of the pettier motives. We laid a path down before Nasser, and he took it. Things might have been otherwise had he been programmed differently.

His role in *our* future depends on the kind of future we are going to have.

And what about our future Game of Nations? I don't know whether the Game Center still exists, although I know that a similar kind of exercise goes on in many of our leading universities. I do believe, however, that our diplomats, who were so naïve about the Middle East of 1947, have come a long way and have developed a whole new perspective. The counterproductive politics of the underdeveloped countries which we used to regard as essential to the democratic process—one which, in turn, we believed to be essential to peace and prosperity—are now viewed with a detachment that we could not muster twenty years ago. We will henceforth look at the politics of a backward country the way a doctor looks at a diseased patient: with concern, but without involvement. In the future, I believe, every embassy will have some third secretary chasing around keeping track of the Mumbo Jumbos versus the Heebie Jeebies, the National Socialists versus the Social Nationalists, and all the rest, but I believe that when his reports reach Washington they will be dealt with by anthropologists rather than by political analysts. We will be concerned exclusively with such questions as, What, if anything, is the Government of Azania doing about its population increase? About modernizing its agriculture? About increasing the productivity of its working force? The guiding thought will be this: A segment of the human race, to wit ourselves, intend to put a man on the moon, to cure cancer and the common cold, and to solve all the problems that overpopulation and waning raw materials are going to present us with. Anyone else who wishes can join in—regardless of race, religion, or color. But anyone who is more concerned with such pursuits as burning down foreign embassies, "rejecting Western materialism," and all else to acquire "freedom from imperialism" can have it with our blessing. After all, freedom from imperialism is one thing we can hand out—in large doses.

Appendix:
Power Problems of a
Revolutionary Government

I: BASIC PRINCIPLES

The essence of government is power, since to govern is not merely to propose measures of public action and decide questions of justice, but to *undertake* public action and *enforce* justice. Hence, in some degree the maintenance of power must be an end in itself for any government, and the selection of means appropriate to this end must be one of its essential concerns.

In constitutional governments, tradition and "fundamental laws" limit the means that may be employed. A constitutional government, for instance, can commonly not arrest the leaders of the opposition on political grounds. But in extraconstitutional or revolutionary governments there are no express limitations on the government's action in preserving and perpetuating its own power.

History teaches two general principles about the maintenance of governmental power. The first of these principles is that power may be based on *repressive* action or on *constructive* action. To these two kinds of action correspond two extreme types of government:

1. a pure tyranny, imposed by force against the will of all the citizens in all it does;

2. a completely "popular" government (not necessarily "democratic" in form) enjoying the support of all the citizens in all it does.

It will easily be seen that these two extremes are theoretical and that no actual government in history has ever been uniquely one or the other. The problem of a revolutionary government is to find a middle ground between the two types, and the proper middle ground is determined by the aims and purposes of the revolution itself.

A revolution that does not intend to establish a simple tyranny, yet aims at being more than a mere "palace intrigue," will necessarily have two purposes:

1. to solve the pressing social and political problems that made the revolution necessary (and possible), thus ending abruptly the previous political system in which these problems had become unsolvable;

2. to evolve a new constitutional system in which the accomplishments of the revolution will be perpetuated without fear of a regression to the ills of the past.

Such being the purposes of a genuine revolution, it follows that the revolutionary government should not rely exclusively on repressive action to hold power, but should seek as many constructive means as possible. Repression—i.e. police and secret-intelligence methods—while frequently indispensable, must be supplemented and eventually superseded by constructive means.

The second principle that history teaches about the maintenance of governmental power is that *everything a government does has an effect on its power base.* By power base is meant, on the one hand, the capacity of the government to restrain opposition and, on the other hand, the acceptance and support the government enjoys among those people it governs. The capacity to restrain opposition is the government's repressive power base; its popular acceptance and support—the capacity of the government to govern without repressive means—is its constructive power base. To say, then, that everything a government does affects its power base means that every governmental policy, and every administrative act, either directly or indirectly renders its repressive power more necessary or less necessary.

Those governmental actions which have a direct effect on the power base are usually intended as such; the preservation and perpetuation of power is their primary purpose. As examples of direct action with respect to the repressive power base, the following can be enumerated: Any measures that tend to increase the efficiency or strengthen the loyalty of the army, intelligence services, police or other paramilitary organizations of the government; any measures making certain kinds of political activity illegal and subjecting those engaging in them to prosecution. Direct actions affecting the constructive power base include: any measure encouraging certain kinds of political activity—e.g., the formation of a mass organization or political party supporting the government; any constitutional provision or enactment, such as an electoral law, that gives certain advantages to groups and classes supporting the government or favoring the aims of the revolution.

Governmental actions that have an indirect effect on the power bases are those measures which, while primarily intended for another purpose (e.g., fostering the economic health of the nation), have nonetheless a political result. Whenever governmental policy destroys the advantages of a powerful economic group or even works a considerable hardship on such a group, this group tends to be alienated from the constructive power base of the government and becomes a breeding ground for active disaffection. Contrariwise, if the economic status of a class is raised by a government policy, or such a policy promises this effect, that class becomes part of the power base, even though it may previously have been politically negligible or even hostile. Public works usually have specific purposes other than political, yet they have obvious effects which tend to integrate groups and even regions into the power base of the government that undertakes them. Likewise with taxation and the enforcement of other government regulations. Even measures designed to have a *direct* effect on the power base also may have certain *indirect* effects as well. If, for example, significant numbers of the army or police have been members of a political group that has been outlawed, this would have an adverse, indirect effect on the repressive power base.

To a greater or lesser extent, then, all governmental acts, whatever their primary intention, have political results. The genius of revolutionary leaders will always manifest itself in the care with which they relate government policy to the requirements of potential power. They seek to rule by constructive action, but they will be prepared to utilize such repressive means as may be necessary.

If the above distinctions are clear, two great rules of power emerge:

1. A revolutionary government should lay down no policy and undertake no actions without evaluating its probable direct and indirect effects on the power base.

2. A revolutionary government should give first priority to the development of a sound base in order to avoid being forced into a disastrous policy of drift and compromise.

No exact rules exist to guide the leaders of a revolutionary government in evaluating actions for their political effects, or in creating and maintaining an adequate power base. Much depends on the local situation, more on the insight and imagination of the leaders, still more on their qualities of initiative and daring. Nevertheless, it is possible to lay down the following general propositions, some of which will be discussed more fully later:

1. Repressive action unavoidably is primary in the early stage of a revolution.

2. "Mere popularity" should not be the goal of any revolution. "Mere popularity" is transitory, elusive. Insofar as "mere popularity" is what counts, anybody or any group can enter the competition, and the government is in danger of finding itself following instead of leading. The quest for "mere popularity" is always a sign of serious—sometimes fatal—weakness in a government's power base.

3. Constructive popular power, as opposed to "mere popularity," rests on the careful development of government policy and the forthright use of government instrumentalities in enlisting the support of large groups and classes of

people by *appealing to their self-interest* as well as to their emotions.

4. The indirect effects of governmental actions can be just as important as direct action in developing the power base.

5. Both in the transition to a constitutional state and during the immediate period of revolution, extragovernmental organizations are of primary importance in the constructive power base. For instance, a mass organization founded during the revolution can become a major political party in the new constitutional system and can be a prime source of government strength during the revolutionary period itself.

6. The new constitutional system should be directly based on the constructive power of the revolution.

7. A well-organized, incorruptible intelligence service is absolutely essential, not only for effective repressive actions, but for accurate analysis of the constructive power base.

II: REVOLUTIONARY PHASE

We are now in a position to examine more concretely the problems a revolutionary government faces in maintaining and perpetuating its power and the resources it possesses for direct and indirect action. It has been said that a revolution that does not intend to establish a pure tyranny has a twofold aim:

1. to solve the pressing social and political problems that made a revolution necessary;

2. to evolve a new constitutional order to perpetuate the accomplishments of the revolution.

These aims correspond roughly with two periods or phases in a revolution, although it would be impossible to specify when one phase ends and the other begins. It would be more correct to say that they are distinguished only by a difference in emphasis, the predominantly "revolutionary" period shading off, almost imperceptibly, into the beginnings of a new constitutional order. Only for purposes of discussion is it possible to mark them clearly, and we shall do so here always keeping in mind that real "constitution making" begins with the first constructive act of the revolution, and some repressive action may be necessary long after the inauguration of a new constitutional order. We shall identify the first phase as the revolutionary phase and the second phase as the preconstitutional phase.

A revolution abrogates some or all of the political institutions in the context of which the country had previously found it impossible to solve pressing political and social problems. This is eminently a time of rapid developments in which groups and classes are dispossessed of institutional political power and held at bay by the overwhelming nature of the overturn, by the militant force behind it, and by the new government's early success in rallying a spontaneous mass of supporters under the banner of reform. These initial events are succeeded by a period of revolutionary consolidation in which the government, having taken a provisional form, settles down to grapple with the hard facts of actual administration and policy.

This is the time of maximum counterrevolutionary danger arising from three general sources:

1. those having vested interests in the previous political system, or an overriding emotional loyalty thereto;

2. political opportunists who always try to profit from the natural tendencies toward instability inherent in any "revolutionary situation";

3. political subversives—e.g., Communists—who wish to "take over" the revolution for their own ends.

From these sources, singly or in combination, arise three specific dangers:

1. the factional coup d'etat, brought about through contact between elements of the army or police and factions "within" the revolutionary government itself;

2. the counterrevolutionary coup d'etat, brought about through contact between elements of the army or police and "outside" political forces, generally those having some capacity for inciting mob demonstrations;

3. the penetration of the revolutionary government by elements hostile to its purposes, with one or more of the following consequences:
   a. the subtle distortion of its program;
   b. the outright sabotage of its program;
   c. the weakening of the government's ability to maintain its power (thus preparing for its eventual overthrow).

The necessary and proper defense against such dangers as these is the forthright use of repressive power. It has already been stated that in the first phase of a revolution repression is primary, and that later constructive action becomes the basis of power. This is the "correct" progression; but, curiously, the actual course of many revolutions follows the reverse order: in the first phase an excessive reliance is placed on what appear to be constructive measures, and only later does repressive power come to assume major importance. This is a disease of revolutions, and one that can be fatal.

It comes about as follows: because initially the revolutionary leaders have not acquired a settled control over the instruments of the government, and have insufficient confidence in the efficacy of their repressive powers, they feel obliged to embark, bit by bit, on a policy of drift and compromise; they seek popularity and tend to evoke a perpetual crisis psychology in the conduct of governmental affairs. While they are maintaining power by these means, the basic purposes of the revolution are either abandoned or allowed to progress as best they can; and as this "bankruptcy" becomes more and more apparent, further drift and compromise become less and less possible. Then the government is forced to fall back on repressive power which it hurriedly begins to develop. If this development is successful, the revolution comes to adopt an excessive reliance on repression just at the time when it should have been prepared to offer the country a new constitutional order. The revolution has, in fact, degenerated into a tyranny. If, on the other hand, the development of sufficient repressive power is found to be impossible (which is usually the case when the effort is begun too late) the government is obliged to "turn over" to a new constitutional regime with most or all of its purposes unachieved—or, worse still, falls victim to a counterrevolution.

Thus it is obvious that drift and compromise are the allies, within the revolution itself, of counterrevolution and subversion. When one remembers that the similar policy of the previous government was probably one of the very factors that made the revolution possible, it becomes clear that such a course favors those who seek to overthrow or undermine the revolution.

The repressive power upon which a revolutionary government must rely when needed is based on the following:

1. legislation
2. police
3. organized intelligence services
4. propaganda facilities
5. organized military force—the army

Legislation: The use of legislation to promote political stability during the revolutionary phase should be obvious; the aim is not only to disband all organized political activity not favored by the government, but to make all subversive and disruptive action illegal; the method is to review extant legislation touching on these matters and to expand, clarify and consolidate it in one widely promulgated decree or a series of decrees. This legislation becomes the foundation of state security; it defines the mission of the police and internal intelligence services, as well as duties and prerogatives of the citizen. Such legislation should be explicit insofar as possible but general enough to allow the government sufficient discretion; it should not appear to discriminate against any group or class or abrogate basic freedoms of discussion, criticism, etc., but should enable the government to take necessary action for its own protection. This legislation should accomplish at least the following: conspiracy to overthrow the government, advocacy of the overthrow of the government, spreading false rumors, spreading alarm or despondency, incitement to violence, revealing official secrets, espionage, sabotage— all should be illegal. The police should be enabled, at their discretion, to require a license for all public meetings and to prohibit any street gatherings of dangerous size. It is assumed that the judicial magistrature is under the control of the revolutionary government, and that all decisions in cases of violation of the security laws will not work against the convenience of the government.

Police: Of all the instruments of the government, the police should receive the most attention from the revolutionary leaders during the early phases of the revolution. The police are the bulwark of the security system and the ultimate guarantors of public order in "crises" not severe enough to require the army. Hence, it is most vital that the police personnel and operations be constantly examined from the viewpoints of loyalty and efficiency. The revolutionary leaders should have absolute confidence in the police chief and *all* his principal subordinates, and the top government leaders should take a personal and direct interest in the development of police efficiency in security operations. This means, essentially, that the police should be "politicized" and should become, to whatever extent is necessary, a partisan paramilitary arm of the revolutionary government.

The particular functions of the security police are the following: the mass gathering of security information on an informant-network basis; the rapid investigation of security cases through the normal methods of surveillance and interrogation; the low-level penetration of suspected anti-government groups; the development of an efficient anti-riot service.

Intelligence: The nerve center of the whole security system of a revolutionary state (or of any state) lies in a secret body, the identity and very existence of which can be safely known only to the head of the revolutionary government and to the fewest possible of the other key leaders. It is the responsibility of this body, disguised within the fabric of the government (or even located outside the government) to provide the head of state with critical intelligence necessary for prompt and efficient action against real counterrevolutionary threats and for the formulation of overall security policy. It is the duty of this body to be aware of all prejudicial activity, incipient or actual, whether outside of the government or within, whether it involves cabinet ministers or a captain in the armed forces.

To accomplish its mission, this body must have access to the "product" of all other security and intelligence services; it must be able (through appropriate "cover" channels) to direct special investigations, surveillances, etc., on the part of the police, and it must have the resources for conducting "high-level" penetrations of any suspected antirevolutionary activity.

Propaganda: Propaganda is an auxiliary weapon and not an absolute one. To regard propaganda as absolute and to rely primarily thereon is to run the risk of finding government policy dictated by the needs of propaganda, instead of the reverse. This is the most direct path to a policy of drift and compromise.

Sound government propaganda during the revolutionary phase should be closely related to the use of repressive power and serve as "justification" for its continued exercise. Its aims should be the exposure of counterrevolutionary elements and Left-revolutionary activity.

The problem of counterpropaganda inspired by opposition forces deserves special mention, since it raises the question of *freedom of the press.* Whether there should or should not be press censorship during the revolutionary phase is a question that cannot be decided apart from specific conditions. In any case, a revolutionary government must be prepared to institute such censorship if it is judged necessary, although control of the press is frequently possible through various forms of government pressure short of actual censorship. For example, it is often sufficient to assign to each newspaper or periodical a press officer who can advise on stories that are to be published and offer government "guidance" with respect to the editorial handling of important and public issues. The authority of these officers can be reinforced when necessary by evoking the security legislation described above, or by threatening the overstrict or "nuisance" enforcement of various other laws or taxes.

Military force: It is hardly necessary to emphasize the importance of a loyal and efficient army. Neither should it be taken for granted. During the revolutionary phase it is essential to build up a countersubversive intelligence system within the armed forces, and it may also be advisable to establish a political education program. Above all, it is important that improvements be introduced in army training and equipment; that the troops be paid regularly and as well as possible; that it be, in short, a "happy army."

Taken together, these constitute a formidable apparatus. Their judicious use should not only guarantee the maintenance of power against counterrevolutionary enemies, but should provide a background of political stability against which the revolutionary government can pursue its constructive ends with maximum efficiency. Based on fundamental social-economic reforms, the revolution can lay the foundation, through a multitude of direct and indirect actions, for a new period of political life in the country. The laying of this foundation, which can commence on the first day of the revolution, is the preconstitutional phase.

III: PRECONSTITUTIONAL PHASE

From the very outset, the leaders of a revolution must begin to foresee the "institutionalization" of their own movement in a new constitutional state. It has been remarked that genuine revolutions do not aim at the establishment of a tyranny, and certainly one of the important elements of the stability of a revolution is the promise, usually explicit, of the promulgation of a new constitutional order at some future time. There is, moreover, the further problem of "succession"; the revolutionary leaders will not live forever, and neither will the "revolutionary spirit" of the country. The most effective means of handing on power in an orderly manner (without another revolution) is through the use of some sort of electoral machinery, and elections necessarily entail a constitutional system of at least a minimal sort.

Since the leaders of a revolution and its supporters wish to perpetuate its accomplishments, it becomes necessary to foresee new sources of danger in the eventual recapture of political power under the succeeding constitutional system by the still-present enemies of the revolution and of its reforms. This can come about quite easily if the revolution has failed to develop the political effectiveness of those groups and classes whose interests the revolution has served and to develop a new constitutional system in which these groups and classes will have predominant influence. The specific dangers are these:

1. The old political parties will revive and become powerful enough to return the enemies of the revolution to power.

2. New political parties will be formed in which the old interests will come to the fore; these parties will become powerful enough to return the enemies of the revolution to power.

3. Politicians serving interests alien to the revolution will, as a result of superior political abilities and experience, become dominant in whatever "revolutionary party" continues into the constitutional period. Thus, although the "revolutionary party" may be in power, the interests of its supporters will be nonetheless betrayed.

4. The new constitutional system may turn out to be such as to encourage a number of parties of approximately equal strength, and in the resultant political instability the parties serving the old interests will be in a position to force the others into "bargaining away" many of the revolutionary gains.

All these dangers can be averted if the revolutionary government, during the period in which it enjoys a monopoly of legal political activity, uses its unique advantages to lay the foundation for a new constitutional system in which one political party will have a decisive role, this one party being the heir of the revolution. To bring about such a state of affairs, the revolutionary government must establish a mass organization which will eventually become a political party, but which in the meantime serves as a training ground for "revolutionary" voters and politicians. And when the time comes it must offer a new constitution for the country that will ensure a maximum opportunity for this revolutionary party.

THE MASS ORGANIZATION

What it is: Whatever it may be called, the mass organization here in view is an extragovernmental association in which the leaders of the revolution, together with other government officials and employees, join with a large mass of private citizens for the declared purpose of supporting and furthering the accomplishments of the revolution. During the period when political parties are illegal and elections suspended, this movement is not called a political party; yet it is organized with strict regard for future elections. It should, indeed, be organized like a political party and should have national, regional and local headquarters (where appropriate); officers having various policy-making, administrative and disciplinary powers; a secretariat having a number of permanent, salaried employees; a propaganda staff; publications, etc.

Its purpose: The declared purpose of the organization would be to provide a "fraternal" type of association for those who support the aims of the revolution. Its real purpose is to create a present propaganda front for the government and to build a political party for the future by attracting new grounds and classes of people into sustained political activity by providing a training ground for such activity and by concretely demonstrating the value of political activity in obtaining the best from one's life in one's community and country.

How these purposes may be accomplished: The secret of the success of this organization would be its close, although unofficial, association with the revolutionary government itself. It should be the only such organization tolerated by the government, and the top leaders of the organization should be for the most part identical with the top leaders of the government. Such being the case, the masses of people whose interests have been served by the revolution, and who feel an emotional loyalty to its leaders, will automatically be attracted to membership. A large "working cadre" can be found in the civil service, for all government employees can and should be required to join on an active basis as the condition of continued government employment. In addition, the vast powers of the government in administrative discretion and in the field of public works can be readily made to serve the interests of the mass organization (an excellent opportunity for *indirect* action on the power base). Within the limits of efficient administration and just national policy, the offices of the mass organization should become the "clearinghouse" for individuals and groups wishing to influence the government or otherwise having dealings with public officials. Any government has many favors to bestow in the routine administration of its affairs, and in the enforcement of laws many citizens can find themselves in special difficulties. It should become apparent to all—although never officially declared—that the active support of the mass organization is the surest way to obtaining "satisfaction" in such cases. In return for these services, the mass organization can expect the adherence of many people who otherwise might remain indifferent, and financial contributions or other types of active support should be much easier to solicit.

Once the basic concept of such a mass organization has been grasped, its precise form and practical scope of activity follow in accordance with the general state of culture within the country, the social and economic status of the groups and classes who may be expected to support it, and their needs in the way of political indoctrination, emotional stimulation, and governmental or quasigovernmental assistance. The activities of such an organization should embrace a wide range of matters, from educational activities (e.g. simple instruction in civics—electoral procedures, governmental organization, political history, etc.) to the publication of a newspaper; from mass demonstrations, "congresses," etc., to simple, direct assistance in getting government or other employment for active organization workers.

The important thing to keep in mind is that the mass organization is the part of the revolutionary power base that survives after the extraordinary tenure of the revolutionary government itself has yielded to the new constitutional order. It becomes the political party that will have the responsibility of carrying on the revolutionary tradition against succeeding generations of reactionary opposition.

THE NEW CONSTITUTION

Just as it is impossible in the abstract to prescribe the precise structure and activity of the mass organization, so it is impossible to lay down exact provisions for the kind of ideal constitutional order that should follow a revolutionary period. Two features of such a constitution are of utmost importance, however, if the revolutionary power base is to be perpetuated with maximum effect:

1. The written constitution should consist of general provisions, with the specific arrangements left to be determined by ordinary law. This will allow necessary flexibility to meet new circumstances and conditions, and since the revolutionary party will be the predominant force it should be in a position for some time to come to "write the constitution" in accordance with its own requirements.

2. The constitution should provide for a strong executive, popularly elected by plurality. If the revolutionary party is to use its numerical preponderance and organizational efficiency to the most advantage, it must be assured of at least control of the executive, and the executive must be in a powerful position *vis-à-vis* the legislature.

It is impossible to overemphasize the importance of these two propositions—that the formal constitution (the "written instrument") should consist of broad general provisions, and that it should provide for a strong executive. A written constitution is intended to be a permanent document defining and regulating the political system of a country. Once adopted, such a document acquires a sacrosanct character and is usually very difficult or impossible to alter. When it contains a multitude of fine details as well as general principles, these details appear to be just as "sacred" as the principles. This is dangerous for two reasons. The details of a governmental system should be flexible, and should be alterable to meet altered conditions; but if they are included in the written constitution they are as permanent as the document itself. Through the working of a detailed provision of a constitution, moreover, it is often possible for a minority to defeat the will of the majority on a critical political issue. For example, at the time of the adoption of a constitution it may have seemed in the general interest to require a two-thirds majority (instead of a simple majority) of a vote in parliament in order to enact a certain kind of legislation. As time goes on, however, it may happen that because of changing circumstances this no longer is wise; yet a minority of the parliamentary votes (perhaps representing a special interest) can still use the constitutional provision to block the will of the majority. Were the provision a mere law, alterable like any other, no such problem would arise.

The provision for a strong executive power is even more important. The great curse of governments in which the legislative is supreme over the executive is the political instability that results from the fragmentation of parliament into many small parties or factions. Since one party—even a revolutionary party! —can rarely command anything like an absolute majority, the executive is at the mercy of the shifting winds of parliamentary coalition. Where the executive, on the other hand, is as strong as or stronger than the legislative (i.e., where the executive is elected directly rather than by the parliament, and where the executive has the power to dissolve the parliament), the situation tends toward a balance. In a strong-executive system, the predominant electoral party can usually control the executive and dominate the parliament, thus providing the country with an inherently stable government.

In sum, a revolutionary government should offer the country a realistic constitution. Such legalistic documents as are produced by constitutional commissions (composed largely of professors and jurists) frequently are drawn up with great regard for complicated concepts of government that appear in textbooks and with the niceties of theoretical justice, but rarely take sufficient account of the practicalities of real political life in the country for which the documents are intended.

IV: CONCLUSION

At the outset it was observed that power is an end in itself for any government. Political power sufficient for the needs of effective government exists actually or potentially in every society, whatever its state of organization. The crux of the problem is that in most stages more power remains potential than is ever actualized. In a constitutional state, the considerations of legality that restrict the government's activities in actualizing political power also restrict the activities of those interests *opposed* to the government. But a revolutionary government knows no legality, a revolution being by its very definition illegal. This is the source of its weakness. No questions of legality limit its activities, yet the residue of political power that always remains potential is likewise unbound by legality and is an ever-present threat to its security.

Two general ways by which a revolutionary government may deal with this threat have emerged. One is dangerous in the extreme although superficially it appears to be the very essence of expediency. This is the policy of drift and compromise, by which a revolutionary government seeks to maintain itself not by actualizing a maximum of power but by forsaking power for popularity.

The other course—and the one advocated in this paper— follows for the purposes of a real revolution and recognizes this fundamental law of revolutionary power: namely, that a revolutionary government must do *whatever is necessary* to actualize more power—repressive and constructive—than is allowed to remain potential. It is hoped that this paper may serve as an introduction to the *art of doing the necessary.*

Suggested Reading List

For a young diplomat or businessman going to the Arab world with room for only one book in his luggage, I would recommend either:

The Passing of Traditional Society, by Daniel Lerner (New York, Free Press, 1958) or
The Arab World Today, by Morroe Berger (New York, Doubleday, 1962).

If he is going to Egypt, or is in any way going to be affected by the Game between Nasser and the Great Powers, I would also recommend that he find room for:

The American Approach to the Arab World, by John Badeau (Council on Foreign Relations, New York, Harper and Row, 1968): I understand that Ambassador Badeau had to rewrite an excellent first draft some five or six times before it finally came up to the Council on Foreign Relations' standards for dullness and pompousness but the end product is an extremely valuable presentation of what is misleadingly called "the pro-Nasser" school of thought in the Department of State. The explanation of American policy toward Yemen is especially worthwhile.

The Arabs and the World, by Charles Cremeans (Council on Foreign Relations, New York, Praeger, 1963): While Cremeans' book also suffers from Council on Foreign Relations disciplines (which apparently prohibit an author from admitting any first-hand knowledge of his subject), it is nonetheless an extremely interesting account of what there is of "Arab" foreign policy coming from one who has spent almost as many hours as I have discussing the question with President Nasser, Vice President Zakaria Mohieddin, Vice President Ali Sabri, and others with whom he enjoyed friendly relations during a special diplomatic assignment to Egypt during 1955.

Most of the current histories of the Middle East one finds in public libraries are by scholars of the great universities who get their information largely by taking in each other's washing, spiced up by infrequent visits to Beirut and Cairo, or by international newsmen who have only a passing familiarity with the area. The exceptional books under this category are as follows:

Egypt, by Tom Little (New York, Praeger, 1958) and *Nasser's Egypt,* by Peter Mansfield (Baltimore, Penguin Books, Inc., 1967): While both of these gentlemen, old hands in the Arab world, have refrained from telling all they know, they have got their facts straight and have included no *mis*information. The same can be said of P. J. Vatikiotis's *The Egyptian Army in Politics* (Ankara University, 1961), although it's a bit more academic and less based on personal observation than the other two.

The Struggle for Syria, by Patrick Seale (New York, Oxford University Press, 1965), and *The Arab Cold War 1958–1964,* by Malcolm Kerr (New York, Oxford University Press, 1965), are, in my opinion, the most intelligent mixtures of scholarship and firsthand information written on Egypt's relations with her neighbors. Both of these gentlemen speak fluent Arabic. While I do not agree with many of Seale's conclusions, I have to admit that he has probably spent more time than all the rest of us put together in talking and arguing with Arab leaders and ideologues.

To anyone seeking an understanding of the buildup toward the Arab-Israeli war of 1967, I highly recommend Walter Laqueur's *The Road to War 1967* (London, Weidenfeld and Nicolson, 1968), which is better understood after a careful reading of Professor Laqueur's *The Soviet Union and the Middle East* (New York, Praeger, 1959). On the other hand, if you are seeking an understanding of the Arabs' reason—and unreasonableness—which took them into the conflict, I recommend *Israel and the Arabs* (Baltimore, Penguin Books, Inc., 1968) by Maxime Rodinson, a French Jew and former Communist who lived in Syria for a number of years.

Empire by Treaty, by M. A. Fitzsimons (Notre Dame, University of Notre Dame Press, 1964): While I am unaware of any firsthand familiarity Professor Fitzsimons may have with the Arab world, I recommend his book as an excellent study of Nasser's relations with the West, mainly Great Britain, as reflected in treaties and the making of treaties. For similar reasons, I found John Campbell's *Defense of the Middle East* (New York, Harper and Row, 1960) very helpful for its view of American problems of policy as seen by Secretary Dulles in the stand-up-and-be-counted days.

John Marlowe's *Arab Nationalism and British Imperialism* (New York, Praeger, 1961), Wilton Wynn's *Nasser of Egypt* (London, Arlington Books, 1959), Keith Wheelock's *Nasser's New Egypt* (New York, Praeger, 1960), and Gordon Torrey's *Syrian Politics and the Military* (Columbus, Ohio State University Press, 1964) are all by authors who know what they are talking about. If I did not refer to them in the text at any great length, it was only because I read them only after I had written my first draft. There is also *Revolution in Iraq*, by someone calling himself "Caractacus," published by Gollancz in 1959, which is fascinating as an eyewitness account of the Iraqi coup, although naïve in the extreme in its estimation of the principal figures and their motives.

There are other books which, although most of them do not deal with Egypt or the Middle East, throw light on the factors involved in behind-the-scenes Egyptian-Western relations. Here are some of them:

The Machiavellians, by James Burnham (New York, John Day, 1943): This is a classic, by one who was a consultant to the CIA during the period covered by the early chapters of this book. As an account of the modern Machiavellians—Mosca, Michels, Parento and others—it is must reading for anyone who would understand the Game of Nations. Similarly, Lord Russell's *Power* (London, Allen and Unwin, latest edition 1960) deals, in concise and readable form, with the main ideas that make the game what it is.

The True Believer, by Eric Hoffer (New York, Harper and Row, 1951): Unfortunately, Eric Hoffer has recently been seen by a large British television audience trying to match wits with David Frost and by an American television audience sounding off unguardedly about Sirhan Sirhan. This is unfortunate, because a reading of his book is perhaps the most convenient way to get an inkling of the kind of fanatic that Nasser finds useful in Egypt for Egypt's Phase Two purposes and elsewhere in the Arab world for general use.

The Ecological Perspective on Human Affairs, by Harold and Margaret Sprout (Princeton, Princeton University Press, 1965): If you can get past the title, you will find this a tremendously readable book for its own sake. I include it here because it inspired Zakaria Mohieddin's thinking on the subject of "environmental engineering"—which, even now that Zakaria has temporarily retired, continues to be referred to as "Zakariaism" in Nasser's innermost circles.

Strategy of Conflict, by Tom Schelling (Cambridge, Harvard University Press, 1960): This is another book that has intrigued Nasser, Zakaria and others.

The Year 2000, by Herman Kahn and Anthony J. Wiener (New York, The Macmillan Company, 1967): To say that this book has "intrigued" Egyptian leaders would be an understatement. To them, it seems to describe the coming science-fiction world which we Westerners intend to dominate thirty years hence. And they do not like it.

Memoirs, 1925–1950, by George Kennan (London, Hutchinson, 1968): This book expresses a number of views, subscribed to by our most effective diplomats, which are highly relevant to the Western-Nasser conflict although they do not refer to it directly.

Diplomat Among Warriors (New York, Doubleday, 1964), by Robert Murphy, one of the most distinguished diplomats, will give the reader a revealing glimpse of what goes on in the minds of our senior official troubleshooters as they travel about making decisions which affect the lives of all of us.

The Anatomy of Revolution, by Crane Brinton (New York, Vintage, 1965): Professor Brinton was not only a historian, but a member of the wartime OSS who kept in touch, through many friends in Washington, with many of the behind-the-scenes developments covered in my book. Kermit Roosevelt considered *Anatomy* so relevant to pre-Ajax deliberations that he made it compulsory reading for all members of his staff.

The Rebels (Boston, Beacon Press, 1960) and *The Struggle for the Third World* (Chester Springs, Pa., Dufour Editions, Inc., 1966), by Brian Crozier: Crozier, who is now sponsoring a series of books on political and military power, is a long-time student of Third World politics in much the same terms as those of my own book. Both of these books are first-rate.

The Boss, by Robert St. John (New York, McGraw-Hill Book Company, Inc., 1960): A child's guide to Nasser, read by newly assigned U.S. Embassy personnel because it gives all sorts of details omitted by the more adult books: Nasser's personal foibles, names of his children, etc.

The Ugly American, by William Lederer and Eugene Burdick (New York, W. W. Norton & Co., Inc., 1959): I include this book in the bibliography only because I have referred to it several times in the text. Actually, if you will reverse the Good Guys and the Bad Guys most of the points it makes are valid.

The Memoirs of Anthony Eden: Volume I, Full Circle (New York, Houghton, 1960): Eden's own account of the Suez crisis.

Finally, in a special category, I must put Edward R. F. Sheehan's *Kingdom of Illusion* (London, Panther Books, Ltd.,

1967), which is "faction" (fact presented in fictional form) built out of Roosevelt's friendship and contest with Nasser between 1952 and 1956. Most of the outrageous incidents recounted in *Kingdom* actually happened, and the characters actually existed—with minor changes, of course, to make the events hold together as an integrated story. Apart from its literary merit, the book is worth the serious attention of any historian trying to get a feel of the spirit in which antics of this part of the Game of Nations were performed.

Index

F
H43   Herrick, William.
         That's life.

ATE	ISSUED TO